PREACHING
THE TEACHING:

Hispanics, Homiletics, and
Catholic Social Justice Doctrine

THE HISPANIC THEOLOGICAL
INITIATIVE SERIES

VOLUME IV

PREACHING
THE TEACHING:

Hispanics, Homiletics, and
Catholic Social Justice Doctrine

KENNETH G. DAVIS, O.F.M. CONV. and
LEOPOLDO PÉREZ, OMI, EDITORS

SCRANTON: UNIVERSITY OF SCRANTON PRESS

© 2005 by:
University of Scranton Press

Library of Congress Cataloging-in-Publication Data

Preaching the teaching : Hispanics, Homiletics, and Catholic social justice doctrine /
   Kenneth G. Davis and Leopoldo Pérez, editors.
    p. cm.
   Includes bibliographical references and index.
   ISBN: 1-58966-072-2(pbk)
    1. Catholic preaching. 2. Hispanic American Catholics. 3. Social justice.
I. Davis, Kenneth G., 1957- II. Pérez, Leopoldo, 1957-

BX1795.P72P74 2004 2005
261.8'088'282--dc22   2003066550

Distribution:

University of Scranton Press
Chicago Distribution Center
11030 S. Langley
Chicago IL 60628

PRINTED IN THE UNITED STATES OF AMERICA

CONTENTS

ACKNOWLEDGEMENTS

The most pleasant part of publishing is thanking those who make it possible. In addition to our essayists, we also thank the ACTA Foundation for funding this book. We are also grateful to the Instituto Nacional Hispano de Litúrgia for their support, and particularly their former executive director Doris Turek, SSND. Daniel Grippo and Richard W. Rousseau, S.J., also deserve our thanks. Of course, it is also an honor to publish the preface of Walter Burghardt, S.J.

We appreciate as well the kind permission of the United States Conference of Catholic Bishops (USCCB) publishing office to reprint these documents of the local church. Those documents are reprinted here with permission and the USCCB retains sole copyrights. The documents may not be reproduced by any means without the explicit permission of the USCCB.

Our respective religious communities and schools, as well as colleagues, have also been most generous and deserve recognition. Finally and foremost, we thank God for the Word Incarnate served by the teaching of the Church. We dedicate this volume to those who serve that Word by preaching the teaching.

PREFACE

I t is almost anticlimactic to say that Hispanics are fast becoming the majority of the Catholic Church of the United States. The 1990 census data and the recent document of the United States Conference of Catholic Bishops (USCCB) *Encuentro y Mission* repeat this axiom. Yet few preachers have carefully considered the phenomenon. And that is why I am delighted to introduce this book.

Since 1983 the church in the United States has called the Hispanic presence a blessing and a challenge. Hispanics represent a linguistic challenge since most speak Spanish, the language of the first Catholics to reach our shores, but still an idiom unfamiliar to most of our preachers. They represent a cultural challenge since they come from twenty-one different mainland countries as well as the Caribbean, each of which bears vestiges of the Iberian Catholicism of the late middle ages, indigenous rituals from the great civilizations of the Aztecs, Mayas, and Incas, as well as the spirituality imported along with the human cargo of the nefarious slave trade. Moreover, Hispanics are at very different stages of acculturation. Some have just crossed the Rio Grande without documents; others are in corporate boardrooms with privilege and power. And finally, Hispanics are a very young community. As our priests age, there is a growing gap between them and young Catholics, an age group which Hispanics are dominating most rapidly.

More importantly, however, Hispanics represent a great blessing for our local church. In their lands was born the first autogenic theology that responded to the wisdom of the Second Vatican Council. Liberation theology reminded the church of the central place of the poor in Scripture as well as in the writings of the post-Apostolic age. In their lands also was born a new way of being church, namely, base communities. Parishes are restructuring around the domestic church and that results in preachers and other leaders necessarily confronting the consequences of faith in the plaza and the marketplace. Finally, Hispanics conserve a Catholic imagination dramatized in their lively devotional life. Their faith is not a private prayer confined to a sanctuary; their faith storms the streets with the Christmas posadas, invades the public square with the Lenten Santo Via Crucis, and bears

xi

witness to its martyrs through candles and *retablos* constantly accompanying the tomb of Oscar Romero.

Preachers in the United States have something to learn from such a faith. And that is why this book was written. The intent of this volume is two-fold. First, to aid and encourage the preacher to proclaim the social justice teaching of our church to an Hispanic congregation in such a way as to instruct and motivate. Second, to help that same preacher listen to the proclamation of the Word found in the Hispanic community's tale of survival and even joy in the face of oppression and migration. In this way, the preacher, like the assembly to which he preaches, will be both a challenge and a blessing.

Walter J. Burghardt, S.J.

INTRODUCTION

O f all the phrases of the Spanish language, one of my favorites is "Están en su casa (you are in your home)." This saying not only conveys to people that they should feel welcome and as comfortable as they would in their own homes, but it also communicates on an emotional level the gracious hospitality of the Hispanic culture. Oh, that the homilies of our Latino parishes would make Hispanics feel so welcome and at home in our churches! And what if we could also foster, along with our gracious welcome, a formation in the social teaching of the church? The result might be the inculturation of our preaching in the lives of our communities, furthering the church's social mission.

Those in the pews are placing increasing emphasis on the homilist's message, voicing a demand for good preaching to accompany religious services. Hispanics are among those groups asking for homilies that speak to their daily lives and aspirations. Also a sign of the present times is the church's prophetic call for gospel themes of social justice to be incorporated into the liturgy (see *Communities of Salt and Light* in this volume). It is therefore with immense hope that we publish this work to help meet the needs of pastors, deacons, and all who prepare homilies for Hispanic congregations.

Catholic social teaching has been called one of the church's best-kept secrets. Our episcopal documents make excellent use of Scripture, doctrine, and social analysis. These are strong messages which advocate on behalf of the poor and marginalized, and deserve to be known and explained to the person in the pew. The purpose of this current book is to offer examples of how to incorporate some of these teachings into our preaching, especially to a Hispanic audience.

To this aim, we have reprinted seven United States Conference of Catholic Bishops documents that deserve to be addressed in U.S. Hispanic parishes. Our choice of these and not others is a limitation of the scale of this present book. The themes we present here include: the Gospel of Life, domestic violence, the social mission of the parish, capital punishment, the economy, racism, and immigration. Some of the finest Hispanic theologians working in the U.S. address these topics from the homilist's perspective. They offer insights into how such messages can be pastorally presented within a Latino community. The chapters by Elizondo, Erevia, and Gonzalez are modifications of presentations first offered at a conference sponsored by the Instituto de Liturgia Hispana entitled *Predicando la Enseñanza/Preaching the Teaching: Preaching the Social Justice Documents of the Church in the Hispanic Context*, held at the Oblate Renewal Center, San Antonio, Texas during February 1998. The other chapters were written by the authors specifically for this book.

The chapters are presented along with the corresponding pastorals and statements of the USCCB. *Living the Gospel of Life: A Challenge to American Catholics* 1998 is addressed by Rev. Arturo Pérez–Rodriguez. *When I Call for Help: A Pastoral Response to Domestic Violence Against Women* (Tenth Anniversary Edition, 2002) is taken up by Most Rev. Ricardo Ramírez of Las Cruces, New Mexico. *Communities of Salt and Light: Reflections on the Social Mission of the Parish* (1994) is addressed by Jorge Presmanes, O.P., and Mark Wedig, O.P. Rev. José Rubio looks at the *Statement on Capital Punishment* (1980). Sr. Angela Erevia, MCDP, spoke on the topic of the economy at the 1998 conference, and her presentation has been translated, edited, and included with the USCCB's *A Decade After "Economic Justice for All": Continuing Principles, Changing Context, New Challenges.* The Most Rev. Roberto González, Archbishop of San Juan, Puerto Rico has allowed us to include a translation of an address he gave at the conference on racism while he was Bishop of Corpus Christi, TX, and we have coupled this with the Bishops' *For the Love of One Another: Special Message on the Occasion of the Tenth Anniversary of Brothers and Sisters to Us* (1989). Rev. Virgil Elizondo's presentation on immigration from the conference has also been translated and is paired with *Welcoming the Stranger Among Us* (2000).

The Lectionary and certain holidays and feast days offer many opportunities to incorporate the social teaching of the church into our liturgies. For this reason, we asked Rev. Jose Lopez to write on each document from the perspective of the Lectionary, suggesting specific Lectionary texts that lend themselves to each document covered. Rev. Raúl Gómez, S.D.S. performed a similar contribution by writing on each document, relating them to civil or liturgical feasts of importance to Latinos. We have also included a general Bibliography to help those who wish to explore the respective subjects in more depth. The Bibliography includes many of the valuable but under-used works which address these topics.

I often hear from homilists that they run out of ideas on how to break open the theme of God's justice when addressing Hispanic congregations. A fresh approach is sometimes well within our reach, if we only know where to turn. It is hoped that this volume will lead preachers to find new reservoirs of creativity in proclaiming God's blessing on those who hunger and thirst for justice. There can be few more privileged moments to do this than in the Church's liturgy.

Leopoldo Pérez, OMI

CHAPTER I

Capital Punishment

United States Bishops' Statement on Capital Punishment
United States Catholic Conference

In 1974, out of a commitment to the value and dignity of human life, the U.S. Catholic Conference, by a substantial majority, voted to declare its opposition to capital punishment. As a former president of the National Conference of Catholic Bishops pointed out in 1977, the issue of capital punishment involves both "profound legal and political questions" as well as "important moral and religious issues."[1] And so we find that this issue continues to provoke public controversy and to raise moral questions that trouble many. This is particularly true in the aftermath of widely publicized executions in Utah and Florida, and as a result of public realization that there are now over 500 persons awaiting execution in various prisons in our country.

The resumption of capital punishment after a long moratorium, which began in 1967, is the result of a series of decisions by the United States Supreme Court. In the first of these decisions, *Furman v. Georgia* (1972), the Court held that the death penalty as then administered did constitute cruel and unusual punishment and so was contrary to the Eighth Amendment to the Constitution. Subsequently in 1976 the Court upheld death sentences imposed under state statutes which had been revised by state legislatures in the hope of meeting the Court's requirement that the death penalty not be imposed arbitrarily. These cases and the ensuing revision of state and federal statutes gave rise to extended public debate over the necessity and advisability of retaining the death penalty. We should note that much of this debate was carried on in a time of intense public concern over crime and violence. For instance, in 1976 alone, over 18,000 people were murdered in the United States. Criticism of the inadequacies of the criminal justice system has been widespread, even while spectacular crimes have spread fear and alarm, particularly in urban areas. All these factors make it particularly necessary that Christians form

1

their views on this difficult matter in a prayerful and reflective way, and that they show a respect and concern for the rights of all.

We should acknowledge that in the public debate over capital punishment we are dealing with values of the highest importance: respect for the sanctity of human life, the protection of human life, the preservation of order in society, and the achievement of justice through law. In confronting the problem of serious and violent crime in our society, we want to protect the lives and the sense of security both of those members of society who may become the victims of crime and of those in the police and in the law enforcement system who run greater risks. In doing this, however, we must bear in mind that crime is both a manifestation of the great mysteries of evil and human freedom and an aspect of the very complex reality that is contemporary society. We should not expect simple or easy solutions to what is a profound evil, and even less should we rely on capital punishment to provide such a solution. Rather, we must look to the claims of justice as these are understood in the current debate and to the example and teaching of Jesus, whom we acknowledge as the Justice of God.

I. Purposes of Punishment

Allowing for the fact that Catholic teaching has accepted the principle that the state has the right to take the life of a person guilty of an extremely serious crime, and that the state may take appropriate measures to protect itself and its citizens from grave harm, nevertheless, the question for judgment and decision today is whether capital punishment is justifiable under present circumstances. Punishment, since it involves the deliberate infliction of evil on another, is always in need of justification. This has normally taken the form of indicating some good which is to be obtained through punishment or an evil which is to be warded off. The three justifications traditionally advanced for punishment in general are retribution, deterrence, and reform.

Reform or rehabilitation of the criminal cannot serve as a justification for capital punishment, which necessarily deprives the criminal of the opportunity to develop a new way of life that conforms to the norms of society and that contributes to the common good. It may be granted that the imminence of capital punishment may induce repentance in the criminal, but we should certainly not think that this threat is somehow necessary for God's grace to touch and to transform human hearts.

The deterrence of actual or potential criminals from future deeds of violence by the threat of death is also advanced as a justifying objective of punishment. While it is certain that capital punishment prevents the individual from committing further crimes, it is far from certain that it actually prevents others from doing so. Empirical studies in this area have not given conclusive evidence that would justify the imposition of the death penalty on a few individuals as a means of preventing others from committing crimes. There are strong reasons to doubt that many crimes of violence are undertaken in a spirit of rational calculation which would be influenced by a remote threat of death. The small number of death sentences in relation to the number of murders also makes it seem highly unlikely that the threat will be carried out, and so undercuts the effectiveness of the deterrent.

The protection of society and its members from violence, to which the deterrent effect of punishment is supposed to contribute, is a value of central and abiding importance; and we urge the need for prudent firmness in ensuring the safety of innocent citizens. It is important to remember that the preservation of order in times of civil disturbance does not depend on the institution of capital punishment, the imposition of which rightly requires a lengthy and complex process in our legal system. Moreover, both in its nature as legal penalty and in its practical consequences, capital punishment is different from the taking of life in legitimate self-defense or in defense of society.

The third justifying purpose for punishment is retribution or the restoration of the order of justice which has been violated by the action of the criminal. We grant that the need for retribution does indeed justify punishment. For the practice of punishment both presupposes a previous transgression against the law and involves the involuntary deprivation of certain goods. But we maintain that this need does not require, nor does it justify, taking the life of the criminal, even in cases of murder. We must not remain unmindful of the example of Jesus, who urges upon us a teaching of forbearance in the face of evil (Matthew 5:38–42) and forgiveness of injuries (Matthew 18:21–35). It is morally unsatisfactory and socially destructive for criminals to go unpunished, but the forms and limits of punishment must be determined by moral objectives which go beyond the mere inflicting of injury on the guilty. Thus we would regard it as barbarous and inhumane for a criminal who had tortured or maimed a victim to be tortured or maimed in return. Such a punishment might satisfy certain vindictive desires that we or the victim might feel, but the satisfaction of such desires is not and cannot be an objective of a humane and Christian approach to punishment. We believe that the forms of punishment must be determined with a view to the protection of society and its members, and to the reformation of the criminal and his reintegration into society (which may not be possible in certain cases). This position accords with the general norm for punishment proposed by St. Thomas Aquinas when he wrote:

> In this life, however, penalties are not sought for their own sake, because this is not the era of retribution; rather, they are meant to be corrective by being conducive either to the reform of the sinner or the good of society, which becomes more peaceful through the punishment of sinners.[2]

We believe that in the conditions of contemporary American society, the legitimate purposes of punishment do not justify the imposition of the death penalty. Furthermore, we believe that there are serious considerations which should prompt Christians and all Americans to support the abolition of capital punishment. Some of these reasons have to do with evils that are present in the practice of capital punishment itself, while others involve important values that would be promoted by abolition of this practice.

II. Christian Values in the Abolition of Capital Punishment

We maintain that abolition of the death penalty would promote values that are important to us as citizens and as Christians. First, abolition sends a message that we can break the cycle of violence, that we need not take life for life, that we can envisage more humane and more hopeful and effective responses to the growth of violent crime. It is a manifestation of our freedom as moral persons striving for a just society. It is also a challenge to us as a people to find ways of dealing with criminals that manifest intelligence and compassion, rather than power and vengeance. We should feel such confidence in our civic order that we use no more force against those who violate it than is actually required.

Second, abolition of capital punishment is also a manifestation of our belief in the unique worth and dignity of each person from the moment of conception, a creature made in the image and likeness of

God. It is particularly important in the context of our times that this belief be affirmed with regard to those who have failed or whose lives have been distorted by suffering or hatred, even in the case of those who by their actions have failed to respect the dignity and rights of others. It is the recognition of the dignity of all human beings that has impelled the Church to minister to the needs of the outcast and the rejected, and that should make us unwilling to treat the lives of even those who have taken human life as expendable or as a means to some further end.

Third, abolition of the death penalty is further testimony to our conviction, a conviction which we share with the Judaic and Islamic traditions, that God is indeed the Lord of Life. It is a testimony which removes a certain ambiguity which might otherwise affect the witness that we wish to give to the sanctity of human life in all its stages. We do not wish to equate the situation of criminals convicted of capital offenses with the condition of the innocent unborn or of the defenseless aged or infirm, but we do believe that the defense of life is strengthened by eliminating exercise of a judicial authorization to take human life.

Fourth, we believe that abolition of the death penalty is most consonant with the example of Jesus, who both taught and practiced the forgiveness of injustice and who came "to give his life as a ransom for many" (Mark 10:45). In this regard we may point to the reluctance which those early Christians who accepted capital punishment as a legitimate practice in civil society felt about the participation of Christians in such an institution[3] and to the unwillingness of the Church to accept into the ranks of its ministers those who had been involved in the infliction of capital punishment.[4] There is and has been a certain sense that even in those cases where serious justifications can be offered for the necessity of taking life, those who are identified in a special way with Christ should refrain from taking life. We believe that this should be taken as an indication of the deeper desires of the Church as it responds to the story of God's redemptive and forgiving love as manifest in the life of his Son.

III. Difficulties Inherent in Capital Punishment

With respect to the difficulties inherent in capital punishment, we note first that infliction of the death penalty extinguishes possibilities for reform and rehabilitation for the person executed, as well as the opportunity for the criminal to make some creative compensation for the evil he or she has done. It also cuts off the possibility for a new beginning and of moral growth in a human life which has been seriously deformed.

Second, the imposition of capital punishment involves the possibility of mistake. In this respect, it is not different from other legal processes; and it must be granted our legal system shows considerable care for the rights of defendants in capital cases. But the possibility of mistake cannot be eliminated from the system. Because death terminates the possibilities of conversion and growth and support that we can share with each other, we regard a mistaken infliction of the death penalty with a special horror, even while we retain our trust in God's loving mercy.

Third, the legal imposition of capital punishment in our society involves long and unavoidable delays. This is in large part a consequence of the safeguards and the opportunities for appeal which the law provides for defendants; but it also creates a long period of anxiety and uncertainty both about the possibility of life and about the necessity of reorienting one's life. Delay also diminishes the effectiveness of capital punishment as a deterrent, for it makes the death penalty uncertain and remote. Death row can be the scene of conversion and spiritual growth, but it also produces aimlessness, fear, and despair.

Fourth, we believe that the actual carrying out of the death penalty brings with it great and avoidable anguish for the criminal, for his family and loved ones, and for those who are called on to perform or to witness the execution. Great writers such as Shakespeare and Dostoyevsky in the past and Camus and Orwell in our time have given us vivid pictures of the terrors of execution not merely for the victim but also for bystanders.[5]

Fifth, in the present situation of dispute over the justifiability of the death penalty and at a time when executions have been rare, executions attract enormous publicity, much of it unhealthy, and stir considerable acrimony in public discussion. On the other hand, if a substantial proportion of the more than five hundred persons now under sentence of death are executed, a great public outcry can safely be predicted. In neither case is the American public likely to develop a sense that the work of justice is being done with fairness and rationality.

Sixth, there is a widespread belief that many convicted criminals are sentenced to death in an unfair and discriminatory manner. This belief can be affirmed with certain qualifications. There is a certain presumption that if specific evidence of bias or discrimination in sentencing can be provided for particular cases, then higher courts will not uphold sentences of death in these cases. But we must also reckon with a legal system which, while it does provide counsel for indigent defendants, permits those who are well-off to obtain the resources and the talent to present their case in as convincing a light as possible. The legal system and the criminal justice system both work in a society which bears in its psychological, social, and economic patterns the marks of racism. These marks remain long after the demolition of segregation as a legal institution. The end result of all this is a situation in which those condemned to die are nearly always poor and are disproportionately black.[6] Thus, 47 percent of the inmates on death row are black, whereas only 11 percent of the American population is black. Abolition of the death penalty will not eliminate racism and its effects, an evil which we are called on to combat in many different ways. But it is a reasonable judgment that racist attitudes and the social consequences of racism have some influence in determining who is sentenced to die in our society. This we do not regard as acceptable.

IV. Conclusions

We do not propose the abolition of capital punishment as a simple solution to the problems of crime and violence. As we observed earlier, we do not believe that any simple and comprehensive solution is possible. We affirm that there is a special need to offer sympathy and support for the victims of violent crime and their families. Our society should not flinch from contemplating the suffering that violent crime brings to so many when it destroys lives, shatters families, and crushes the hopes of the innocent. Recognition of this suffering should not lead to demands for vengeance, but to a firm resolution that help be given to the victims of crime and that justice be done fairly and swiftly. The care and the support that we give to the victims of crime should be both compassionate and practical. The public response to crime should include the relief of financial distress caused by crime and the provision of medical and psychological treatment to the extent that these are required and helpful. It is the special responsibility of the Church to provide a community of faith and trust in which God's grace can heal the personal and spiritual wounds caused by crime and in which we can all grow by sharing one another's burdens and sorrows.

We insist that important changes are necessary in the correctional system in order to make it truly conducive to the reform and rehabilitation of convicted criminals and their reintegration into society.[7] We also grant that special precautions should be taken to ensure the safety of those who guard convicts who are too dangerous to return to society. We call on governments to cooperate in vigorous measures against terrorists who threaten the safety of the general public and who take the lives of the innocent. We acknowledge that there is a pressing need to deal with those social conditions of poverty and injustice which often provide the breeding grounds for serious crime. We urge particularly the importance of restricting the easy availability of guns and other weapons of violence. We oppose the glamorizing of violence in entertainment, and we deplore the effect of this on children. We affirm the need for education to promote respect for the human dignity of all people. All of these things should form part of a comprehensive community response to the very real and pressing problems presented by the prevalence of crime and violence in many parts of our society.

We recognize that many citizens may believe that capital punishment should be maintained as an integral part of our society's response to the evils of crime, nor is this position incompatible with Catholic tradition. We acknowledge the depth and the sincerity of their concern. We urge them to review the considerations we have offered which show both the evils associated with capital punishment and the harmony of the abolition of capital punishment with the values of the Gospel. We urge them to bear in mind that public decisions in this area affect the lives, the hopes, and the fears of men and women who share both the misery and the grandeur of human life with us and who, like us, are among those sinners whom the Son of Man came to save.

We urge our brothers and sisters in Christ to remember the teaching of Jesus who called us to be reconciled with those who have injured us (Matthew 5:43–45) and to pray for forgiveness for our sins "as we forgive those who have sinned against us" (Matthew 6:12). We call on you to contemplate the crucified Christ who set us the supreme example of forgiveness and of the triumph of compassionate love.

NOTES

[1] *Statement on Capital Punishment*, Archbishop Joseph L. Bernardin, President National Conference of Catholic Bishops, January 26, 1977. Cf. *Community and Crime*, Statement of the Committee on Social Development and World Peace, United States Catholic Conference, February 15, 1978, p. 8.

[2] Thomas Aquinas, *Summa Theologiæ*, II–II, 68, 1; tr. Marcus Lefebure, O.P. (London: Blackfriars, 1975).

[3] Tertullian, *De Idolatria*, c. 17.

[4] *Code of Canon Law*, Canon 984.

[5] William Shakespeare, *Measure for Measure*, Act II, Scene 1; Fyodor Dostoyevsky, *The Idiot*; George Orwell, "A Hanging"; Albert Camus, "Reflections on the Guillotine."

[6] Cf. Charles Black, Jr., *Capital Punishment* (New York: Norton, 1974), pp. 84–91.

[7] Cf. *The Reform of Correctional Institutions in the 1970s*, Statement of the United States Catholic Conference, November 1973.

Reflections on the Bishops' Statement
on Capital Punishment

José Antonio Rubio

Currently, a significant debate is taking place in the public arena that involves religious leaders, the arts, the media, the courts, the polls, politicians, and the general public. But, although the issue deeply affects the Latino community, Latino voices are not prominent in this debate. I am referring to the debate over the use of capital punishment in this country.

The issue, which has been in the press for the past few years, gained more prominence after the September 11 terrorist attacks. But in reality the issue was already in the public forum. Some three years ago, former Governor George Ryan of Illinois called for a moratorium on the death penalty in his state. The following year, U.S. Supreme Court Justice Sandra Day O'Connor questioned the fairness of the death penalty, citing the growing number of cases that involved unqualified trial lawyers. (Nationwide, two of every three death sentences are so flawed that an appellate court overturns them.)

Two decisions by the U.S. Supreme Court in June 2002 once again brought the issue to the fore. The first decision, by a 6–3 majority, ruled against the execution of mentally retarded offenders; it could affect about 200 inmates. The second was a 7–2 decision declaring it unconstitutional for judges, rather than jurors, to impose the death sentence. This decision affects over 800 inmates in nine states where judges decide who should die, including Florida, Arizona, and Colorado, which have significant Latino populations. Most recently, a dissenting opinion in August 2002 by three Supreme Court justices questioned the constitutionality of imposing the death penalty on people who committed capital crimes while juveniles. Currently, about 80 inmates are on death row for crimes committed at 16 or 17 years of age. All told, there are about 3,700 people on death row in this country, including 54 women.

But this is not just a debate going on in the courts. It is going on in the popular culture as well. Two recent movies have contributed to this debate. One is *The Green Mile* and the other is *Dead Man Walking.* This last movie was based on the work and book of Sr. Helen Prejean, C.S.J. It even has been made into a highly acclaimed opera with music by Jake Heggie and text by Terrence McNally, bringing the issue not only to moviegoers but also to opera lovers.

Most importantly, this is a debate going on in the streets, even among strangers. My car has a bumper sticker that reads, "The Death Penalty is Dead Wrong." In December 2001, with September 11 still on people's minds, I took my car to a garage for an oil change. The mechanic read my bumper sticker aloud and said, "Surely you don't mean that to apply to Osama bin Laden, do you?" We got into a discussion about the death penalty right there in the garage. And while polls show that a majority of the people in this country still supports capital punishment, they also indicate that this support is eroding. Momentum is growing to address the issue, and sentiment is evolving to abolish it.

We may well wonder where the Christian voice is on the issue. The Catholic voice in the United States on the morality of the death penalty has been heard at least since 1974, when the U.S. Catholic Conference first voted to declare its opposition to capital punishment. Since then, the U.S. Bishops have issued several significant statements. In November 1980 the Conference issued the *U.S. Bishops' Statement on Capital Punishment.* In 1999, the statement *A Good Friday Appeal to End the Death Penalty* appeared. The 2000 Bishops' Statement on Criminal Justice, *Responsibility, Rehabilitation, and Restoration: A Catholic Perspective on Crime and Criminal Justice*, reiterated the bishops' opposition to the death penalty.

Many state conferences have also issued statements. For example, in 1985 the California Catholic Conference issued its statement, *A Call to Discipleship*, reissued in 1989. All told, over 150 bishops' conferences and individual bishops in this country have issued statements on the death penalty, as have many religious orders of both women and men. The Catholic voice is also heard through the work of Sr. Helen Prejean and through the Holy Father, both in his encyclical letter, *The Gospel of Life*, (*Evangelium Vitæ*) and in his highly publicized appeals for clemency for individual convicts. Among these was the appeal during his January 1999 visit to St. Louis, where he persuaded Missouri Governor Mel Carnahan to commute the sentence of a condemned man. Since then, the Holy Father, through the

Papal Nuncio, has been writing to governors of every state before each execution and pleading with them to reconsider.

Most of the statements that have been issued follow the arguments put forth in the *U.S. Bishops' Statement on Capital Punishment* of November 1980. This statement begins by declaring the bishops' intention to apply "the example and teaching of Jesus" to the issue (2). It affirms that Catholic teaching has always accepted the death penalty in principle, but wonders whether it is justifiable under the present circumstances (3). This is consistent with our understanding of what it means to be a Christian: to take the teachings of Jesus and apply them to our situation, which may be very different from what it was in the time of Jesus. The bishops conclude, "we believe that in the conditions of contemporary American society, the legitimate purposes of punishment do not justify the imposition of the death penalty"(5).

The bishops cite several important Christian values that would be preserved by the abolition of capital punishment. First, abolishing capital punishment would "break the cycle of violence"(7). The bishops aver that order cannot come from violence, and that violence can never be suppressed with more violence. Violence can only breed more violence and at some point the cycle has to be broken. The second Christian value that would be served by abolishing capital punishment is the dignity of the human person. "It is particularly important," the bishops declare, "that this belief be affirmed with regard to those who have failed . . . "(7). The third important value is "the sanctity of all human life in all its stages." Vital to a Catholic opposition to abortion is a consistent life ethic that opposes the taking of all human life in all instances. Finally, they argue that working to abolish capital punishment is "most consonant with the example of Jesus"(8).

The bishops then go on to cite several difficulties inherent in the administration of capital punishment. Among them is the possibility of error. This is particularly important for us today, when DNA testing has resulted in at least 100 death row inmates being acquitted. This raises a further problem: what is an appropriate level of error in the taking of a human life?

Another difficulty that was cited in the statement is the unavoidable anguish for the family and loved ones of the convicted criminals. If capital punishment is not "cruel and unusual punishment" for the convict, is it not so for his or her family and loved ones, who have committed no crime? I am often asked, "How would you feel if a loved one were murdered? Wouldn't you want the person who killed your loved one executed?" I usually reply, "How would you feel, God forbid, if your son were convicted of murder? Would you want your child executed?"

Capital punishment is not just a Catholic issue; this is an important ecumenical and interfaith issue as well. Official statements opposing the death penalty have been issued by the American Baptist Churches in the U.S.A., the Christian Church (Disciples of Christ), the Church of the Brethren, the Episcopal Church, the Evangelical Lutheran Church, the Mennonite Church, the Moravian Church in America, the Orthodox Church in America, the Presbyterian Church (U.S.A.), the Reformed Church in America, the Reorganized Church of Jesus Christ of the Latter Day Saints, the United Church of Christ, the United Methodist Church, and the National Council of the Churches of Christ in the U.S.A.

Fruitful ecumenical and interfaith dialogue on the local level could be based on a study of these various statements, along with the Catholic statements. In December 1999 the National Jewish/Catholic Consultation, which includes the National Conference of Catholic Bishops and the National Council of Synagogues, issued a statement agreeing to work together to end the death penalty. The eloquent statement could easily form the basis of a local Catholic-Jewish dialogue.

Like the bishops' statements, the Jewish/Catholic statement also acknowledges that the Scriptures mandate capital punishment for certain offenses. We need to look at this point seriously for two important reasons. First, care needs to be taken to avoid any type of "death penalty snobbery," that is, those of us who oppose the death penalty cannot have an attitude of moral superiority over those who support it. Sincere Christians can disagree. So the question is not whether it is wrong to support the death penalty, but whether the Holy Spirit is leading us to a new understanding of the Scriptures today.

This brings us to the second reason to look at Scripture's mandate of capital punishment; we cannot ignore the Biblical tradition. It becomes important, then, to acknowledge that the Hebrew Scriptures, what we call the Old Testament, clearly endorse capital punishment, but that the Christian Scriptures, the New Testament, are actually silent on the point. If anything, they call for clemency. Matthew 5:38–45, Jesus' commentary on the law of the talion, is one example, as is the petition in the Our Father, "Forgive us . . . as we forgive others." The parable of the unforgiving servant that follows Jesus' admonition to forgive not seven times but seventy times seven (Matthew 18:21–35) is still another. These examples are all cited in the *U.S. Bishops' Statement*.

There is talk of punishment for murders in the New Testament— in two parables of judgment—but it's "the King," that is, God who punishes. In the parable of the wicked tenants we read, "He [the King, God] will bring the wicked crowd to a bad end" (Matthew 21:41, cf. Mark 12:9 and Luke 20:16). The parable of the wedding banquet says, "At this the King grew furious and sent his army to destroy those murderers and burn their city" (Matthew 22:7). In the Book of Revelation there is punishment for murders, but it will be meted out by the "One who sits on the throne," i.e., God. God will send them to "the fiery pool of burning sulfur" (Revelation 21:8), and they will be outside the city (22:15). Yet even behind these words of condemnation, we hear Jesus' last words on the cross: "Father, forgive them; they do not know what they are doing" (Luke 23:34). And we ask ourselves, "Where is the Holy Spirit leading us?"

At one time, no one questioned the morality of slavery. The whole Bible took it for granted, both the Hebrew Scriptures and the New Testament. Yet no one today would say that God approves of slavery. It would seem that the Holy Spirit has moved us beyond the biblical acceptance of slavery to an understanding that it is contrary to God's will. Could the Holy Spirit be moving us beyond the biblical acceptance of capital punishment? After all, Christians are the followers of an innocent victim of capital punishment, imposed by both the civil and religious authorities of his day. Peter, Paul—and how many others whom we see as saints and martyrs today—were victims of capital punishment imposed by the civil authorities of their day.

One hundred and six nations do not allow the death penalty today; 30 have abolished it since 1990. Pope John Paul II, the Catechism of the Catholic Church, and the U.S. bishops all question whether the application of the death penalty is morally justifiable today. As Catholics, we affirm the sanctity of life from the moment of conception to its natural end for all human beings. All this has led many people to consider that even if the death penalty were applied equally to all racial, ethnic, and economic groups, and even if only the guilty were executed, it would still be morally unjustifiable today.

Latinos are painfully aware that a disproportionate number of Latinos are on death row in this country. We are also aware that the countries of Latin America do not permit the death penalty. We also realize that many of us are not U.S. citizens. However, non citizens can still help form public opinion. We can still participate in the debate at work, in our parishes, in garages. We can say that in our countries of origin we do not have the death penalty and that we do not have more murders than in this country. When someone asks us how we would feel if our child was murdered, we can answer by asking how they would feel if their child were sentenced to die. And, most importantly, we can say that capital punishment is a moral issue that needs to be seen in the light of the teachings of our Church and in the light of the teaching and example of Christ.

When we talk among ourselves, we help form public opinion, and as public opinion forms, laws are changed. We can participate in the debate. We can be part of a growing movement that seeks to address the issue of capital punishment, and of an evolving sentiment to abolish it, a sentiment that may well be where the Spirit is calling us as followers of a victim of capital punishment.

Statement on Capital Punishment (1980)
Suggestions for Civil/Liturgical Occasions

Rev. Raúl Gómez

This statement addresses the themes of the sanctity of human life, its protection, the preservation of order, justice through law, and retribution. Though the number of civil occasions lending themselves to preaching on these themes is limited, a number of liturgical occasions provide an opportunity for approaching the topic of capital punishment and the themes of this statement.

The anniversaries of the Oklahoma City bombing and the attacks of September 11 are occasions for addressing the topic of retribution. Particularly worth considering are those times when the debate on capital punishment is evident in the public forum, be it in newspapers, news programs, or legislative sessions. Pending executions are especially fitting times to deal with retribution.

Because the events surrounding Christ's Passion and execution on the cross provide fit starting points, Holy Week is liturgically the most opportune time to address the themes of this statement. For example, the seven last words of Christ on Good Friday, or a *pésame a la virgen* service, when participants ritually express their condolences to the Virgin who has lost her son, can call for preaching on capital punishment. In addition, the memorial of the martyrdom of John the Baptist, the feasts of the Holy Cross (September 14), Our Lady of Sorrows (September 15), Saint Lawrence (August 10), and the Solemnities of the Body and Blood of Christ and of Christ the King also provide openings.

Statement on Capital Punishment
Suggested LectionaryTexts

Rev. José A. López

Reference: United States Conference of Catholic Bishops, Lectionary for Mass, Second Typical Edition, Vol. I–IV. Chicago: Liturgy Training Publications, 2002.

Texts

IV:938	Lamentations 3:17–26
IV:939–1	Romans 8:18–30
IV:939–2	Romans 8:31b–39
IV:939–4	Revelation 21:1–5a, 6b–7
II:365	Matthew 5:38–42
II:380	Matthew 9:1–8
I:130	Matthew 18:21–35

These Scripture texts call the community to reflect on their response to God's love toward creation. The bishops urge all to consider that:

> public decisions in this area affect the lives, the hopes and the fears of men and women who share both the misery and the grandeur of human life with us and who, like us, are among those sinners whom the Son of Man came to save. (U.S. Bishops' Statement on Capital Punishment, pg. 12)

In the Hispanic community, the preacher's task is to bring to the people those hopes and fears of the families facing the death of a loved one. Often poor, with little resources, they depend on the community for sustenance. If the community is to be aware and to be able to respond, the preacher cannot but bring this concern to all. Hope is not the province of a few. Hope is extended to all, especially to families who have no other option but their brothers and sisters. "And hoping for what we cannot see means awaiting it with patient endurance" (Rom 8:25).

CHAPTER II

For the Love of One Another

For the Love of One Another: A Special Message on the Occasion of the Tenth Anniversary of Brothers and Sisters to Us

Bishops' Committee on Black Catholics
National Conference of Catholic Bishops
September 1989

In November 1984, the Most Reverend Joseph A. Francis, S.V.D., presented the following statement to the bishops of the United States during their fall meeting:

"November 1984 marked the fifth anniversary of the promulgation of the pastoral on racism, *Brothers and Sisters to Us*, by the Catholic Bishops of the United States. Having been intimately involved in the production and issuance of that pastoral letter, I feel that it is proper for me to reflect on the past five years in the light of the pastoral on racism.

"It would be comforting to millions of people of all races if it could relate that the pastoral on racism has made a significant difference in the racial attitudes and practices of sisters and brothers in the Catholic Church in the United States. I fear that it has not. In fact, I have often called it the 'best kept secret in the U.S. Church.' Had our words been taken seriously by clergy, religious, and laity, millions of Blacks and other racial minorities in our country and perhaps around the world would really have something to celebrate on this fifth anniversary. How encouraged we would be if this pastoral on racism had received the attention accorded the pastoral on war and peace, also issued by the conference of bishops.

"The pastoral on racism speaks of devastation of peoples of the past, the present, and the future. The pastoral on war and peace speaks to us of a devastation not yet upon us, but close enough and possible enough to move the entire nation and even the world to action on behalf of peace. Yet both pastorals speak to the dignity of individuals and groups of human beings. Both pastorals have to do with survival and dignity. Both pastorals flow from the same concern for the sanctity of life. The important message of the pastoral on racism is that racism is a sin and racism is a reality in our country and within our Church. As difficult as it may be for one to envision, we may well be faced with the terrible truth that the finger on the trigger of nuclear war is that of racism. Survival in the wake of a nuclear war, if this is possible, will surely be conditioned by racism. It is inconceivable that people denied their rights in normal times and under somewhat favorable conditions will enjoy any rights at all in a time of national global chaos if they happen to be Black.

"A positive celebration for this fifth anniversary of the pastoral *Brothers and Sisters to Us* could lead us to reflect seriously on our relationship as sisters and brothers, with God as our Father and Jesus as our Brother. A fitting celebration would be to take up the pastoral on racism and make it a lived reality in our homes, churches, and communities. It is not too late to seek out and isolate the terrible virus of racism in our midst. To do so would place us squarely in the center of a fight for life. Racism is anti-life. Racism is anti-Christian. For the past five years, I have reflected daily on the final paragraph of the pastoral on racism. I have concluded every major address of the last five years with the words of that final paragraph:

> There must be no turning back along the road of justice,
> no sighing for bygone times of privilege, no nostalgia for
> simple solutions from another age. For we are children of
> the age to come, when the first shall be last and the last
> first, when blessed are they who serve Christ the Lord in
> all his brothers and sisters, especially those who are poor
> and suffer injustice.[1]

Five years later in 1989, we were delighted to receive the Pontifical Justice and Peace Commission's document, *The Church and Racism: Towards a More Fraternal Society*. We read and reread certain sections and felt that our message—the message of the American bishops, which has been like "voices crying in the wilderness" and literally "proclaimed from the roof tops" for such a long time—was now being proclaimed forthrightly and unapologetically by the pope's own Commission on Justice and Peace in 1989. There is a powerful, providential, perhaps even prophetic message in the timing of this document for the Church in the United States. The pontifical statement on racism comes just ten years after the National Conference of Catholic Bishops issued our own pastoral on racism entitled *Brothers and Sisters to Us: U.S. Bishops' Pastoral Letter on Racism in Our*

Day, which the pontifical document on racism calls "the most important document of the last decade."[2] That pontifical statement arouses in us feelings of joy and pride, but also of sadness.

In September 1976, at the Call to Action Convocation in Detroit, our brother bishop, Archbishop Eugene A. Marino, S.S.J., of Atlanta read a resolution calling for the National Conference of Catholic Bishops to issue a pastoral statement on the sin of racism in the Church and in society. While many Catholics express dissatisfaction with the results of the Call to Action Convocation, some consider it to be one of the greatest moments of real dialogue and openness in the history of the Catholic Church in the United States. The convocation did propose some resolutions that were nonnegotiable, but it also aroused the institutional and individual consciences of U.S. Catholics to a level never before achieved. Framed in the historical perspective of the nineteenth-century Church's tragic response to the question of slavery, and the subsequent years of the effective and affective growth of institutional racism in the Church and in society, the Call to Action Convocation was a happening whose time had come to respond to so many critical issues in the U.S. Church, especially that of racism.

Following the Call to Action Convocation, the U.S. bishops selected those resolutions that were most in need of attention and established an ad hoc committee to address them. The resolution calling for a pastoral letter on racism was given to the Committee on Social Development and World Peace, which in turn established a committee to produce the pastoral letter. In the process of writing the pastoral on racism, the committee, in conjunction with the USCC staff, sought the widest possible consultation from individuals and groups around the country.

The letter was finally put into excellent literary form by Reverend Cyprian Davis, O.S.B. The presentation, discussions, and voting on the pastoral were not an easy task. The vote of approval for *Brothers and Sisters to Us* was overwhelming. Our National Conference of Catholic Bishops established an *ad hoc* committee to oversee the implementation of the Call to Action Resolutions. Nonetheless, what so many of us feared was that *Brothers and Sisters to Us* would suffer the same fate of previous statements produced by the Church, even the documents of Vatican II. The promulgation of the pastoral on racism was soon forgotten by all but a few. A survey by the *ad hoc* committee on the implementation of Call to Action projects undertaken by the U.S. bishops revealed a pathetic, anemic response from archdioceses and dioceses around the country when they were asked to report on social action programs. The pastoral on racism had made little or no impact on the majority of Catholics in the United States.

Thus, we have reason to be sad along with thousands of minorities as we approach the tenth anniversary of *Brothers and Sisters to Us*. The pastoral suggests that "crude and blatant expressions of racist sentiment, though they occasionally exist, are today considered bad form."[3]

How we wish this was the reality. Today, both individual and corporate institutional racism is on the rise in our country. We experience and hear about blatant forms of racism on the campuses of our colleges and universities—Catholic colleges are not exempt. In our cities, in government agencies, in the political arena, in corporate boardrooms and, in some instances, in our church-related high schools and elementary schools, the ugly head of racism surfaces. During the past eight years, ground has been lost and hard-won civil rights have suffered greatly due to a lack of legislative support. False and misleading information about affirmative action initiatives and practices was fed to the public, with our apology. Housing developers and real estate agencies, along with many municipalities, adopted exclusionary policies and practices, even in defiance of state and federal regulations. It has been discovered that some of the most active Ku Klux Klan members are Catholics. Neo-Nazis, young and old, enjoy a resurgence that is hard to understand.

The question of why we have receded into a blatantly racist society this late in the twentieth century looms larger than life itself. Why has the Church been so vocal nationally and so silent locally? A part of the answer relates to racism in the Church itself, as well as in other societal institutions. A significant passage in the pontifical document on racism captured our attention. It is to be found in Part I, Section 7. This section speaks to the ultimate in modern racism—that of the Nazis. It reads:

> Such theses had considerable resonance in Germany. It is well known that the National-Socialist totalitarian party made a racist ideology the basis of its insane programme, aimed at the physical elimination of those it deemed belonging to 'inferior races.' This party became responsible for one of the greatest genocides in history. This mur-

derous folly struck first and foremost the Jewish people in unheard of proportions, as well as other peoples such as the Gypsies and the Tziganes, and also categories of persons such as the handicapped, [homosexuals], and the mentally ill. It was only a step from racism to eugenics, and it was quickly taken.

The Church did not hesitate to raise her voice. Pope Pius XI clearly condemned Nazi doctrines in his encyclical, *Mit brennender Sorge*, stating in particular: "Whosoever takes race, or the people or the State . . . or any basic value of the human community . . . in order to withdraw them from [their] scale of values . . . and deify them through an idolatrous cult, overturns and falsifies the order of things created and established by God." On 13 April 1938, the Pope had the Sacred Congregation for Seminaries and Universities address a letter to all Rectors and Deans of Faculties, asking all professors of theology to refute, using the method proper to each discipline, the scientific pseudo-truths with which Nazism justified its racist ideologies.[4]

The reality of racism in 1989 vis-à-vis theological considerations on the subject forcefully challenges our consciousness. In spite of all that has been said and written about racism in the last twenty years, very little—if anything at all—has been done in Catholic education; such as it was yesterday, it is today. Should not there be a call in 1989 by the pope and by the episcopate to theologates, seminaries, and religious institutes asking of the educators and persons in formation to educate their charges on the moral and ethical implications of racism in our day? Should not the subjects of such education be members of our seminaries, our religious congregations, our parishes? We have good reason to ask: How many seminarians in our theologates have read or even heard of *Brothers and Sisters to Us*? How many professors have even considered the question and reality of racism in their institutions? We wonder how many of these same academicians will take the pontifical document on racism seriously, let alone read it.

A few of us have "played the flute for you, but you did not dance, we sang a dirge but you did not mourn."[5] We are tempted to cry out with Jeremiah: "Is there no balm in Gilead?"[6]

This Special Message is not meant to repeat what *Brothers and Sisters to Us* has said, nor what the pontifical document paints in much broader strokes. The purpose is to share in some small way our hopes, disappointments, joys, and pain—perhaps, too, in a larger way our faith. We do have faith in good people everywhere in this country who would care, if only they knew. If only they would become conscious of the devastation, the tragedies, and the alienation, especially in the Church, that racism has caused and is causing. Good people would react positively if they realized, too, that "freedom for the victims of racism is a right–to–life issue." We believe that good women and men would come together and profess, if only to themselves, their racism—conscious or otherwise.

What we have tried to do is to ask our readers to reflect on the price they would pay to eradicate racism from the institutions to which they belong, the most basic institution being the family. At the heart of all we have tried to write is the command given by Jesus to love one another, even when love seems impossible. We write this message joined in the episcopacy by a number of African-American Catholic bishops. We write with the voices of those who have lived and continue to live with racism ever at their side. It is a companion no one should have to live with, let alone accommodate in our Church. We believe the pontifical document on racism says it best in speaking of the Church:

> The Catholic Church encourages all these efforts. The Holy See has its role to play in the context of its specific mission. All Catholics are invited to work concretely side by side with other Christians and all others who have this same respect for persons. The Church wants first and foremost to change racist attitudes, including those within her own communities. She appeals first of all to the moral and religious sense of people. She states exigencies but uses fraternal persuasion, her only weapon. She ask God to change hearts. She offers a place for reconciliation. She would like to see promoted initiatives of welcome, of exchange and of mutual assistance as regards men and women belonging to other ethnic groups. Her mission is to give soul to this immense undertaking of human fraternity. Despite the sinful limitations of her members, yesterday and today, she is aware of having been constituted a

witness to Christ's charity on earth, a sign and instrument
of the unity of humankind. The message she proposes to
everyone, and which she tries to live is: "Every person is
my brother or sister."[7]

Summary

Of the 53 million American Catholics, only 2 million are of African-
American descent. History reveals that racism has played a powerful
role in discouraging African Americans from the Catholic Church as
a spiritual home. The commemoration of the tenth anniversary of
*Brothers and Sisters to Us: U.S. Bishops' Pastoral Letter on Racism
in Our Day* is another opportunity for the Church to speak out against
racism, welcome our African-American sisters and brothers, their
culture, and the gifts of their "Blackness."

The Working Document of the National Black Catholic Congress
entitled *Our Pastoral Vision* (a reflection paper on the status of evangelization from an African-American perspective, enjoying the participation of more than 35,000 Black Catholics) has indicated *racism
as the key "evangelization deterrent"* within the African-American
community.

As the Catholic Church prepares for the Fifth Centenary of
Evangelization on these shores, the National Conference of Catholic
Bishops' Committee on Black Catholics encourages dioceses to discern the implications of racism in both the ecclesiastical and secular
segments of society, and to provide a Christian response to this dehumanizing and violent social sin.

> *Wake me up Lord, so that the evil or racism / finds no
> home within me. / Keep watch over my heart Lord, / and
> remove from me any barriers to your grace / that may
> oppress and offend my brothers and sisters. / Fill my voice
> Lord, with the strength to cry freedom. / Free my spirit
> Lord, so that I may give services of / justice and peace./
> Clear my mind Lord, and use it for your glory. / And final-
> ly, remind us Lord that you said / "blessed are the peace-
> makers, / for they shall be called children of God." /
> Amen.*

Suggested Ways to Become Involved

DESIGNATE a Diocesan Task Force on Racism to assist parishes and diocesan leadership in their discernment and consequent response to racism. To assist the members of the task force in their work, the following resources are recommended for reading and discussion:

National Conference of Catholic Bishops. *Brothers and Sisters to Us: U.S. Bishops' Pastoral Letter on Racism in Our Day* (Washington, D.C.: USCC Office of Publishing and Promotion Services, 1979). Publication No. 653-0.

Pontifical Commission Justitia et Pax. *The Church and Racism: Towards a More Fraternal Society* (Washington, D.C.: USCC Office of Publishing and Promotion Services, 1989). Publication No. 277-2.

"America's Original Sin—The Legacy of White Racism," *Study Guide on White Racism* (Washington, D.C.: Sojourners Resource Center, November 1987).

COLLECT from diocesan archives and media centers, resources exploring the topic of racism and make them available for parish and diocesan use.

CONTACT the National Black Catholic Congress delegates and Implementation Team leaders in your diocese to solicit input on this topic.

PUBLISH provocative articles on racism in your local Catholic newspaper.

DISTRIBUTE the statement of the Bishops' Committee on Black Catholics in your diocese or parish.

ENCOURAGE diocesan directors and staffs to explore and evaluate the effects of racism on diocesan policies, decisions, hiring practices, promotions, purchasing, and other actions and activities.

ENCOURAGE and support the empowerment of indigenous leaders. (Suggested Resources: National Catholic Conference for Interracial Justice [Affirmative Action Program and Affirmative Action Booklet]; USCC Ad Hoc

Commit-tee on the Implementation of the Pastoral Letter on the U.S. Economy.)

HEIGHTEN the awareness of racism, its sinfulness, and its dehumanizing effects on today's society at evangelization, religious education, and social justice institutes and forums.

ENCOURAGE youth dialogue on this topic at youth forums and social gatherings. Challenge them to oppose racist and ethnic persecution at school, social, and recreational programs.

PARTICIPATE in national forums that challenge racism, such as the National Teleconference on Racism, held in November 1989 by the Black Catholic Television Network.

ENCOURAGE Catholics throughout the dioceses to pray for the demise of racial oppression.

NOTES

[1] National Conference of Catholic Bishops, *Brothers and Sisters to Us: U.S. Bishops' Pastoral Letter on Racism in Our Day* (Washington. D.C.: USCC Office of Publishing and Promotion Services, 1979), p. 15.

[2] Pontifical Commission Justitia et Pax, *The Church and Racism: Towards a More Fraternal Society* (Washington, D.C.: USCC Office of Publishing and Promotion Services, 1989), p. 41, footnote 71.

[3] *Brothers and Sisters to Us*, p. 6.

[4] *The Church and Racism*, p. 14.

[5] Matthew 11:17.

[6] Jeremiah 8:22.

[7] *The Church and Racism*, pp. 44–45.

Reflections on "For the Love of One Another"

Most Rev. Roberto O. Gonzalez, O.F.M.

Preaching on social justice is of vital importance for the world and for the Church. It is an essential component of evangelization, as countless documents of the magisterium since the Second Vatican Council have insisted. The "New Evangelization" to which the Church calls us today, therefore, requires an adequate understanding of how it is that the social teaching of the Church is inseparable from her preaching about Jesus Christ. The Church has no other purpose for existence than being the sacrament of Christ's presence and its fruits in this world. Evangelization is about Christ and his powerful presence in the world. The Church's social justice teachings originate in her faith and experience of the presence in the world of the One for Whom it was created.

Before taking up the specific topic of preaching about racism, I'd like to begin with a brief reflection on the pope's homily in Havana on Sunday, January 25, 1998. It seems to me that this homily is an example of how to integrate preaching about social justice and human rights into both a doctrinal context and the cultural context of a people. The text of the pope's homily in Havana begins by citing the book of Nehemiah: "This day is holy to the Lord your God; do not mourn or weep" (Nehemiah 8:9). He continues:

> With great joy I preside over this Holy Mass in this Plaza de José Martí on Sunday, the Lord's Day, which should be dedicated to rest, prayer and family life" (John Paul II, 177).

Many might be surprised by the fact that the Pope's most awaited homily in Cuba, preached in the presence of President Fidel Castro and the top officials of the revolutionary government, began with a reference to the holiness of Sunday as a day of "rest, prayer, and family life." It was preached at the Plaza de José Martí, one of the great patriots and founders of Cuba. After the Revolution, the government changed the name of the plaza to the Plaza of the Revolution. By referring to that plaza by its original name the pope is already sending a significant message. In a sense he is pointing out that the revolution—any revolution—cannot be regarded as the ultimate source of a society's well-being, especially one that excludes from its programs the link with infinity, with the Mystery, with the "Holy," which is the reason for the dignity of the human person, a dignity that is the basis for the social teachings of the Church. In Cuba, Sunday is not a day of rest or of prayer. It is a compulsory workday. The pope, very clearly but in a respectful manner, is also beginning to speak about the most important of human rights, upon which all others depend: the right to religious expression.

After this kind of "prologue," the Holy Father reminded those present that before being citizens of a particular society, human beings are called to belong to the universal people of God—the people being formed from all nations to be the way Christ is present in the world to bring about the redemption of the world. "Cubans are part of this great universal family that is the Church," he said. "Therefore, the Church in Cuba does not stand alone, or in isolation; rather, it is part of the universal Church spread around the world." The mission of the Church is to continue the mission of Christ, who applied to himself the words of the prophet: "The Spirit of the Lord is upon me, because he has anointed me to preach good news to the poor" (cf. Luke 4:18). It is in fulfillment of this mission that the pope is addressing the Cuban people. "Every minister of God has to make those words spoken by Jesus of Nazareth his own in his personal life," he said:

> For this reason as I am among you, I wish to give you the Good News of hope in God. As a servant of the Gospel I bring you this message of love and solidarity that Jesus Christ, by His coming, offers to human beings of all times. It is absolutely not a matter of an ideology or a new economic or political system; rather it is a path of authentic peace, justice, and freedom.

> (Translation by the author)

In the social doctrine of the Church, these words are key: *hope, solidarity, love, peace, justice, and freedom*. These words are mentioned with such frequency today that they are in danger of becoming clichés. We need to reflect again on their meaning in the social doctrine of the Church. Above all, it is important to realize that these words express the fruits of Christ's presence and not the outcome of ideological thinking. For example, solidarity, justice, peace, and liberation have been defined by economic and ideological criteria based on confrontation and class struggle. These ideologies have conditioned the way many think about man and society in a profound way. Some of these economical and ideological systems have sought to reduce religion to the merely individual sphere, depriving it of its social fruitfulness and relevance.

Therefore, it is necessary to remember that the State should promote a respectful social climate and adequate legislation that permits each person and each religious denomination to live their faith, and to be sure these can utilize their available means and facilities to bring to the life of the nation their spiritual, moral, and civic riches.

After this introduction, the Holy Father pointed out that lack of religious freedom leads to the abuse of power in other areas of social life, including those countries under the capitalist neo-liberal system that abandon the human person and submit the development of peoples to the mercy of the blind forces of the market, burdening with unbearable loads the less-developed countries.

In this context, the Holy Father referred to the problem of the external debt of the Third World countries, mentioning the great burden imposed by the developed countries on the less-developed countries of the world, especially in the Latin American continent and Africa. Unrealistic economic programs are often imposed on nations as conditions for receiving aid. This leads to an increasing gap between the immense wealth of a few nations and the growing impoverishment of the many.

The pope continued:

> Dear brothers and sisters: the Church is a teacher in humanity. Faced with these systems, she presents a culture of love and of life, restoring hope to humanity, hope in the transforming power of Love lived in the unity willed by Christ. For this to happen, it is necessary to follow a path of reconciliation, dialogue and fraternal welcoming of the neighbor.

Having established the perspective, the point of departure, and the basis for his teaching, the Holy Father was able to speak on the urgent social issues without fear of appearing to impose politically inspired personal or ideological views.

There was also an informal side to the pope, not only in Havana, but also in the homilies he gave elsewhere, in which he let his personal side show—his sense of humor, and above all, referring to the actual condition of his health. The pope brought a very personal element to his words. This is something we need in our preaching, whether it is formal preaching as in the liturgy of the Eucharist, catechetical preaching, or preaching in a para-liturgical service. This personal element is important precisely because it shows how faith is the response to a personal experience, the encounter with Jesus Christ through the life of the Church. Christ's revelation of the mystery of his identity and mission is, at the same time, the revelation of the mystery of the human person and the meaning and purpose of human life. Evangelization, including its social justice dimension, loses all its credibility and becomes propaganda without this personal testimony of the evangelizer. It is for this reason that "the Church is the teacher of humanity," as the pope said.

The anthropology of the Church is an anthropology that unites the human person to God. A human being does not exist without God. In fact, a society like that of our sister Cuba is in crisis fundamentally as the model of a system that excludes God, the love of God, and the mercy of God. The fundamental failure of this system, and of all similar systems, is that they become systems that focus on human beings in an egotistical manner, creating a rupture between the person and God. Therefore, the Church as teacher of humanity presents a vision of life that, above all, focuses on the dignity of the human being as God's creature. A person finds fulfillment together with other human beings only in the measure in which the person establishes his or her roots and grows in the mystery of the love of God.

Unlike these systems, the Church proposes the culture of love and of life. When we speak of overcoming the barriers and prejudices of racism and discrimination, for example, the Church asks us to deal with these at their cultural roots, where they can be recognized as indicative of an overall attitude towards life that needs to be changed through the process known as "conversion." Evangelization is always a call to conversion, to "metanoia," a profound change of heart. This is the only way to eliminate racism and discrimination at their roots. As the pope says: "Hope in the transforming power of love must be returned to humanity." The only power that we should possess in the

Church is the transforming power of love, which transforms human hearts. This applies to all our preaching about issues of social justice, whether it concerns migration, racism, abortion, work, or any other theme. The house of society is built on the little house of each one of us, on the heart of each man and woman. For this we need to traverse the path of reconciliation, of dialogue, and of fraternal acceptance of the neighbor.

These are the goals that we must seek as the consequences of an inner awakening, of conscience-forming in our people concerning the dignity and rights that we all should enjoy. Unfortunately, even today when an interracial couple wishes to marry there are not a few people, even among our Hispanic brothers and sisters, who either oppose it or are hostile to that couple. She may be Black or he white or the other way around, or the color may be brown or mestizo. As a people, we have not yet overcome this attitude against interracial marriage. Yet it has to be said that the interracial marriage is today one of the most powerful symbols we have of the unity that is ours as brothers and sisters in Jesus Christ. The interracial marriage says something unique about how we overcome differences, and how the differences embrace and surrender themselves in the mystery of Love, and of the most sublime love there is upon the earth, which is the love between spouses. The path of reconciliation, of dialogue, and of fraternal acceptance of the neighbor and of every neighbor: this is the path to follow.

I would like to refer to two documents of the Conference of United States Bishops. The first reference is to the document entitled *Brothers and Sisters to Us*, a pastoral letter from the bishops on racism in the United States. This pastoral was approved in 1979. What it says still applies today. The bishops begin the pastoral with the words: "Racism is an evil which endures in our society and in our Church" (1). They condemn racism, saying: "Racism is a sin" (3). It is a sin that divides the people of God, the human family, and violates the human dignity of the children of the same Creator. Racism erases the image of God in some specific members of that family, and it violates the fundamental human dignity of those called to be sons and daughters of the same Creator. Racism is the sin that alleges that some human beings are superior and others inferior because of their color.

We cannot put aside our great responsibility as teachers of humanity. For as the Church is teacher of humanity so each one of us, members of the Church, ought to be teachers of humanity wherever we fulfill our obligations in daily life. Therefore it seems to me that the challenge is very great for us to welcome this understanding of our mission by means of workshops, public dialogue, and seminars to study this matter once again, and to put our convictions into practice in our pastoral ministry. After the racial disturbances in some Los Angeles neighborhoods a few years ago, Bishop Curtis, who was chairman of the Committee for Afro-American Affairs of the Bishops' Conference, and myself, as chairman of the Committee for Hispanic Affairs, decided to prepare a document on reconciliation and on the racism that exists in our communities, and to indicate some ways of overcoming it. The combined work of our two committees was the document, *Reconciliados por Cristo (Reconciled Through Christ)* whose theme was reconciliation and greater collaboration between Afro-American and Hispanic Catholics.

Apart from the text of the bishops, the document contains a brief history of pastoral activity between Afro-American and Hispanic Catholics. There is also statistical data on the Hispanic and Black population in different parts of the country according to diocese. There is much information here for use in studies, for reflection, in preparing homilies, and so forth. There is a section toward the end that contains specific recommendations at the national, diocesan, and parochial levels. For example, at the national level it is recommended that formal relations among representatives of both the Hispanic and Afro-American bishops continue, and this continuity has been maintained. In 1989 the first meeting between all the Hispanic and Afro-American bishops was held. We began a dialogue on racism. We wanted to ensure that at every national assembly of either group, a bishop from the other group should be present. A series of recommendations were also made at the national and diocesan levels. These include the following:

1. To encourage Hispanic and Black bishops to meet together at least once a year.

2. To reply jointly to discrimination, especially when it exists in ecclesial ministries and structures.

3. To promote dialogue between Afro-American and Hispanic leaders, and between secular leaders, and to support interdisciplinary preparation for collaboration in ministry, for instance in the

Mexican-American Cultural Center and in the Institute for Black Catholics.

4. To increase the opportunities for Afro-American and Hispanic Catholic leaders and personnel members to meet to examine common concerns, campaigns in common, and to examine the situation of juvenile prisoners.

5. Parish recommendations include the following: To encourage the holding of informal meetings of parish leaders, Hispanic and Afro-American, to listen to their stories and to exchange life experiences, both of joy and sorrow.

When I was pastor of Holy Cross Parish in the Bronx, we tried to follow this policy in our parish, but with three groups: Afro-Americans, Hispanics, and two English-speaking groups of Irish and Italian origin, the latter being quite numerous. The purpose was to promote communication, with the hope that this would lead to mutual understanding, and eventually to collaboration. The three key words in interpersonal relations are communication, understanding, and collaboration. These are the fundamental means to overcome barriers among different ethnic and racial groups. Within the parish, it is important to promote meetings between priests, deacons, men and women religious and lay leaders, so they can share their faith in an environment free from competition and without feeling threatened. The words "without competition" appear important to me because when what is done arises from faith, they are not posing a threat to each other. This perception of competition actually is the common denominator in the trauma experienced by the Hispanic and Afro-American peoples.

Each of us carries within us the burdens of the past. This is especially true of Afro-Americans, who carry with them the legacy of the trauma of slavery. In the psychology of the Afro-American the consciousness is still maintained that their great-grandparents, or their parents before them, perhaps even people they knew, came to this country as slaves or were sons or daughters of slaves. There are still Afro-Americans who can remember forbearers who were slaves. So we ourselves ought to have a keener sensitivity for this trauma, so as to live in solidarity with our brothers and sisters of the Afro-American race. When I was in Boston, the Archdiocese of Boston began a project between the Office of Hispanic Ministry and the Office of Black Catholics. For the feast of Saint Martin de Porres, we held a bilingual mass to foster reconciliation. I believe that it was a very fruitful experience for our communities. We both identified very closely with Saint Martin de Porres. How fulfilling it was to come and celebrate the Eucharist together—praying in each other's language and singing each other's songs.

The Gospel for the Feast of St. Martin de Porres, Nov. 3, begins:

> One of the Pharisees, a lawyer, in an attempt to trip Jesus up, asked him 'Teacher, which commandment of the law is the greatest?' Jesus said to him: 'You shall love the Lord your God with your whole heart, with your whole soul, and with all your mind. This is the greatest and first commandment. The second is like it: You shall love your neighbor as yourself.' On these two commandments the whole law is based, and the prophets as well (Mt. 22: 34–40).

There are many things that we human beings do instinctively. But there are others that we cannot do instinctively, that are quite difficult for us, such as to forgive. Also, to love as God loves us. We can love many people, but to love as God loves and do it instinctively, this we cannot do, because of the distance between our Creator and ourselves. For that reason, there is a need in each of our hearts to enter more fully into the practice of conversion. We need to make more space for God, for his Word, his Grace, and in this way to grow in the path of holiness. Growing in holiness, we can grow in God's life, and if that life fills us, it will manifest itself in expressions of love and solidarity. In the measure in which we also are growing in this solidarity, we will seek ways of realizing this service, this love, and this reconciliation.

Jesus poured out his blood on the cross for the salvation of humanity. And the blood that Jesus poured out from the cross is the same blood that runs in the veins of each one of us. We know that blood type varies among people, but the texture or the essence of blood is the same. An African can give blood to an Australian, he or she can give blood to an Egyptian, he or she can give blood to a Hispanic, he or she can give blood to anyone at all. In other words, helping another person by giving blood, race is not a factor. The reason is that every human being has been created in the image of the Firstborn who poured out his blood on the cross for everyone, for each one of us, for all peoples, for all races, for all nations, for all time.

It is a tragedy that prejudice, discrimination, hate, friction, and tension still exist between races. All this is the fruit of sin and division. Unity between us in Jesus is something to be sought after by all. In the mystical body of Christ, one person's color is everybody's color. We have a long way to go, a lot to correct and to renew in our hearts, to allow the grace of God to convert us, and proceed to change our attitudes, because every human being has something in himself or herself to improve and purify. We have to follow the example of Christ, who has given all the races a rightful place; and if He has done so, we his servants have the great challenge, the great responsibility and task to fulfill: to bring to completion what Paul says; namely, to complete Christ's mission here on earth!

REFERENCES

John Paul II, "The Doctrine of Freedom and Solidarity: Homily of Pope John Paul II at the Mass Celebrated in Havana's Revolution Plaza" (January 25,1998). In *The Pope Speaks*, Vol. 43, 177–180.

NCCB, *Brothers And Sisters to Us: U.S. Bishops' Pastoral Letter on Racism in Our Day.* Washington, D.C.: USCC, 1979.

_____, *For the Love of One Another: A Special Message on the Occasion of the Tenth Anniversary of Brothers and Sisters to Us.* Washington, D.C.: USCC, 1989.

_____, *Reconciled Through Christ: On Reconciliation and Greater Collaboration Between Hispanic Catholics and African American Catholics.* Washington, D.C.: USCC, 1989.

For the Love of One Another (1989)
Suggestions for Civil/Liturgical Occasions

Rev. Raúl Gómez

The theme of persistent racism addressed by this statement lends itself to various occasions that speak of human relationships. In terms of events in civil life, the most obvious have to do with those that promote greater intercultural understanding and acceptance. Liturgical events are less precise, but opportunities abound throughout the liturgical year.

Clearly months dedicated to honoring the various ethnic and racial groups of the United States provide good opportunities for preaching on this theme. In addition to Black History Month, Hispanic Heritage Month, and ethnic festivals celebrated in many places throughout the country, the commemoration of Martin Luther King, Jr. is another obvious occasion.

Liturgically, the various memorials and feast days dedicated to the commemoration of saints who have worked for the poor, the disenfranchised, and the outcast are especially suitable. In particular the memorials of Saints Peter Claver, Martín de Porres, Benedict the Moor, Frances Xavier Cabrini, Katherine Drexel, and others can provide a point of departure for addressing the issue of racism. Patronal feast days, such as *la Virgen de la Caridad del Cobre* or *el Cristo Negro de Esquipulas*, also provide an opening for addressing cultural and racial themes. Whenever liturgical readings speak of love of one another, the treatment of the least, service to widows and orphans, the Good Samaritan, or the conflict between Greek-and Hebrew-speaking Christians in the early Church, the preacher can make references to this statement and its predecessor, *Brothers and Sisters to Us: U.S. Bishops' Pastoral Letter on Racism in Our Day* (1979).

For the Love of One Another:
10th Anniversary of Brothers and Sisters to Us
Suggested Litergical Texts

Rev. José A. López

Reference: United States Conference of Catholic Bishops, Lectionary for Mass, Second Typical Edition, Vol. I–IV. Chicago: Liturgy Training Publications, 2002.

Texts

III:379	Amos 5:14–15, 21–24
I:95	Galatians 3:26–29
III:474	Ephesians 2:12–22
III:337	James 1:19–27
I:227	Matthew 7:7–12
I:160	Matthew 25:31–46

The Scripture passages above call us to reflect on the dignity of every person, for Saint Paul declares that each one of us is a child of God because of our faith in Christ Jesus (Gal. 3:26). In addressing this concern to the Hispanic community, the preacher must focus on two areas. One is that most Hispanics have experienced discrimination in their lives in many ways. They understand that racism may not be as blatant as others have experienced, but Hispanics do not have to describe what they know and feel: "Many times the new face of racism is the computer printout, the graph of profits and losses, the pink slip, the nameless statistic" (*Brothers and Sisters to Us*, 6). These scripture passages give strength, hope, and determination to those who live in the midst of racism and strive to live out Paul's claim that "There does not exist among you Jew or Greek . . . All are one in Christ Jesus" (Gal 3:28).

The other is that in Christ Jesus the "barrier of hostility that kept us apart" (Eph 2:14) is no longer there. It is important to note this, because even in the Hispanic community there is often hostility to other minorities and the immigrant, especially those of one's own ethnicity. It is many times directed to the poor, the homeless, and the powerless. To preach to this requires a strong sense of unity, of the challenge to welcome the stranger, of the need to incorporate those who are different. To incorporate them is truly to make those feel welcome in the body of Christ. Racism can affect all of us, even toward those who bear our same image and ethnicity or race.

For all of us, the prophet Amos cries out for justice to prevail, for justice to surge (15:24): "There must be no turning back along the road to justice, no sighing for bygone times of privilege, no simple solutions from another age" (*For the Lofe of One Another*, no. 4).

CHAPTER III

Communities of Salt and Light

Communities of Salt and Light: Reflections on the Social Mission of the Parish

National Conference of Catholic Bishops
1994

Introduction

The parish is where the Church lives. Parishes are communities of faith, of action, and of hope. They are where the gospel is proclaimed and celebrated, where believers are formed and sent to renew the earth. Parishes are the home of the Christian community; they are the heart of our Church. Parishes are the place where God's people meet Jesus in word and sacrament, and come in touch with the source of the Church's life.

One of the most encouraging signs of the gospel at work in our midst is the vitality and quality of social justice ministries in our parishes. Across the country, countless local communities of faith are serving those in need, working for justice, and sharing our social teaching as never before. Millions of parishioners are applying the gospel and church teaching in their own families, work, and communities. More and more, the social justice dimensions of our faith are moving from the fringes of parishes to become an integral part of local Catholic life.

We welcome and applaud this growing recognition of and action on the social mission of the parish. We offer these brief reflections to affirm and support pastors and parish leaders in this essential task, and to encourage all parishes to take up this challenge with renewed commitment, creativity, and urgency.

In the past decade, we have written major pastoral letters on peace and economic justice and issued pastoral statements on a number of important issues touching human life and human dignity. But until now, we have not specifically addressed the crucial role of parishes in the Church's social ministry. We offer these words of support, encouragement, and challenge at this time, because we are convinced that the local parish is the most important ecclesial setting for sharing and acting on our Catholic social heritage. We hope that these reflec-

44

tions can help pastors, parish staffs, parish councils, social concerns committees, and other parishioners strengthen the social justice dimensions of their own parish life. This focus on the social mission of the parish complements and strengthens the call to evangelization found in our statement *Go and Make Disciples: A National Plan and Strategy for Catholic Evangelization in the United States.*

We offer a framework for integration rather than a specific model or new national program. We seek to affirm and encourage local parish commitment and creativity in social ministry. We know pastors and parish leaders do not need another program to carry forward or more expectations to meet. We see the parish dimensions of social ministry not as an added burden, but as a part of what keeps a parish alive and makes it truly Catholic. Effective social ministry helps the parish not only do more, but be more—more of a reflection of the gospel, more of a worshiping and evangelizing people, more of a faithful community. It is an essential part of parish life.

This is not a new message, but it takes on new urgency in light of the increasing clarity and strength of Catholic social teaching and the signs of declining respect for human life and human dignity in society. We preach a gospel of justice and peace in a rapidly changing world and troubled nation. Our faith is tested by the violence, injustice, and moral confusion that surround us. In this relatively affluent nation, a fourth of our children under six grow up in poverty.[1] Each year in our nation, 1.6 million children are destroyed before birth by abortion.[2] And every day, 40,000 children die from hunger and its consequences around the world.[3] In our streets and neighborhoods, violence destroys the hopes, dreams, and lives of too many children. In our local communities, too many cannot find decent work, housing, health care, or education. In our families, parents struggle to raise children with dignity, hope, and basic values.

Our faith stands in marked contrast to these grim realities. At a time of rampant individualism, we stand for family and community. At a time of intense consumerism, we insist it is not what we have, but how we treat one another that counts. In an age that does not value permanence or hard work in relationships, we believe marriage is forever and children are a blessing, not a burden. At a time of growing isolation, we remind our nation of its responsibility to the broader world, to pursue peace, to welcome immigrants, to protect the lives of hurting children and refugees. At a time when the rich are getting richer and the poor are getting poorer, we insist the moral test of our society is how we treat and care for the weakest among us.

In these challenging days, we believe that the Catholic community needs to be more than ever a source of clear moral vision and effective action. We are called to be the "salt of the earth" and "light of the world" in the words of the Scriptures (cf. Matthew 5:13–16). This task belongs to every believer and every parish. It cannot be assigned to a few or simply delegated to diocesan or national structures. The pursuit of justice and peace is an essential part of what makes a parish Catholic.

In urban neighborhoods, in suburban communities, and in rural areas, parishes serve as anchors of hope and communities of caring, help families meet their own needs and reach out to others, and serve as centers of community life and networks of assistance.

The Roots of Parish Social Mission

The roots of this call to justice and charity are in the Scriptures, especially in the Hebrew prophets and the life and words of Jesus. Parish social ministry has clear biblical roots. In the Gospel according to Luke, Jesus began his public life by reading a passage from Isaiah that introduced his ministry and the mission of every parish. The parish must proclaim the transcendent message of the gospel and help:

> bring "good news to the poor" in a society where millions lack the necessities of life;

> bring "liberty to captives" when so many are enslaved by poverty, addiction, ignorance, discrimination, violence, or disabling conditions;

> bring "new sight to the blind" in a culture where the excessive pursuit of power or pleasure can spiritually blind us to the dignity and rights of others; and

> "set the downtrodden free" in communities where crime, racism, family disintegration, and economic and moral forces leave people without real hope (cf. Luke 4:18).

Our parish communities are measured by how they serve "the least of these" in our parish and beyond its boundaries—the hungry, the homeless, the sick, those in prison, the stranger (cf. Matthew 25:31). Our local families of faith are called to "hunger and thirst for justice" and to be "peacemakers" in our own communities (cf. Matthew 5:6, 9). A parish cannot really proclaim the Gospel if its message is not reflected in its own community life. The biblical call to charity, justice, and peace claims not only each believer, but also each community where believers gather for worship, formation, and pastoral care.

Over the last century, these biblical mandates have been explored and expressed in a special way in Catholic social teaching. The central message is simple: our faith is profoundly social. We cannot be called truly "Catholic" unless we hear and heed the Church's call to serve those in need and work for justice and peace. We cannot call ourselves followers of Jesus unless we take up his mission of bringing "good news to the poor, liberty to captives, and new sight to the blind" (cf. Luke 4:18).

The Church teaches that social justice is an integral part of evangelization, a constitutive dimension of preaching the gospel, and an essential part of the Church's mission. The links between justice and evangelization are strong and vital. We cannot proclaim a gospel we do not live, and we cannot carry out a real social ministry without knowing the Lord and hearing his call to justice and peace. Parish communities must show by their deeds of love and justice that the gospel they proclaim is fulfilled in their actions. This tradition is not empty theory; it challenges our priorities as a nation, our choices as a Church, our values as parishes. It has led the Church to stand with the poor and vulnerable against the strong and powerful. It brings occasional controversy and conflict, but it also brings life and vitality to the people of God. It is a sign of our faithfulness to the gospel.

The center of the Church's social teaching is the life, dignity, and rights of the human person. We are called in a special way to serve the poor and vulnerable; to build bridges of solidarity among peoples of differing races and nations, language and ability, gender and culture. Family life and work have special places in Catholic social teaching; the rights of the unborn, families, workers, immigrants, and the poor deserve special protection. Our tradition also calls us to show our respect for the Creator by our care for creation and our commitment to work for environmental justice. This vital tradition is an essential resource for parish life. It offers a framework and direction for our social ministry, calling us to concrete works of charity, justice, and peacemaking.[4]

The Social Mission of the Parish: A Framework of Integration

In responding to the Scriptures and the principles of Catholic social teaching, parishes are not called to an extra or added dimension of our faith, but to a central demand of Catholic life and evangelization. We recognize the sometimes overwhelming demands on parish leadership and resources. We know it is easier to write about these challenges than to carry them out day by day. But we believe the Church's social mission is an essential measure of every parish community, and it needs more attention and support within our parishes.

Our parishes are enormously diverse—in where and who they serve, in structures and resources, in their members and leaders. This diversity is reflected in how parishes shape their social ministry. The depth and range of activity are most impressive. Across our country, parishioners offer their time, their money, and their leadership to a wide variety of efforts to meet needs and change structures. Parishes are deeply involved in meeting their members' needs, serving the hungry and homeless, welcoming the stranger and immigrant, reaching out to troubled families, advocating for just public policies, organizing for safer and better communities, and working creatively for a more peaceful world. Our communities and ministries have been greatly enriched and nourished by the faith and wisdom of parishioners who experience injustice and all those who work for greater justice.

There has been tremendous growth of education, outreach, advocacy, and organizing in parishes. From homeless shelters to prayer services, from food pantries to legislative networks, from global education programs to neighborhood organizing, parishes are responding. But in some parishes the social justice dimensions of parish life are still neglected, underdeveloped, or touch only a few parishioners.

We have much to learn from those parishes that are leading the way in making social ministry an integral part of parish ministry and evangelization. We need to build local communities of faith where our social teaching is central, not fringe; where social ministry is integral, not optional; where it is the work of every believer, not just the mission of a few committed people and committees.

For too many parishioners, our social teaching is an unknown tradition. In too many parishes, social ministry is a task for a few, not a challenge for the entire parish community. We believe we are just beginning to realize our potential as a community of faith committed to serve those in need and to work for greater justice.

The parishes that are leaders in this area see social ministry not as a specialized ministry, but as an integral part of the entire parish. They weave the Catholic social mission into every aspect of parish life—worship, formation, and action. They follow a strategy of integration and collaboration, which keeps social ministry from becoming isolated or neglected.

A framework of integration might include the following elements:

1. Anchoring Social Ministry: Prayer and Worship

The most important setting for the Church's social teaching is not in a food pantry or in a legislative committee room, but in prayer and worship, especially gathered around the altar for the Eucharist. It is in the liturgy that we find the fundamental direction, motivation, and strength for social ministry. Social ministry not genuinely rooted in prayer can easily burn itself out. On the other hand, worship that does not reflect the Lord's call to conversion, service, and justice can become pious ritual and empty of the Gospel.

We support new efforts to integrate liturgy and justice, to make clear that we are one people united in faith, worship, and works of charity and justice. We need to be a Church that helps believers recognize Jesus in the breaking of the bread and in those without bread. Eucharist, penance, confirmation, and the other sacraments have essential social dimensions that ought to be appropriately reflected in how we celebrate, preach, and pray. Those who plan and preside at our worship can help the parish community understand more clearly the spiritual and scriptural roots of our pursuit of justice without distorting or imposing on the liturgy.

Our social ministry must be anchored in prayer, where we uncover the depths of God's call to seek justice and pursue peace. In personal prayer, the reading of the Scriptures, and quiet reflection on the Christian vocation, we discover the social mission of every believer. In serving those in need, we serve the Lord. In seeking justice and peace, we witness to the reign of God in our midst. In prayer, we find the reasons, the strength, and the call to follow Jesus in the ways of charity, justice, and peace.

2. Sharing the Message: Preaching and Education

We are called to share our social teaching more effectively in our parishes than we have. Our social doctrine is an integral part of our faith; we need to pass it on clearly, creatively, and consistently. It is a remarkable spiritual, intellectual, and pastoral resource that has been too little known or appreciated even in our own community.

Preaching that reflects the social dimensions of the gospel is indispensable. Priests should not and need not impose an agenda on the liturgy to preach about justice. Rather, we urge those who preach not to ignore the regular opportunities provided by the liturgy to connect our faith and our everyday lives, to share biblical values on justice and peace. Week after week, day after day, the lectionary calls the community to reflect on the scriptural message of justice and peace. The pulpit is not a partisan rostrum and to try to make it one would be a mistake, but preaching that ignores the social dimensions of our faith does not truly reflect the gospel of Jesus Christ. Our social doctrine must also be an essential part of the curriculum and life of our schools, religious education programs, sacramental preparation, and Christian initiation activities. We need to share and celebrate our common social heritage as Catholics, developing materials and training tools that ensure that we are sharing our social teaching in every educational ministry of our parishes. Every parish should regularly assess how well our social teaching is shared in its formation and educational ministries.

3. Supporting the "Salt of the Earth": Family, Work, Citizenship

Our parishes are clearly called to help people live their faith in the world, helping them to understand and act on the social dimensions of the gospel in their everyday lives. National statements, diocesan structures, or parish committees can be useful, but they are no substitute for the everyday choices and commitments of believers—acting as parents, workers, students, owners, investors, advocates, policy makers, and citizens.

For example, parishes are called to support their members in:

> building and sustaining marriages of quality, fidelity, equality, and permanence in an age that does not value commitment or hard work in relationships;

> raising families with gospel values in a culture where materialism, selfishness, and prejudice still shape so much of our lives;

> being a good neighbor; welcoming newcomers and immigrants; treating people of different races, ethnic groups, and nationalities with respect and kindness;

> seeing themselves as evangelizers who recognize the unbreakable link between spreading the gospel and working for social justice;

> bringing Christian values and virtues into the marketplace;

> treating coworkers, customers, and competitors with respect and fairness, demonstrating economic initiative, and practicing justice;

> bringing integrity and excellence to public service and community responsibilities, seeking the common good, respecting human life, and promoting human dignity;

> providing leadership in unions, community groups, professional associations, and political organizations at a time of rising cynicism and indifference.

In short, our parishes need to encourage, support, and sustain lay people in living their faith in the family, neighborhood, marketplace, and public arena. It is lay women and men, placing their gifts at the service of others (cf. 1 Peter 4:10), who will be God's primary instruments in renewing the earth by their leadership and faithfulness in the community. The most challenging work for justice is not done in church committees, but in the secular world of work, family life, and citizenship.

4. Serving the "Least of These": Outreach and Charity

Parishes are called to reach out to the hurting, the poor, and the vulnerable in our midst in concrete acts of charity. Just as the gospel tells us our lives will be judged by our response to the "least of these," too our parishes should be measured by our help for the hungry, the homeless, the troubled, and the alienated—in our own community and beyond. This is an area of creativity and initiative with a wide array of programs, partnerships with Catholic Charities, and common effort with other churches. Thousands of food pantries, hundreds of shelters, and uncounted outreach programs for poor families, refugees, the elderly, and others in need are an integral part of parish life. The parish is the most significant place where new immigrants and refugees are welcomed into our Church and community. A Church that teaches an option for the poor must reflect that option in our service of those in need. Parish efforts to meet human needs also provide valuable experience, expertise, and credibility in advocating for public policy to address the forces that leave people in need of our charity.

Catholic teaching calls us to serve those in need and to change the structures that deny people their dignity and rights as children of God. Service and action, charity and justice are complimentary components of parish social ministry. Neither alone is sufficient; both are essential signs of the gospel at work. A parish serious about social ministry will offer opportunities to serve those in need and to advocate for justice and peace. These are not competing priorities, but two dimensions of the same fundamental mission to protect the life and dignity of the human person.

5. Advocating for Justice: Legislative Action

Parishes need to promote a revived sense of political responsibility calling Catholics to be informed and active citizens, participating in the debate over the values and vision that guide our communities and nation. Parishes as local institutions have special opportunities to develop leaders, to promote citizenship, and to provide forums for discussion and action on public issues. Religious leaders need to act in public affairs with a certain modesty, knowing that faith is not a substitute for facts, that values must be applied in real and complex situations, and that people of common faith and good will can disagree on specifics. But parishioners are called to use their talents, the resources of our faith, and the opportunities of this democracy to shape a society more respectful of the life, dignity, and rights of the human person. Parishes can help lift up the moral and human dimension of public issues, calling people to informed participation in the political process.

The voices of parishioners need to be heard on behalf of vulnerable children—born and unborn—on behalf of those who suffer discrimination and injustice, on behalf of those without health care or housing, on behalf of our land and water, our communities and neighborhoods. Parishioners need to bring our values and vision into the debates about a changing world and shifting national priorities. Parishes and parishioners are finding diverse ways to be political without being partisan, joining legislative networks, community organizations, and other advocacy groups. In election years, parishes offer nonpartisan voter registration, education, and forums to involve and inform their members. This kind of genuine political responsibility strengthens local communities as it enriches the witness of our parishes.

6. Creating Community: Organizing for Justice

Many parishes are joining with other churches and groups to rebuild a sense of community in their own neighborhoods and towns. Parish leaders are taking the time to listen to the concerns of their members and are organizing to act on those concerns. These kind of church-based and community organizations are making a difference on housing, crime, education, and economic issues in local communities. Parish participation in such community efforts develops leaders, provides concrete handles to deal with key issues, and builds the capacity of the parish to act on our values.

The Campaign for Human Development has provided vital resources to many self-help organizations, empowering the poor to seek greater justice. Parish support and participation in these organizations help put Catholic social teaching into action and to revitalize local communities.

7. Building Solidarity: Beyond Parish Boundaries

Parishes are called to be communities of solidarity. Catholic social teaching more than anything else insists that we are one family; it calls us to overcome barriers of race, religion, ethnicity, gender, economic status, and nationality. We are one in Christ Jesus (cf. Galatians 13:28)—beyond our differences and boundaries.

Parishes need to be bridge-builders, reminding us that we are part of a Universal Church with ties of faith and humanity to sisters and brothers all over the world. Programs of parish twinning, support for Catholic Relief Services, mission efforts, migration and refugee activities, and other global ministries are signs of solidarity in a shrinking and suffering world. Advocacy on human rights, development and peace through legislative networks, and other efforts are also signs of a faith without boundaries and a parish serious about its social responsibilities. A key test of a parish's "Catholicity" is its willingness to go beyond its boundaries to serve those in need and work for global justice and peace. Working with others for common goals across religious, racial, ethnic, and other lines is another sign of solidarity in action.

We hope these seven elements of the social mission of parishes can serve as a framework for planning and assessing parish social ministry. The more practical resources that accompany these reflections may offer some help and assistance in meeting these challenges. National and diocesan structures have materials, resources, and personnel to help parishes assess and strengthen their social ministry.

Lessons Learned

Many parishes have found their community life enriched and strengthened by a serious effort to integrate more fully the social justice dimensions of our faith. They have also learned some lessons.

Rooting Social Ministry in Faith

Parish social action should flow clearly from our faith. It is Jesus who calls us to this task. Social ministry is an expression of who we are and what we believe; it must be anchored in the Scriptures and Church teaching. With the eyes of faith, we see every "crack baby" or person with AIDS, every Haitian refugee or Salvadoran immigrant, every victim of unjust discrimination, and every person combating addiction as a child of God, a sister or brother, as Jesus in disguise. These are not simply social problems, economic troubles, or political issues. They are moral tragedies and religious tests. Parish social ministry is first and foremost a work of faith.

The social mission of the parish begins in the gospel's call to conversion; to change our hearts and our lives; to follow in the path of charity, justice, and peace. The parish is the place we should regularly hear the call to conversion and find help in answering the Lord's call to express our faith in concrete acts of charity and justice.

Respecting Diversity

We are a very diverse community of faith—racially, ethnically, economically, and ideologically. This diversity should be respected, reflected, and celebrated in our social ministry. For example, what works in a predominately African-American parish in an urban neighborhood may not be appropriate for a largely white suburban or rural congregation. The issues, approaches, and structures may differ, but our common values unite us. Social justice coalitions across racial, ethnic, and geographic lines can be an impressive sign of the unity of the Body of Christ.

Leadership: Pastors, Councils, Committees, and Educators

While pursuing social justice is a task for every believer, strengthening parish social ministry depends on the skill and commitment of particular parish leaders. Pastors and parish priests have special responsibilities to support integral social ministry. By their preaching, participation, and priorities, they indicate what is important and what is not. They can make it clear that social justice is a mission of the whole parish, not a preoccupation of a few. They are called to teach the authentic social doctrine of the universal Church.

Other parish staff members and leaders play crucial roles in shaping the quality of parish social ministry. Parish councils in their important planning and advisory functions can help place social ministry in the center of parish life. Councils can be a means of collaboration and integration, bringing together liturgy, formation, outreach, and action into a sense of common mission. Councils can play a valuable role in assessing current efforts, setting priorities for the future, and building bridges between parish ministries.

Many parishes have special committees focused on social concerns. These structures can play crucial roles in helping the parish community act on the social justice dimensions of its overall mission. Some parishes have staff members who coordinate social ministry efforts. This is a promising development. These committees and coordinators best serve parishes by facilitating and enabling the participation of the parish community, rather than simply doing the work on behalf of the parish.

Educators in parish schools, religious education, and formation efforts have special responsibility to share our tradition of social justice as an integral part of our faith. They shape the leaders of the future, and by their teaching and example share the social dimensions of our Catholic faith.

Creative and competent leaders—clerical and lay, professional and volunteer—are indispensable for effective parish social ministry. They deserve more assistance, encouragement, financial support, and tools to help them fulfill these demanding roles. Leadership development efforts and ongoing training help parishes strengthen their social ministry capacity.

Links to Diocesan Structures

No parish functions totally by itself. Parish leaders often look to other parishes and diocesan social justice structures for help in fulfilling these responsibilities. Almost all dioceses have social justice structures that offer resources and training for parishes. These structures are diverse, including justice and peace commissions, social action offices, CHD funding and education efforts, rural life offices, and parish social ministry programs of Catholic Charities. Other diocesan groups also offer opportunities for service and action for parishes: for example, Councils of Catholic Women, St. Vincent DePaul Society, Ladies of Charity, ecumenical advocacy and outreach efforts. Many dioceses offer specific "handles" for parish action—legislative networks, work on specific issues or needs, convening parish leaders, providing educational programs coordinating outreach, and so forth. For the most part, parishes cannot go it alone in this area. It is just as clear that diocesan social action can only be effective if it builds parish capacity. Good ties between diocesan and parish efforts are indispensable.

Practicing What We Preach

We also need to try to practice in our own parishes what we preach to others about justice and participation. Too often we are better at talking about justice than demonstrating it, more committed to these values in the abstract than in our everyday ministry. We acknowledge this not to minimize our common efforts, but to acknowledge how far we have yet to go before we fully close the gap between our principles and our performance.

Sensitive, competent, and compassionate pastoral care is an expression of justice. Parish plans and priorities—as well as the use of parish facilities—that reflect the social mission of the Church are expressions of justice. Investing parish resources in social justice and empowering the poor are also expressions of justice. Just personnel policies, fair wages, and equal opportunity efforts are expressions of justice. Respecting and responding to the cultural and ethnic diversity of the communities we serve is an expression of justice. Recognizing the contributions and welcoming the participation of all members of the parish whatever their race, gender, ethnic background, nationality, or disability—these are integral elements of parishes seeking justice.

Some Difficulties and Dangers

In reflecting on the social mission of the parish, the opportunities seem clear; so do some of the difficulties. One danger is the tendency to isolate social ministry, to confine it to the margins of parish life. Another is for social action leaders to isolate themselves, treating the parish as a target rather than a community to be served and empowered.

Another danger is potential partisanship, the temptation to try to use the parish for inappropriate political objectives. We need to make sure our faith shapes our political action, not the other way around. We cannot forget that we pursue the kingdom of God, not some earthly vision or ideological cause.

A significant challenge is to avoid divisiveness; to emphasize the common ground among social service and social action, education and advocacy, pro-life and social justice, economic development and environmental commitment. We need to work together to reflect a comprehensive concern for the human person in our parish.

Another danger is to try to do too much on too many issues, without clear priorities and an effective plan of action. Not everyone can do everything, but the parish should be a sign of unity in pursuing a consistent concern for human life and human dignity.

The final and most serious danger is for parish leaders to act as if the social ministry of the Church was the responsibility of someone else. Every believer is called to serve those in need, to work for justice, and to pursue peace. Every parish has the mission to help its members act on their faith in the world.

A Final Word of Appreciation, Support, and Challenge

We close these brief reflections with a word of support and encouragement for pastors and parish leaders. The social ministry of the Church is not just another burden, another set of expectations to feel bad about, though in these demanding days it may sometimes seem that way.

The social ministry is already a part of your ministry and leadership. We hope these reflections help you and those you work with to explore how best to carry out this part of your parish's mission. What is strong already? What can be further developed? What needs greater attention? How, given limited time and resources and other obligations, can our parish better share and act on the social justice demands of the gospel?

The Catholic community has been making steady progress in this area. We seek to build on and share these achievements. We know from experience that parishes that strengthen their social ministry enrich every aspect of their parish, bringing increased life and vitality, greater richness, and community to their entire family of faith.

We offer our gratitude and admiration to those who are leading and helping our parishes act on their social mission. We pledge our support to those who pursue this important challenge with new commitment and energy.

In the gospel, we read how John the Baptist's followers came to Jesus and asked, "Are you the one who is to come, or should we look for another?" Jesus responded in this way: "Go and tell John what you hear and see: The blind regain their sight, the lame walk, lepers are cleansed, the deaf hear, the dead are raised, and the poor have the good news proclaimed to them" (Matthew 11:3–5).

These are still the signs of Christ among us—parishes across our country who in their own ways are caring for the sick, opening eyes and ears, helping life overcome death, and preaching the good news to the poor.

Today, more than ever, our parishes are called to be communities of "salt" and "light"; to help believers live their faith in their families, communities, work, and world. We need parishes that will not "lose their flavor" nor put their "light under a basket." We seek to build evangelizing communities of faith, justice, and solidarity, where all believers are challenged to bring God's love, justice, and peace to a world in desperate need of the seasoning of the gospel and the light of Catholic teaching.

NOTES

[1] U.S. Department of Commerce, Bureau of the Census, 1990.

[2] Allan Guttmacher Institute, 1991.

[3] UNICEF, *State of the World's Children*, 1992.

[4] For a more extensive treatment of Catholic social teaching, see *A Century of Social Teaching: A Common Heritage, A Continuing Challenge. A Pastoral Message of the Catholic Bishops of the United States on the 100th Anniversary of "Rerum Novarum"* (Washington, D.C.: United States Catholic Conference, 1990).

Reflections on "Communities of Salt and Light": Preaching the Social Mission of the Church in the Hispanic/Latino Parish

Jorge L. Presmanes, O.P. and Mark E. Wedig, O.P.

In its document *Communities of Salt and Light,* the National Conference of Catholic Bishops in the United States carefully crafted a framework for establishing the social mission of the parish in the United States. The document anchors social ministry in prayer and worship, delineates ways to integrate the message of justice and peace in preaching and education, describes methods for a parish to conduct social outreach and advocate for social justice, and demonstrates ways to build solidarity with communities beyond the parish boundaries. Overall it helps the pastoral minister and community to understand the integral role that social mission plays in everything the parish community does.

Communities of Salt and Light reminds the preacher that social concerns are never peripheral, but reflective of the very nature of people who bear the Word of God for the world. Therefore, the preacher seldom refrains from seeing the social implications of the gospel in all aspects of parish life. Social mission is not an occasional theme or a special focus of preaching but the fundamental link between the Word of God and Christian living.

With all its helpful insights into the integrity of social mission in the life of the parish, *Communities of Salt and Light* lacks specific directives pertaining to the inculturation of that mission. For example, those of us who preach the good news in a Hispanic/Latino parish in the U.S. every week know that social justice and social concerns are not matters of generic faith put into action, but pertain to a particular experience and expression of the Church. Social justice is not simply a generalized phenomenon, but a matter of a particular mediation of the faith linked to the story of a specific people whose lives are uniquely related to the gospel. Therefore for the sake of clarifying the particular way the social mission is preached and lived in the U.S. Hispanic/Latino context, we want to describe the characteristics of the context itself and the fundamental substance of the message.

60

We will use the example of our parish in Miami. While recognizing the great diversity of the people themselves, we will first address what we see as the two poles of parish life and the overarching expression and character of the Hispanic/Latino parish in the United States. Second, we will show how that common expression, characterized by the phenomena of exile, leads to experiencing social consciousness as accompaniment. The social mission of the parish in the Hispanic/Latino context cannot be separated from the popular and communal resources of the culture, necessitating that people walk with people and not simply profess abstract concepts and ideas. We demonstrate how these resources directly affect the preacher. The gospel must be preached in ways that show a practical solidarity with the poor and marginalized.

The Hispanic/Latino Parish Context in the United States

To speak simply about a single Hispanic/Latino experience of church in the United States is, at face value, to deny the diverse and multi-faceted reality of the peoples originally from Mexico, Central America, South America, and the Caribbean who make up the Catholic Church in a large and complex country. The social, cultural, and religious differences that characterize the Hispanic/Latino peoples in the U.S. cannot be glossed over by sweeping generalizations. The racial, economic, and political diversity within national and linguistic identities are merely nuances of what it means to be a Hispanic or a Latino.

These differences are lived out through differing stories of immigration and exile, racial and linguistic struggle and enduring frustrations about assimilation, and triumphant successes about identity and liberation achieved. Furthermore, social, political, and economic factors are intermeshed with the religious horizon of the Catholic Church and other Christian denominations. The journey of a people finds its completion in stories about Jesus, Mary, and the saints who give access to a God who does not abandon or forsake them, but accompanies them in their estrangement and suffering. The Church evangelizes and lives out its mission by sanctifying, establishing, and extending the paschal drama of salvation and promise. The Church becomes the intersection of intensified remembrance between the story of a people and the story of God saving a people from slavery, exile, and death.

The Two Poles of Parish Life

The Catholic parish community in the U.S. Hispanic/Latino context cannot be properly understood without seeing how these complex dramas of faith mediate local church life. Therefore, the religious life of the parish, as we see it, is encountered at the intersection of two poles of parish life: the Sunday assembly and the popular religious life that accompanies the people in their cultural and religious liberation.[1] Both Sunday assembly and popular religiosity together embody the Paschal Mystery and the heart of a people. In other words, for the Hispanic/Latino parish in the U. S., both the church as a eucharistic assembly and the church as a shrine intermingle to embody the great paschal remembrance of the Christian faith.

St. Dominic Church in Miami represents a microcosm of that experience of the U.S. Hispanic/Latino parish. Located in a working-class section of the western part of the city, the parish is composed of people from Nicaragua, Cuba, Colombia, Puerto Rico, Guatemala, Honduras, and Mexico, as well as a small Anglo membership. Furthermore, the people represent a diversity of economic and political profiles. As Dominican Friars, the authors view the role of the parish uniquely in terms of its preaching. As leaders and presiders of the community, we see our role to be one that integrates and helps organize the ways in which the local church preaches and lives out the gospel. Engendering the ebb and flow of parish life through preaching in the eucharistic assembly—and all its attendant ministries—and preaching to the religious life that stems from the popular devotion of the people best achieve these tasks. These two poles do not necessarily mean two distinct assemblies, but designate two unique facets of a people's religious life.

Therefore, parish life in the Hispanic/Latino context is best realized when great sensitivity is given to ways in which these two poles of religious life intersect in the lives of the parishioners. Often the point or place of that integration is not obvious. The two realities can exist in seeming contradiction to each other, especially as lived out in the extremes of the religious life of the parish. Devotional practices can be seen to take away from a gathered assembly. Certain catecheses concerning the ecclesial reforms following Vatican II put at odds these two aspects of the people's spirituality. The role of the parish leader, especially in the Hispanic/Latino context, is to help engender the simultaneity of these facets in one preaching. In the Dominican tradition, originating in the late Middle Ages, preaching these two aspects of the people's religious life was achieved both by the friars' promotion of popular devotions, such as the rosary, eucharistic adoration, and avid storytelling missions, and advocacy of religious life through participation in official and canonical celebrations of our covenants and the cathedrals.[2]

Preaching from the Common Experience of Exile

Such pastoral sensitivity will help the community as a whole avoid overlooking the diversity of the peoples of the parish. Attentiveness to feasts and festivals pertaining to particular religious-cultural identities, to the individual stories that embody them, and to the specific hurts and struggles linked to those stories—all are necessary for the enhancement of the religious life of the local church. Moreover, in the parish, cultural and social differences can be the cause of strife and tension between peoples and thwart the achievement of the harmony and cohesion necessary for healthy parish life. Nevertheless, even with these differences among peoples, there remains a commonality that binds the U.S. Hispanic/Latino religious experience. It is from that common place that preaching and ministry flow in the parish. A sense of shared marginality evokes the paschal drama of people's lives in unique ways.

The shared experience of a cultural and religious estrangement unique to U.S. Hispanic/Latino peoples is brought about by their common experience of exile. Despite differences, U.S. Hispanic/Latino peoples share the common experience of estrangement from family, homeland, and church. Frequently, political and economic factors have driven people from their familiar environments, and it is often difficult or impossible for them to return there. Even though they have found new places to live, and perhaps to prosper, various social and religious obstacles in the dominant U.S. culture continue to underscore their exile. The phenomenon of second-class citizenry, whereby one's native language and culture remain foreign to the dominant Anglo culture, characterizes the people's experience of alienation. In addition, another form of exile is illustrative of the double-estrangement of not being accepted as fully American and at the same time no longer belonging to the land where one originated, rendering the person betwixt and between land of origin and new homeland. This double-exile from both the family of origin and the dominant U.S. culture renders one alien from self and surrounding culture.

In order for preaching and pastoral ministry in U.S. Hispanic/ Latino parish life to be successful, it must address the sense of exile that punctuates the lives of the people. It must speak to how a common experience of alienation divides families and is covered over by various forms of socio-cultural denial and compensation. In a more positive vein, healing and reconciliation arise in the face of remembrance, often unmasking the causes of alienation. In the case of our parish life, preaching and social mission serve as especially important sources for healing "dangerous memories." For instance, sensitivity to how language and the liturgical life of the parish function can mend painful tensions between generations.

We have found that careful and intelligible revision of popular religious devotion in the life of the parish serves especially as one of the most important ways that religious and social identity is revived. Once again, preaching plays a singularly important place in these celebrations. This means creatively retelling the narrative of exile as it is embodied in the popular stories of faith. Jesus, Mary, and the saints deliver an exiled and wandering people from their alienation. In U.S. contexts, these devotions come alive with new richness. Preaching about God's accompaniment in the awkward and lonely frontier of non-acceptance and estrangement revives the paschal dramas of Christian suffering and hope. We retell the story of God's promise to a people rendered alien and foreign, a people who are saved by a God who shows preference for the exiled.

Social Mission of the Parish as Accompaniment

The experience of walking with another as a community of exiled persons is tested by how that community responds to those in need. Advocacy for social justice and social mission in Hispanic/Latino communities remains not as abstract principles to be lived out, but as concrete relationships with others who have been exiled by political and economic estrangement. Fundamental to social mission is the tremendous desire to help those who are in need, likened to the way God has accompanied them in their exile.

Roberto Goizueta speaks of this "particularity of accompaniment" in his description of social advocacy in the Hispanic/Latino community:

> A necessary precondition of authentic community is a preferential identification with particular poor persons, whose perspective—precisely as particular—is not merely "one among equally valid others," but, since it is the one presently excluded from community, is the one without which no authentic community is possible. In other words, the particularity of the poor is the most accurate perspective from which to view the community as a whole—and from which to "opt for" *all* persons.[3]

Universality of concern occurs in the particularity of involvement. In the Hispanic/Latino context, social mission emanates from the strong sense of community that occasions the particularity of encounter.

An organization that has strongly affected the social ministry of our parish for the past 30 years helps us illustrate the concept of social mission as accompaniment. *Amor en Acción* was born out of the desire of a group of Cuban exiles in Miami to help others. Their experience of the poverty of exile gave them a sensibility for the universal issues of injustice and oppression. Their increased awareness of the faith of the poor also drew them more deeply into a realization of their own faith. From the onset, the organization was designed so that a relationship with the poor would contribute as much to the missionaries' transformation as to the quality of life for the poor.

For three decades, *Amor en Acción* has invited mature young men and women in their last years of high school to travel, with more experienced leaders, on mission trips to Haiti and the Dominican Republic, primarily to meet people radically different yet radically the same as themselves. The purpose of *Amor en Acción* is to develop relationships and not to fix situations. That is not to say that the leaders of the organization would not take on the expressed mission of improving people's lives and sharing faith, but the primary purpose remains accompaniment.

Preaching and Accompaniment

We have learned what it means to preach accompaniment from one of the mission leaders of the parish who herself struggled with how the symbolic encounter of ritual and preaching represented an authentic response to what she had encountered in the Dominican Republic. This leader returned from what she experienced while on mission and wondered how the rituals, especially the eucharistic celebration in

Miami, could parallel that experience. And what she learned about the sacramentality of the sign and the Word was the direct result of her accompaniment of a poor and abused woman she had come to know in the village where she ministered year after year. The insight was simple yet profound. She told us with great satisfaction that the eucharistic bread she ate with the woman in the village was indeed the same bread she ate in Miami and the same word shared as well. Her catechesis for other young missionaries, she announced, from now on would be about the bread and Word shared in the accompaniment of a person.

The context of Hispanic/Latino community teaches us that preaching social mission is about sharing the sign and word encountered in accompaniment. It is catechesis about the shared experience between communities, the bridging of worlds separated by exile. It is about the redeeming experience of reencountering our suffering and loss in the poverty of others who suffer greatly. In addition, the context of the U. S Hispanic/Latino community instructs the Christian about ways to reimagine the Church's response to the suffering of our neighbors.

Preaching social mission also throws one back to the popular narratives that have saved exiled people. Hispanic/Latino religious and church experience teaches us that proclaiming the good news of social mission with integrity depends on the imaginative resources of popular devotion that have provided ritual space for a people's deliverance from alienation. In order to preach popular religion one must critically retrieve these rituals for their intrinsic value for self and community. One must understand how popular feasts and devotions keep the Paschal Mystery alive in the lives of exiled people. What it means for a people to ritually walk with Jesus, Mary, and the saints in their journey from exile to homeland remains an essential aspect of the preacher's task.

Conclusion

In the document *Communities of Salt and Light*, the U.S. bishops have emphasized the integral reality of social mission in the ministry of the parish. Advocacy for social justice and the needs of the poor should not manifest itself as a peripheral concern of the local church community. Instead, social mission must emanate from the heart of the people's Christian vocation. From the liturgy, religious education, and other communal activities of the parish, a clear focus on social mission should flow.

What we have tried to show in this chapter is that the bishops' document, though helpful in setting up a clear framework for parish social mission, lacks specific guidelines for attending to the inculturation of that mission. For the U.S. Hispanic/Latino assembly, preaching a just word relies on shaping a practical solidarity with others in need. It necessitates understanding the importance of popular religiosity in the lives of the people. Moreover, the proclamation of social mission depends on understanding the dominant metaphors of the community itself and how memory is kept. In the case of the Hispanic/Latino assembly, social consciousness relies on the accompaniment of communities and the profound importance of people sharing a common direction in the saving mystery of overturning their exile.

NOTES

[1] Mark E. Wedig, "The Visual Hermeneutics of Hispanic/Latino Popular Religion and the Recovery of the Image in Christian Praxis," *Journal of Hispanic/Latino Theology* vol. 8:3 (February 2001): 6–17.

[2] John Van Engen, "Dominic and the Brothers: *Vitæ* as Life–Forming *Exempla* in the Order of Preachers," in *Christ Among the Medieval Dominicans*, Dent Emery, Jr. and Joseph P. Wawrykow, eds. (Notre Dame: University of Notre Dame Press, 1998), 7–25.

[3] Roberto S. Goizueta, *Caminemos Con Jesús: Toward a Hispanic/Latino Theology of Accompaniment* (Maryknoll: Orbis, 1995), 183.

REFERENCES

Jorge L. Presmanes, "The Juxtaposition of Dangerous Memories: Towards a Latino Theology of Preaching from the Underside of the Diaspora Experience," in *Preaching and Culture in Latino Congregations*, Kenneth G. Davis and Jorge L. Presmanes, eds. (Chicago: Liturgy Training Publications, 2000).

Fernando F. Segovia, "In the World but Not of It: Exile as Locus for a Theology of the Diaspora," H*ispanic/Latino Theology: Challenge and Promise*, Ada María Isasi–Díaz and Fernando F. Segovia, eds. (Minneapolis: Fortress Press, 1996), 195–217.

Communities of Salt and Light: Reflections on the Social Mission of the Parish (1993): Suggestions for Civil/Liturgical Occasions

Rev. Raúl Gómez

T he liturgy throughout the year provides ample opportunities to connect faith to everyday life, and the gospel readings describing Jesus' ministry offer chances to preach on social outreach and justice. Blessings on special occasions of those involved in activities embodying the church's social mission help focus attention on questions of justice and peace. Special prayer services advocating for justice, creating community, building solidarity, or respecting diversity are other ways *Communities of Salt and Light* can have an impact on the faith community.

Civil events lending themselves to celebrations of the Church's social mission include commemorations of Martin Luther King, Jr. in January, the anniversary of the death of labor leader César Chávez on April 23, and the martyrdom of El Salvadoran Archbishop Oscar Romero on March 24. Black History Month in February, Hispanic Heritage Month in September-October, and *El Día de la Raza* (October 12), celebrating the Hispanic heritage of the Americas, provide good occasions to address social justice concerns. Labor Day, Memorial Day, and Veteran's Day are other apt occasions.

Several liturgical events provide opportunities as well. The Feast of Saint Francis of Asissi on October, with its stress on service to the poor and respect for the earth, is a good time for preaching on social justice. Good Shepherd Sunday, Divine Mercy Sunday, the Feast of the Holy Family in December, and the two feasts honoring Saint Joseph on March 19 and May 1 are also times to preach on this topic. Many dioceses have an annual "Red Mass" for those who work as lawyers and judges, as well as special liturgies honoring Respect Life Sunday.

Communities of Salt and Light:
Reflections on the Social Mission of the Parish

Rev. José A. López

Reference: United States Conference of Catholic Bishops, Lectionary for Mass, Second Typical Edition, Vol. I–IV. Chicago: Liturgy Training Publications, 2002.

Texts

I:14	Isaiah 9:1–6
II:413	Deuteronomy 10:12–22
II:440	Colossians 3:12–15
III:341	James 3:13–18
I:73	Matthew 5:13–16
I:160	Matthew 25:31–46
I:69	Luke 4:14–21

Our challenge, says the *Parish Resource Manual*,

> is to preach the social importance of the biblical message in a more effective way to ensure that God's word is heard in this congregation as the salt of our wisdom and as light for our action. (no. 7)

This manual offers rich resources for consideration in our preaching on this document. The communities who have reflected on God's actions in the world begin with the first to be called out of the land of Ur: Abraham, Sarah, and their communities. There was no other way to bring out the saving deeds of God except in the community's experience. Oral tradition has continued even to this day.

For the Hispanic, one of the great treasures is oral tradition, telling the story of their lives based on the experience of the ones who came before, *los sabios*, the wise ones, and the keepers of the story. Through *leyendas* (legends), *corridos* (folk stories set to music), and *cuentos* (tales and fables), one can sense the story of the people joined to the story of God. What a joyful opportunity for the preacher in the Hispanic community! With the proper approach to the narrative in Hispanic history, Isaiah's triumphant cry of the people's seeing a great light (9:1) joins the community's sense of earthiness (salt) that gives *sabor* (taste) to the gospel stories in which Scripture is fulfilled in our hearing.

To seek justice, to right wrongs, and to keep faith has been the story of the Hispanic in this country. Whether the Church has been with them or not, the social context has always played a role in the faith of the people. To be salt and light is to be faithful to the calling to bring solidarity and hope to a people. The challenge to preach justice, peace, and righteousness is to tell the story of God in the context of the story of a people seeking the fulfillment of Scripture in their story. The words of James ring out when our preaching invites action: "The harvest of justice is sown in peace for those who cultivate peace" (3:18).

A Decade After "Economic Justice for All": Continuing Principles, Changing Context, New Challenges

A Pastoral Message on the Tenth Anniversary of The Economic Pastoral

National Conference of Catholic Bishops

1997

The challenge of this pastoral letter is not merely to think differently, but also to act differently. A renewal of economic life depends on the conscious choices and commitments of individual believers who practice their faith in the world . . . . This letter calls us to conversion and common action, to new forms of stewardship, service, and citizenship. The completion of a letter such as this is but the beginning of a long process of education, discussion, and action.

—*Economic Justice for All* (nos. 25, 27, 28)

Introduction

Almost ten years ago our Bishops' Conference adopted the pastoral letter *Economic Justice for All*. This letter was an effort to proclaim the Gospel of Jesus Christ in the midst of our complex and powerful economy. Our pastoral letter insisted that the measure of our economy is not only what it produces, but also how it touches human life, whether it protects or undermines the dignity of the human person, and how it promotes the common good. We emphasized that economic decisions have human consequences and moral content; they help or hurt people, strengthen or weaken family life, advance or diminish the quality of justice in our land. Our letter was not an economic blueprint, but a moral challenge and a call to action. We called for a "New American Experiment" of participation and collaboration for the common good that has yet to be really tried in our land.

Ten years after *Economic Justice for All*, the nation needs to hear its message once again and respond to its continuing challenges. At a time of great national debate, the Catholic community must continue to speak for poor children and working families. Our nation must reduce its deficits, reform welfare, reshape its foreign assistance, and reorder national priorities. However, the fundamental moral measure of these policy choices is how they touch the poor in our midst, especially children and families who struggle against economic, social, and moral pressures that leave them poor and powerless.

Poor children, workers, and families may not have the most powerful lobbies, but they have the greatest needs. We welcome a broad debate on economic life, but we cannot support a retreat in the fight against poverty and economic injustice.

Therefore, at this time of national choices, we ask the Catholic community's help in assessing how far we have come and where we need to go to realize the promise of our nation and to be faithful to our Catholic teaching on economic life. Much has changed in this decade—in our economy and our world, our churches and our communities. But much remains the same—there is still too much poverty and not enough economic opportunity for all our people.

In this anniversary message, we renew our call to greater economic justice in an economy with remarkable strength and creativity, but with too little economic growth distributed too inequitably. The power and productivity of the U.S. economy sometimes seems to be leading to three nations living side by side:

> One is prospering and producing in a new information age, coping well with new economic challenges.

> A second is squeezed by declining real incomes and global economic competition. They wonder whether they will keep their jobs and health insurance, whether they can afford college education or Catholic schools for their children.

> A third community is growing more discouraged and despairing. Called an American underclass, their children are growing up desperately poor in the richest nation on earth. Their question at the end of the month is whether they can afford the rent or groceries or heat.

As people of faith, we believe we are one family, not competing classes. We are sisters and brothers, not economic units or statistics. We must come together around the values of our faith to shape economic policies that protect human life, promote strong families, expand a stable middle class, create decent jobs, and reduce the level of poverty and need in our society. We need to strengthen our sense of community and our pursuit of the common good. A decade after the pastoral, it remains clear that the moral test of our society is how the poor, the weak, and the vulnerable are faring. And by this standard we are falling far short.

We believe the best way to prepare for this anniversary is not to develop a major new document, but to offer an urgent call to renewed Catholic dialogue and action in pursuit of a more just, productive, and human economy. As we mark this anniversary, we ask the Catholic community in its ongoing activities to:

> *look back* at the economic justice letter and its major themes;

> *look around* at the U.S. economy a decade later, noting progress and continuing problems;

> *look ahead* at future challenges in light of our developing Catholic teaching.

A Look Back

The economic justice pastoral was an enormous undertaking. Years in preparation, it generated wide discussion, occasional controversy, and much activity. But it produced remarkable consensus and unity— all but nine bishops voted for the final letter. The process of consultation, listening, and dialogue strengthened the letter and enriched the Church. In parishes, schools, universities, think tanks, and a wide variety of *ad hoc* efforts, the Church's teaching was shared and discussed and its implications debated. In the years after the pastoral, nine of every ten dioceses conducted education sessions in parishes; 60 percent strengthened legislative advocacy; more than half held sessions with businesses, labor, or farm representatives; and a majority assessed their personnel policies.

While much of the news coverage focused on policy directions, the heart of the letter remains its scriptural roots and Catholic principles. The greatest contribution of our economic justice pastoral was to remind us that the pursuit of economic justice is a work of faith and an imperative of the Gospel. For some Catholics this message was an affirmation of long-held principle. For others, it was a jarring exposure to part of the Catholic tradition they had never encountered. The call to economic justice is not a political preference or ideological choice, but a response to the Scriptures and a requirement of Catholic teaching.

We hope this anniversary period will be a time of increased focus on economic justice in our parishes, institutions, families, and society. A brief resolution cannot communicate the full substance of the letter, but its central message might be summarized in this way:

> The economy exists to serve the human person, not the other way around.

> Economic life should be shaped by moral principles and ethical norms.

> Economic choices should be measured by whether they enhance or threaten human life, human dignity, and human rights.

> A fundamental concern must be support for the family and the well-being of children.

> The moral measure of any economy is how the weakest are faring.

In the last decade, the Church has continued to share and apply its social doctrine. Pope John Paul II continues to be a powerful voice for solidarity and justice in a world often lacking both. His defense of the poor, workers, family life, and the victims of injustice is a constant theme of his travels and teaching. In his 1991 encyclical, *Centesimus Annus*, our Holy Father offered a sweeping moral analysis of the economic and global challenges of our times, reaffirming the principles of our tradition, and developing new themes. This encyclical offers particular challenges for U.S. Catholics. While it recognizes the vital contributions of democratic values and market economics, it insists that these be guided by the common good and be at the service of human dignity and human rights. He reviewed the failed, empty promises of communism, as he warned against a capitalism that neglects the human and moral dimensions of economic life. The *Catechism of the Catholic Church* reaffirms the Church's teaching that economic life must be directed to the service of persons and be subject to the limits of the moral order and the demands of social justice.

Our own Conference has sought to apply Catholic principles in a variety of statements and initiatives that build on our economic pastoral. Our reflections on children and families, environmental justice, international responsibility, stewardship, welfare, health care, and violence in our land offer examples of our commitment to continuing education and advocacy on issues of economic justice.

Our economic justice pastoral and the broader Catholic social teaching that shaped it are complex and nuanced. They do not lend themselves to simple ideological identification. Some in our own community welcome the tradition's teaching on private property, the limits of the state, the advantages of free markets, and the condemnation of communism, but resist the focus on the poor, the defense of labor unions, the recognition of the moral limits of markets, and the responsibilities of government. Others welcome the teaching on the "option for the poor," the duties of government to protect the weak, the warnings against unbridled capitalism, but seem to ignore the centrality of family, the emphasis on economic initiative, and the warnings against the bureaucratic excesses of a "social assistance" state. Our social tradition is a moral framework, not a partisan platform or ideological tool. It challenges both right and left, labor and management to focus on the dignity of the human person and the common good, rather than their own political or economic interests.

In the words of *Centesimus Annus*, we promote: "*a society of free work, of enterprise, and of participation*. Such a society is not directed against the market, but demands that the market be appropriately controlled by the forces of society and by the State, so as to guarantee that the basic needs of the whole of society are satisfied" (no. 35).

A Look Around

In this brief message, we do not offer an overall assessment of our economy, but we need to acknowledge that some things have changed and some have not. As reported in the *Statistical Abstract of the United States*:

> Americans living in poverty have increased from 33 million to almost 37 million, even though our economy has been growing in recent years. Economic forces, family disintegration, and government action and inaction have combined to leave more than a fifth of our children growing up poor in one of the richest nations on earth.

Joblessness, hunger, and homelessness still haunt our nation. Millions of people are actively looking for work and cannot find it. Over the past ten years there has been a sharp increase in the percentage of people who work full-time but cannot lift their family out of poverty. At present this represents 18 percent of all workers.

The poor and the middle class face growing economic insecurity. Wages are stagnating despite recent gains in productivity, and companies seeking to cut costs are turning to part-time and temporary workers, often at the expense of family income.

In the past ten years, some 234,000 family farms have been lost, and the overall poverty rate for farmers continues to hover around 20 percent.

Some rural towns are disappearing, and agricultural land and food processing have become increasingly concentrated in fewer and fewer hands.

Discrimination, lack of jobs, poor education, and other factors have left African-Americans and Hispanics far more likely to be jobless and poor.

Forty-four percent of African-American children and 36 percent of Hispanic children are growing up poor.

Over the past 15 years, the gap between rich and poor in America has grown wider. In 1993, it is reported the highest-earning 20 percent of households saw their income increase by about $10,000. In contrast, the 20 percent of households at the bottom of the income range saw their income decrease by $1,200. At a time of modest economic growth, many families are experiencing declining real wages.

Family and social factors continue to contribute to poverty and economic stress. It is reported that a child born to a mother who is married, with a high school diploma, whose husband works or has a job herself, has an 8 percent chance of growing up in poverty. A child born to a mother who is not married, without a high school education, and without a job in the family has an 80 percent chance of growing up in poverty. Clearly, the disintegration of families, the absence of fathers, high divorce rates, the failures of education, and the reality of joblessness are crucial factors in our economic problems. And just as clearly, strong families contribute to the economic, social, and moral health of our nation.

>The nation continues to pile up debt, burdening both our economy and our children. Government deficits, corporate speculation, and excessive consumerism contribute to an ethic of "buy now-pay later" that violates principles of stewardship and responsibility. The gross federal debt has grown from $1.8 trillion in 1985 to $4.7 trillion in 1994.
>
>Economic issues are increasingly global issues with growing foreign competition, interdependence, and trade. In a post-Cold War world, much has changed, but for many it is still a world of too much poverty and not enough development. The number of chronically hungry people has risen from 500 million in 1985 to 800 million in 1995. Almost 1.3 billion people, many of them children, live in desperate poverty around the world.

Our current economy is marked by considerable paradox. Profits and productivity grow, while many workers' real income and sense of security decline. Parents, of even modest means, wonder whether their children will live as well as they do.

Some businesses cut jobs and prosper while their workers pay the price for downsizing. Government seems to pile up debt, cut programs, and feed public cynicism all at once. At a time of diminishing government help for poor workers and families, congressional spending for new weapons exceeds the Pentagon's request, justified more by employment needs than defense criteria. We seem a very long way from "economic justice for all."

There is no consensus on what explains these trends. The decline of manufacturing jobs, rapid technological change, the globalization of the economy, the diminished influence of labor and trade unions, the erosion of the minimum wage, and the costs of health insurance all have contributed to the declining real family income. A growing income gap is fed by economic decisions that put profits ahead of people and lead to inadequate wages, reduced benefits, fewer jobs, and less job security. Meanwhile, individual choices and immoral behavior that contribute to increasing out-of-wedlock births, violence, drug use, and the changing family structure are having a significant impact on both families and the economy. We know poverty and economic injustice result from discrimination *and* destructive personal behavior, from unwise decisions of corporations *and* the unresponsive behavior of the public sector.

Our Catholic tradition speaks to these concerns. Ten years after *Economic Justice for All*, our community's greatest challenge is to encourage those with economic power to shape their decisions by how they affect the stability of families and the opportunities of people who are poor, while at the same time calling on all individuals to make personal choices that strengthen their families and contribute to the common good.

A Look Ahead: Questions for the Future

As we observe this anniversary, we wish to encourage lively dialogue and principled action on a wide variety of issues and concerns, including:

> How can our nation work together to overcome the scandal of so much poverty in our midst, especially among our children?

> How can our Church take a leadership role in calling those in positions of power to promote economic growth, job security, decent wages, and greater opportunities?

> How can our community shape the priorities of our culture to promote greater personal responsibility and better economic choices?

> What are the moral responsibilities and limitations of markets, the state, and the voluntary sector? How can business, labor, various levels of government, and mediating structures like churches, charities, and voluntary groups work together to overcome economic injustice and exploitation in our communities?

> How can the dignity and rights of workers be protected and enhanced in an economy where increasing competition, frequent downsizing, and less unionization have left many workers at risk?

> How can U.S. workers and enterprises survive and thrive in a world where other nations compete by offering their workers subsistence wages and minimal benefits?

> How can our nation's economic power in the world be used to build a more just global economy? How can trade and development policies offer hope to a still hungry and suffering world?

How can we address the enormous economic pressures that undermine families and the family factors (e.g., absent fathers, teenage mothers, high rates of divorce) that leave so many children poor? How can we support families in their essential moral, social, and economic roles?

How can our society make concern for "the least among us" and the common good the central consideration in the development of budget, environmental, and other national policies?

How can we assess our own work ethic, productivity, consumption, and lifestyles in light of the needs of a hungry world?

How can the nation address the diverse social and economic forces that leave both inner-city and rural communities as places of disproportionate poverty and discouragement?

How can we address the racial discord that exists in our nation today?

How can we overcome the growing racial and ethnic distance between different communities and the continuing impact of discrimination in economic life?

How can the Church practice in its own life and institutions what it preaches to others about economic justice, human dignity, and the rights of workers?

There are many more questions that could be raised, but these are examples of issues where Catholics can apply the Church's teaching, share our experience, and voice our hopes in civil dialogue and principled action on economic justice. In addressing these and other questions, we believe the Catholic community can be a bridge-builder in several ways. Our community crosses lines of class and race, politics and ideology. Catholics are at the center and fringes of U.S. economic life. We are CEOs and senators, union leaders and small-business owners, migrant farmworkers, and homeless children. Ten years after the pastoral, we need to help our Church renew its sense of solidarity and our society rediscover a sense of national community, pursuing the common good rather than our own narrow economic and other interests.

In addition, our tradition emphasizes both rights *and* responsibilities, promotes increased charity *and* insists on greater justice, and advocates greater personal responsibility *and* broader social responsibility. We recognize the vital roles *and* limits of markets, government, and voluntary groups. We hope in this anniversary year we can get beyond some of the false choices and ideological polarization in the economic debate and join in a renewed search for the common good.

We can be the advocates of a renewed social contract between employers and employees, between recipients and providers of assistance, between investors and managers, that seeks long-term progress over short-term gains, that offers respect and security in exchange for responsibility and hard work, and that protects the vulnerable, especially our children.

A Call to Renewed Commitment

We hope that this anniversary period can be a time of prayer and reflection, discussion and dialogue, advocacy and action. Economic justice begins in our homes and families, in our individual choices and household priorities. Unless we teach our children basic values of honesty, compassion, and initiative they will not be equipped to deal with the "counter values" of selfishness, consumerism, and materialism so prevalent in our society.

We urge Catholic publications to refocus on economic issues and their moral and human implications. We also urge Catholic educational institutions to redouble their efforts to share our teaching, to help their students develop concern for the poor and for justice, and to contribute to the common good by their research and educational activities. We urge national and diocesan organizations to integrate themes of economic justice in their ongoing meetings, publications, advocacy, and other activities. And most especially, we encourage Catholic parishes to continue to weave our teaching on economic life into their prayer and preaching, their education and formation, their outreach and advocacy.

We do not ask Catholic communities to set aside their ongoing ministry to focus on economic justice. Rather, we ask leaders to further integrate these principles and tasks into the worship, formation, and service they offer on a daily basis. The pursuit of economic justice is not an option or add-on for Catholics; it is part of who we are and what we believe.

The Catholic community will continue to carry out the message of the pastoral in many different ways—in the service and advocacy of Catholic Charities, the relief and development efforts of Catholic Relief Services, the empowerment and education of the Campaign for Human Development, to cite a few.

Through our own national Conference, our state and diocesan structures, the Catholic community is to continue to educate and advocate for children and families on issues ranging from real welfare reform to school choice, the rights of workers to sustainable development. We need to strengthen and build on these and other impressive efforts.

However, it has always been clear that the pursuit of greater economic justice is not carried out primarily by the statements of religious bodies, but in the broader marketplace—where investments are made, contracts are negotiated, products are created, workers are hired, and policies are set. The search for economic justice is also carried forward in the public square. In this election year, while others are campaigning for office, let us campaign for the poor and vulnerable and for greater economic justice. Let us ask those who seek to lead and represent us how they will govern and vote on key issues of human life, human dignity, and economic justice. And let us as citizens and believers continue to advocate for people who are poor and vulnerable in our communities, nation, and world.

We renew our pastoral's call for believers to shape their choices in the marketplace and public arena according to the values of the Scriptures and the moral principles of the Catholic Church. Whatever our economic status, political identification, or ideological preferences, we are called as Catholics to work for an economy more respectful of human life and human dignity. In our work and citizenship, our economic, political, and personal choices, we must reach out to "the least among us" and seek the common good.

We may differ on specifics and priorities, but let us come together across economic, ideological, and ethnic lines—to work for a society and economy offering more justice and opportunity, especially for the poor. Differences over how to move forward will give rise to legitimate debate, but indifference to the need to build a more just and open economy is not an option for Catholics. Every Christian is called to follow Jesus in his mission—and ours—of bringing "good news to the poor, new sight to the blind, liberty to captives and to set the downtrodden free" (Luke 4:18). That was the call of our pastoral letter almost ten years ago and still is our task today.

Reflections on "Economic Justice for All"

Sister Angela Erevia

W e live in a world full of conflicts, violence, and abuse at every level. Even so, we can still be encouraged by the text of John 3:16: "God so loved the world that he gave us his only Son, that whoever believes in him may not die but may have eternal life." And eternal life consists in knowing the true heavenly Father. After being sent by the Father, Jesus sends us out with the words:

> Go therefore, and make disciples of all the nations. Baptize them in the name of the Father, and of the Son, and of the Holy Spirit. Teach them to carry out everything I have commanded you. And know that I am with you always, until the end of the world!   (Matthew 28:19–20)

It is with confidence in this promise of Jesus that we can go about preaching and doing our mission. The United States Bishop's pastoral letter, *Economic Justice for All*, helps us in this mission by giving us norms, centered on "human dignity, realized in community with others and with the whole of God's creation" (no. 25), by which to judge all our institutions. As Catholics, the bishops tell us, we have inherited a strong tradition of justice. Beginning with the gospel—the message of Jesus about the kingdom of God—the central theme of Jesus' preaching was justice. We know that evangelization means to proclaim to people everywhere the Word of God that has become the focus of our own lives. The second part of the process is to denounce the injustice in our economic and political systems. It does not seem that this second part of the process has held its proper place in our preaching and teaching.

I would like to explore the ways some of the documents' themes can be used in homilies. The first principle of the bishops' document is that "every economic decision and institution must be judged in light of whether it protects or undermines the dignity of the human person" (Introduction, no. 13). All of us in institutional structures ought to protect the poor, those who have no voice, and the dispossessed. We need to protect them the way we protect our own family

84

members. Churchgoers intuitively know in their everyday lives that the family is the most basic structure of society. For this reason, one way to apply the principle of human dignity in our preaching, in ways people can understand, is to relate it to the family; its culture, language, beliefs, values, and rituals.

What is the family today? What motivates families today to continue forward with their heads held high, despite all their suffering? We talk about injustice and the lack of dignity. There are many families who have built up their households from the lowest economic level and have remained very close to the Church. They have not allowed their ties to the Church to weaken. We need to learn from the example of these forbearers of ours. We need to learn from their struggles to maintain self-worth and then judge every economic decision on whether it protects their human dignity.

We know our families, with their values and beliefs. We also know the secrets of the family and its imperfections, and we continue to believe in the dignity of each person created in the image of God (Genesis 1:27). The principle of human dignity in *Economic Justice for All* is used to weave all these realities together, examining how they influence, help, or hinder the family.

The second principle of the bishops' pastoral letter informs us that "human dignity can be realized and protected only in community" (Introduction, no. 14). It's not possible to work alone for justice; we need to work in community. All have the right to share in the economic life of society. Even the poorest need to be given the opportunity in their employment to use their talents and special aptitudes. For this reason, we must ask if our economic life enhances or threatens us as a community.

The Greek word *koinonia* or "community/fellowship," can help us better understand this communal principle: Jesus commanded us to be a welcoming community. When I speak to Hispanic communities, I ask them what message they want to send to other Hispanic communities. I ask questions like: What is it you want me to say about you? What kind of community are we? Do I say we are a happy, welcoming community, that we are a community of faith, a community that celebrates its traditions and culture? We have to bring this message from one Hispanic community to another as the first apostles did, so that one community might learn from the other. *Koinonia* means to be community, to be followers of Jesus. Here we are dealing with behavior. If someone preaches to me and teaches me that the gospel says we have to be brothers and sisters because we are all children of the same Creator, then I have to do something, I have to behave in a certain way.

Here in the U.S. many of us know well enough in our heads what the Church requires of us, but this knowledge has not reached our hearts. If we are a community following Christ, then we will appreciate the presence of Jesus in liturgical celebrations and in the sacraments. We celebrate his presence in our earthly journey as a community, where we are all companions in the faith. And if we are followers of Jesus, let us come to the churches to celebrate his presence in the liturgy, for we are all welcomed, we are all recognized.

Through songs and films we communicate what we have learned in life about human dignity. When we celebrate a birthday by singing *Las Mañanitas*, we give a clear message to the person who is celebrating: *"El día en que tu naciste, nacieron todas las flores"* ("The day of your birth, all the flowers were born"). A priest I know celebrates something special with his community. The first Sunday of the month, all who are celebrating birthdays are recognized. On the second Sunday, all who have any kind of anniversaries are honored. The third Sunday, all parents who have a child or a newborn. And on the fourth Sunday, prayers are offered for all who have lost a loved one. In this way, each week the needs, the joys, and the troubles and the pain of the community are acknowledged. This is what being a good pastor is all about.

The third principle of the bishops' pastoral is that "all people have a right to participate in the economic life of society" (Introduction, no. 15). This reminds us that any unfair discrimination in employment or economic life is wrong. If people are excluded unfairly when they are able and willing to work but cannot get a job, then they cannot take part in God's creative activity.

In making a commitment to the Church (in Baptism, Confirmation, and the other sacraments) we become part of the official Church. We also have to recognize the Church of the people with its personal beliefs and distinctive styles of piety, such as we find in the peoples of Guatemala, Puerto Rico, Cuba, Chile, and other Latino countries. We should recognize and appreciate the Church of the people that makes up the domestic Church. So also should we recognize that every person who is willing to work should be helped by society to find their productive place in an economy that needs their participation. If we eat and are part of the economy, then we have to pay our way. The teaching we have for the individual is that our work is God's creative work. We seek a place where we can discover our talents and personal gifts in the workplace—a place where they pay just wages.

The fourth principle of the economic pastoral is: "All members of society have a special obligation to the poor and vulnerable" (Introduction, no. 16). All community members, both poor and rich, have a responsibility for helping those who are poor or weak in some way. To be poor implies the need to have access to education. Our mission is to fight against all unjust systems—economic, political, or any other kind. We need to defend the rights of the voiceless, the poor, the abandoned.

Although I had the opportunity to go to a university, I always remember that as a child, I was a cotton–picker. On returning from our vacations, our teachers used to ask us what we had done during our time at home. I was not ashamed to say what I had done because I did not know I was poor. The poor person is ashamed of the work she does. My parents did not marry in church, but they did teach me to give to others and share with them. This is much like what the bishops' economic document teaches us: ". . . to speak for the voiceless, to defend the defenseless, to assess lifestyles, policies, and social institutions in terms of their impact on the poor" (ibid).

We used to have the idea that a good Catholic was one who went to Mass on Sunday, handed in his contribution envelope, brought her child to religion classes, and if there was a Catholic school sent their child there. I did not experience that way of being Catholic. But there is another kind of Catholic or Christian way that I experienced. We visited the sick, went to novenas, walked in candlelight processions, and visited my two nephews in prison. That is the way the Lord makes us humble! That is the Lord who proclaims, "He has sent me to bring glad tidings to the poor" (Luke 4:18b).

The document's fifth principle is "human rights are the minimum conditions for life in community" (Introduction, no. 17). The basic human rights it mentions include "the rights to life, food, clothing, shelter, rest, medical care, and basic education" (no. 80). The document also puts a great deal of stress on the right to a just working environment where workers can form unions to protect their rights (no. 104). There are so many instances where people do not have access to these rights. One example of the absence of the right to basic education is the right to learn and celebrate the values of our culture, which is restricted in many of our public schools. For example, I was in a large southern city, in one of the school districts. They had a ban on singing Christmas carols or celebrating the season. A teacher came and asked me for information about *Las Posadas*, and I told her about them. Yet they are celebrated only in the parish and seldom in schools. Although this is all part of our tradition, we seldom ask to celebrate them in public places. We must work to ensure that all rights to cultural education are protected in society. We Hispanics are a blessing for the Church and the society in the United States. We should get to know our families better and educate them in our traditions and religious devotions.

The system of education has to prepare students to function properly in the world around them. Many of our children do not have access to quality education. A few years back, John Naisbitt wrote *Megatrends*, where he predicted that in the year 2000 we had to be able to speak three languages: English, Spanish, and "Computerese." I mention Spanish, because many of our people have decided to learn and speak only English so as to avoid trouble when they or their children go to school. We should challenge our families not to lose their language, traditions, and rituals.

I would like to conclude my observations by putting a human face on the message of *Economic Justice for All*. Just a few years ago, one of my nephews died. He worked in highway construction, and at the time of his death his younger daughter was three and one-half years old. When I was able to be united with the family in its sorrow, I talked with the young girl and explained to her the value of the work her father had been doing. I told her his work was building highways, roads that people could use to come and go safely. To build roads is something quite important, a job of great dignity. So also should we appreciate the work we do in society.

We have spoken about being created in the image of God. We have the power to love, to think, to act. Human rights include the right to be born, the right to life, the right to have a roof over one's head, the right to nourishment, the right to medical care, to education, and to work. The human rights document of the United Nations also adds that we have the right to live where we choose.

I have given you an outline of human rights as set forth in the bishops' document. The Christian vision of economic life can be found in the perspectives presented in the bishops' pastoral. But the most important things of all to remember are these: we are created in God's image, we are the people of the Covenant, and the reign of God and God's justice are part of our reality.

A Decade After "Economic Justice for All" (1995) Suggestions for Civil/Liturgical Occasions

Rev. Raúl Gómez

This pastoral message stresses the themes of stewardship, the common good, just wages, and the dignity of human persons, among others. Occasions lending themselves to incorporating passages or concepts from this message include a variety of civil and liturgical events throughout the year. Principal among these are civil holidays dedicated to the American values of prosperity and power as well as social-religious holidays that lend themselves to promoting the economy.

As for civil occasions, Labor Day, Thanksgiving, and the commemoration of Martin Luther King, Jr. come immediately to mind. Other occasions lending themselves to preaching on these themes are the anniversaries of the death of César Chávez on April 23 and of the September 11 terrorist attacks.

Other occasions, though principally religious and liturgical in nature, have entered the realm of popular culture as incentives for shopping and growing the economy. These include Christmas and Easter. The readings for Advent and Lent provide many points of departure to address this challenge.

Liturgical or religious occasions that provide opportunities for preaching on the themes of this pastoral message include the feasts of Saint Joseph on March 19 and May 1, the commemorations of Saints Isidore the Farmer on May 15 and Juan Diego on December 9, or the Solemnity of Our Lady of Guadalupe on December 12. Other opportunities can appear during *Las Posadas* devotion in December or when reflecting on the early Christian community in Jerusalem at the onset of the Easter season. Collections for stewardship campaigns are also opportune moments.

Economic Justice for All
Suggested Liturgical Texts

Rev. José A. López

Reference: United States Conference of Catholic Bishops, Lectionary for Mass, Second Typical Edition, Vol. I–IV. Chicago: Liturgy Training Publications, 2002.

Texts

IV:882–1	Genesis 1:26–2:3
IV:882–2	Genesis 2:4b–9, 15.
IV:882–8	Isaiah 32:15–18
IV:882–9	Isaiah 58:6–11
IV:883–1	Acts 11:27–30
IV:883–4	2 Corinthians 9:6–15
IV:883–7	Colossians 3:9b–17
IV:883–8	Timothy 6:6–11, 17–19
IV:883–10	James 4:1–10
IV:886–1	Matthew 5:1–12a
IV:886–2	Matthew 5:20–24
IV:886–3	Matthew 5:38–48
II:446	Luke 7:36–50
IV:886–7	Luke 12:15–21
IV:886–11	Luke 22:24–30

Chapter 2 of the bishops' pastoral letter presents a comprehensive biblical perspective of the Christian view of economic life, wherein the bishops rightly say that the heart of the letter is its "scriptural roots and Catholic principles" (Tenth Anniversary Edition of *Economic Justice for All*, pg. 5). The preacher is given a plethora of scriptural guides for preaching. The letter also demands repeated reading and reflection for the preacher. Because the letter has lost none of its richness for today's Catholic, one would do well to use the letter as a resource for study, action, and preaching in the Hispanic context. It has not been a factor in either preaching or teaching for the Hispanic community. Perhaps it is time for us to go back to those roots that echo the prophetic justice of Isaiah, fulfilled in Jesus Christ.

This is a case where our preaching in the Hispanic community requires action and community involvement. While Hispanics struggle to make life viable, we need to call them to see the need to expand one's horizons, to see the vision of Christ in the fulfillment of his kingdom for all. To preach in this context is difficult yet prophetic.

CHAPTER V

Living the Gospel of Life

Living the Gospel of Life:
A Challenge to American Catholics
A Statement by the Catholic Bishops
of the United States

Secretariat for Pro-Life Activities
United States Conference of Catholic Bishops
3211 4th Street, N.E., Washington, DC
20017-1194 (202) 541-3070
November 11, 2002

> Now the word of the LORD came to me saying, /
> Before I formed you in the womb I knew you, / and before
> you were born I consecrated you; / I appointed you a
> prophet to the nations.   —Jeremiah 1:5

Brothers and Sisters in the Lord:

At the conclusion of the 1998 *Ad Limina* visits of the bishops of the
United States, our Holy Father Pope John Paul II spoke these words:

> Today I believe the Lord is saying to us all: do not hesi-
> tate, do not be afraid to engage the good fight of the faith
> (cf. 1 Timothy 6:12). When we preach the liberating mes-
> sage of Jesus Christ we are offering the words of life to the
> world. Our prophetic witness is an urgent and essential
> service not just to the Catholic community but to the
> whole human family.

In this statement we attempt to fulfill our role as teachers and pastors
in proclaiming the Gospel of Life. We are confident that the proclamation of the truth in love is an indispensable way for us to exercise
our pastoral responsibility.

I. The American Century

> Your country stands upon the world scene as a model of a
> democratic society at an advanced stage of development.

94

Your power of example carries with it heavy responsibilities. Use it well, America!

—Pope John Paul II, Newark, 1995

When Henry Luce published his appeal for an "American century" in
1941, he could not have known how the coming reality would dwarf
his dream. Luce hoped that the "engineers, scientists, doctors. . .
builders of roads [and] teachers" of the United States would spread
across the globe to promote economic success and American ideals:
"a love of freedom, a feeling for the quality of opportunity, a tradition
of self-reliance and independence and also cooperation."[1] Exactly
this, and much more, has happened in the decades since. U.S. economic success has reshaped the world. But the nobility of the
American experiment flows from its founding principles, not from its
commercial power. In this century alone, hundreds of thousands of
Americans have died defending those principles. Hundreds of thousands more have lived lives of service to those principles—both at
home and on other continents—teaching, advising, and providing
humanitarian assistance to people in need. As Pope John Paul has
observed, "At the center of the moral vision of [the American] founding documents is the recognition of the rights of the human person.
. . ." The greatness of the United States lies "especially [in its] respect
for the dignity and sanctity of human life in all conditions and at all
stages of development."[2]

2. This nobility of the American spirit endures today in those who
struggle for social justice and equal opportunity for the disadvan-
taged. The United States has thrived because, at its best, it embodies
a commitment to human freedom, human rights and human dignity.
This is why the Holy Father tells us: ". . . [As] Americans, you are
rightly proud of your country's great achievements."[3]

3. But success often bears the seeds of failure. U.S. economic and
military power has sometimes led to grave injustices abroad. At
home, it has fueled self-absorption, indifference, and consumerist
excess. Overconfidence in our power, made even more pronounced
by advances in science and technology, has created the illusion of a
life without natural boundaries and actions without consequences.
The standards of the marketplace, instead of being guided by sound
morality, threaten to displace it. We are now witnessing the gradual
restructuring of American culture according to ideals of utility, pro-

ductivity, and cost-effectiveness. It is a culture where moral questions are submerged by a river of goods and services, and where the misuse of marketing and public relations subverts public life.

4. The losers in this ethical sea of change will be those who are elderly, poor, disabled, and politically marginalized. None of these pass the utility test; and yet, they at least have a presence. They at least have the possibility of organizing to be heard. *Those who are unborn, infirm, and terminally ill have no such advantage.* They have no "utility," and worse, they have no voice. As we tinker with the beginning, the end, and even the intimate cell structure of life, we tinker with our own identity as a free nation dedicated to the dignity of the human person. When American political life becomes an experiment on people rather than *for* and *by* them, it will no longer be worth conducting. We are arguably moving closer to that day. Today, when the inviolable rights of the human person are proclaimed and the value of life publicly affirmed, the most basic human right, "the right to life, is being denied or trampled upon, especially at the more significant moments of existence: the moment of birth and the moment of death" (Pope John Paul II, *The Gospel of Life [Evangelium Vitae],* 18).

5. The nature and urgency of this threat should not be misunderstood. Respect for the dignity of the human person demands a commitment to human rights across a broad spectrum: "Both as Americans and as followers of Christ, American Catholics must be committed to the defense of life in all its stages and in every condition."[4] The culture of death extends beyond our shores: famine and starvation, denial of health care and development around the world, the deadly violence of armed conflict, and the scandalous arms trade that spawns such conflict. Our nation is witness to domestic violence, the spread of drugs, sexual activity which poses a threat to lives, and a reckless tampering with the world's ecological balance. Respect for human life calls us to defend life from these and other threats. It calls us as well to enhance the conditions for human living by helping to provide food, shelter, and meaningful employment, beginning with those who are most in need. We live the Gospel of Life when we live in solidarity with the poor of the world, standing up for their lives and dignity. Yet abortion and euthanasia have become preeminent threats to human dignity because they directly attack life itself, the most fundamental human good and the condition for all others. They are committed against those who are weakest and most defenseless, those

who are genuinely "the poorest of the poor." They are endorsed increasingly without the veil of euphemism, as supporters of abortion and euthanasia freely concede these are killing even as they promote them. Sadly, they are practiced in those communities which ordinarily provide a safe haven for the weak—the family and the healing professions. Such direct attacks on human life, once crimes, are today legitimized by governments sworn to protect the weak and marginalized.

6. It needn't be so. God, the Father of all nations, has blessed the American people with a tremendous reservoir of goodness. He has also graced our founders with the wisdom to establish political structures enabling all citizens to participate in promoting the inalienable rights of all. As Americans, as Catholics, and as pastors of our people, we write therefore today *to call our fellow citizens back to our country's founding principles, and most especially to renew our national respect for the rights of those who are unborn, weak, disabled, and terminally ill.* Real freedom rests on the inviolability of every person as a child of God. The inherent value of human life, at every stage and in every circumstance, is not a sectarian issue any more than the Declaration of Independence is a sectarian creed.

7. In a special way, we call on U.S. Catholics, especially those in positions of leadership—whether cultural, economic, or political—to recover their identity as followers of Jesus Christ and to be leaders in the renewal of American respect for the sanctity of life. "Citizenship" in the work of the Gospel is also a sure guarantee of responsible citizenship in American civic affairs. Every Catholic, without exception, should remember that he or she is called by our Lord to proclaim His message. Some proclaim it by word, some by action, and all by example. But every believer shares responsibility for the Gospel. Every Catholic is a missionary of the Good News of human dignity redeemed through the cross. While our personal vocation may determine the form and style of our witness, Jesus calls each of us to be a leaven in society, and we will be judged by our actions. No one, least of all someone who exercises leadership in society, can rightfully claim to share fully and practically the Catholic faith and yet act publicly in a way contrary to that faith.

8. Our attitude toward the sanctity of life in these closing years of the "American century" will say volumes about our true character as a nation. It will also shape the discourse about the sanctity of human life in the next century, because what happens here, in our nation, will

have global consequences. It is primarily U.S. technology, U.S. microchips, U.S. fiber optics, U.S. satellites, U.S. habits of thought and entertainment, which are building the neural network of the new global mentality. What America has indelibly imprinted on the emerging global culture is its spirit. And the ambiguity of that spirit is why the pope appealed so passionately to the American people in 1995. "It is vital for the human family . . . that in continuing to seek advancement in many different fields—science, business, education and art, and wherever else your creativity leads you—America keeps compassion, generosity, and concern for others at the very heart of its efforts."[5] That will be no easy task.

II. The Abolition of Man

> In our time, political speech and writing are largely the defense of the indefensible.
>
> —George Orwell, *Politics and the English Language*

Nations are not machines or equations. They are like ecosystems. A people's habits, beliefs, values, and institutions intertwine like a root system. Poisoning one part will eventually poison it all. As a result, bad laws and bad court decisions produce degraded political thought and behavior, and vice versa. So it is with the legacy of *Roe vs. Wade*. *Roe* effectively legalized abortion throughout pregnancy for virtually any reason, or none at all. It is responsible for the grief of millions of women and men, and the killing of millions of unborn children in the past quarter century. Yet the weaknesses of the Supreme Court's 1973 reasoning are well known. They were acknowledged by the Supreme Court itself in the subsequent 1992 *Casey* decision, which could find no better reason to uphold *Roe* than the habits *Roe* itself created by surviving for 20 years.[6] The feebleness and confusion of the *Casey* decision flow directly out of *Roe's* own confusion. They are part of the same root system. Taking a distorted "right to privacy" to new heights, and developing a new moral calculus to justify it, *Roe* has spread through the American political ecology with toxic results.

    10. *Roe* effectively *rendered the definition of human personhood flexible and negotiable*. It also implicitly excluded unborn children from human status. In doing so, *Roe* helped create an environment in which infanticide—a predictable next step along the continuum of

killing—is now open to serious examination. Thanks ultimately to *Roe*, some today speculate publicly and sympathetically why a number of young American women kill their newborn babies or leave them to die. Even the word "infanticide" is being replaced by new and less emotionally charged words like "neonaticide" (killing a newborn on the day of his or her birth) and "filicide" (killing the baby at some later point). Revising the name given to the killing *reduces its perceived gravity.* This is the ecology of law, moral reasoning, and language in action. Bad law and defective moral reasoning produce the evasive language to justify evil. Nothing else can explain the verbal and ethical gymnastics required by elected officials to justify their support for partial-birth abortion, a procedure in which infants are brutally killed during the process of delivery. The same sanitized marketing is now deployed on behalf of physician-assisted suicide, fetal experimentation, and human cloning. Each reduces the human person to a problem or an object. Each can trace its lineage in no small part to *Roe.*

11. Obviously *Roe* is only one of several social watersheds which have shaped the America of the late 1990s. But it is a uniquely destructive one. In the 25 years since *Roe*, our society's confusion about the relationship of law, moral reasoning, and language has created more and more cynicism in the electorate. As words become unmoored from their meaning (as in "choice" or "terminating a pregnancy"), and as the ideas and ideals which bind us together erode, democratic participation inevitably declines. So too does a healthy and appropriate patriotism.

12. At Baltimore's Camden Yards, Pope John Paul spoke prophetically when he said: "Today the challenge facing America is to find freedom's fulfillment in truth; the truth that is intrinsic to human life created in God's image and likeness, the truth that is written on the human heart, the truth that can be known by reason and can therefore form the basis of a profound and universal dialogue among people about the direction they must give to their lives and their activities."[7]

III. We Hold These Truths to Be Self-Evident

> For the power of Man to make himself what he pleases means, as we have seen, the power of some men to make other men what they please.
>
> —C.S. Lewis, *The Abolition of Man*

We believe that universal understandings of freedom and truth are "written on the human heart." America's founders also believed this to be true. In 1776 John Dickinson, one of the framers of our Constitution, affirmed: "Our liberties do not come from charters; for these are only the declaration of pre-existing rights. They do not depend on parchments or seals, but come from the king of kings and the Lord of all the earth."[8] The words of the Declaration of Independence speak of the "Laws of Nature and of Nature's God," and proceed to make the historic assertion: "We hold these truths to be self-evident, that all men are created equal, that they are endowed by their Creator with certain inalienable Rights, that among these are Life, Liberty and the pursuit of Happiness. . . ." Today, more than two centuries of the American experiment have passed. We tend to take these words for granted. But for the founders, writing on the brink of armed revolution, these phrases were invested not just with their philosophy but with their lives. This is why they closed with a "firm reliance on the protection of divine Providence." The words of the Declaration of Independence illuminate the founding principles of the American Republic, principles explicitly grounded in unchanging truths about the human person.

14.   The principles of the Declaration were not fully reflected in the social or political structures of its own day. Then human slavery and other social injustices stood in tension to the high ideals the founders articulated. Only after much time and effort have these contradictions been reduced. In a striking way, we see today a heightening of the tension between our nation's founding principles and political reality. We see this in diminishing respect for the inalienable right to life and in the elimination of legal protections for those who are most vulnerable. There can be no genuine justice in our society until the truths on which our nation was founded are more perfectly realized in our culture and law.

15.   One of those truths is our own essential creatureliness. Virtual reality and genetic science may give us the illusion of power, but we are not gods. We are not our own, or anyone else's, creator. Nor, for our own safety, should we ever seek to be. Even parents, entrusted with a special guardianship over new life, do not "own" their children any more than one adult can own another. And therein lies our only security. *No one but the Creator is the sovereign of basic human rights—beginning with the right to life.* We are daughters and sons of the one God who, outside and above us all, grants us the freedom,

dignity, and rights of personhood which no one else can take away. Only in this context, the context of a Creator who authors our human dignity, do words like "truths" and "self-evident" find their ultimate meaning. Without the assumption that a Creator exists who has ordained certain irrevocable truths about the human person, no rights are "inalienable," and nothing about human dignity is axiomatic.

16.   This does not make America sectarian. It does, however, underline the crucial role God's sovereignty has played in the architecture of American politics. While the founders were a blend of Enlightenment rationalists and traditional Christians, generations of Jews, Muslims, other religious groups, and non-believers have all found a home in the United States. This is so because the tolerance of our system is rooted in the Jewish-Christian principle that even those who differ from one another in culture, appearance, and faith *still share the same rights.* We believe that this principle still possesses the power to enlighten our national will.

17.   The Second Vatican Council, in its *Pastoral Constitution on the Church in the Modern World* (*Gaudium et Spes*), praises those women and men who have a vocation to public office. It encourages active citizenship. It also reminds us that "the political community . . . exists for the common good: this is its full justification and meaning and the source of its specific and basic right to exist. The common good embraces the sum total of all those conditions of social life which enable individuals, families and organizations to achieve complete and efficacious fulfillment" (74). In pursuing the common good, citizens should "cultivate a generous and loyal spirit of patriotism, but without narrow-mindedness . . . [they must also] be conscious of their specific and proper role in the political community: they should be a shining example by their sense of responsibility and their dedication to the common good . . ." (75).

18.   As to the role of the Church in this process: ". . . The political community and the church are autonomous and independent of each other in their own fields. They are both are devoted to the personal vocation of man, though under different titles . . . [yet] at all times and in all places, the Church should have the true freedom to teach the faith, to proclaim its teaching about society, to carry out its task among men without hindrance, *and to pass moral judgment even in matters relating to politics, whenever the fundamental rights of man or the salvation of souls requires it*" (76).

19. Pope John Paul II elaborates on this responsibility in his 1988 apostolic exhortation, *The Vocation and the Mission of the Lay Faithful in the Church and in the World* (*Christifideles Laici*): "The inviolability of the person, which is a reflection of the absolute inviolability of God, finds its primary and fundamental expression in the *inviolability of human life*. Above all, the common outcry, which is justly made on behalf of human rights—for example, the right to health, to home, to work, to family, to culture—is false and illusory if *the right to life*, the most basic and fundamental right and the condition of all other personal rights, is not defended with maximum determination . . . . The human being is entitled to such rights, *in every phase of development*, from conception until natural death; and *in every condition*, whether healthy or sick, whole or handicapped, rich or poor . . . . [Moreover, if,] indeed, everyone has the mission and responsibility of acknowledging the personal dignity of every human being and of defending the right to life, some lay faithful are given particular title to this task: such as *parents, teachers, healthworkers and the many who hold economic and political power*" (no. 38).

20. We believe that the Gospel of Jesus Christ is a "Gospel of life." It invites all persons and societies to a new life lived abundantly in respect for human dignity. We believe that this Gospel is not only a complement to American political principles, but also the cure for the spiritual sickness now infecting our society. As Scripture says, no house can stand divided against itself (Luke 11:17). We cannot simultaneously commit ourselves to human rights and progress while eliminating or marginalizing the weakest among us. Nor can we practice the Gospel of life only as a private piety. American Catholics must live it *vigorously and publicly*, as a matter of national leadership and witness, or we will not live it at all.

IV. Living the Gospel of Life: the Virtues We Need

It is impossible to further the common good without acknowledging and defending the right to life, upon which all the other inalienable rights of individuals are founded and from which they develop.

—Pope John Paul II, *Evangelium Vitae* (no. 101)

21. Bringing a respect for human dignity to practical politics can be a daunting task. There is such a wide spectrum of issues involving the protection of human life and the promotion of human dignity. Good people frequently disagree on which problems to address, which policies to adopt, and how best to apply them. But for citizens and elected officials alike, the basic principle is simple: *We must begin with a commitment never to intentionally kill, or collude in the killing, of any innocent human life, no matter how broken, unformed, disabled, or desperate that life may seem.* In other words, the choice of certain ways of acting is *always and radically incompatible* with the love of God and the dignity of the human person created in his image. Direct abortion is *never* a morally tolerable option. It is *always* a grave act of violence against a woman and her unborn child. This is so even when a woman does not see the truth because of the pressures she may be subjected to, often by the child's father, her parents, or friends. Similarly, euthanasia and assisted suicide are *never* acceptable acts of mercy. They *always* gravely exploit the suffering and desperate, extinguishing life in the name of the "quality of life" itself. This same teaching against direct killing of the innocent condemns all direct attacks on innocent civilians in time of war.

22. Pope John Paul II has reminded us that we must respect every life, even that of criminals and unjust aggressors. It is increasingly clear in modern society that capital punishment is unnecessary to protect people's safety and the public order, so that cases where it may be justified are "very rare, if not practically non-existent." No matter how serious the crime, punishment that does not take life is "more in conformity with the dignity of the human person" (*Evangelium Vitæ* 56–7). Our witness to respect for life shines most brightly when we demand respect for each and every human life, including the lives of those who fail to show that respect for others. The antidote to violence is love, not more violence.

23. As we stressed in our 1995 statement *Political Responsibility*: "The application of gospel values to real situations is an essential work of the Christian community." Adopting a consistent ethic of life, the Catholic Church promotes a broad spectrum of issues "seeking to protect human life and promote human dignity from the inception of life to its final moment."[9] Opposition to abortion and euthanasia does not excuse indifference to those who suffer from poverty, violence, and injustice. Any politics of human life must work to resist the violence of war and the scandal of capital punishment. Any politics of

human dignity must seriously address issues of racism, poverty, hunger, employment, education, housing, and health care. Therefore, Catholics should eagerly involve themselves as advocates for the weak and marginalized in all these areas. Catholic public officials are obliged to address each of these issues as they seek to build consistent policies which promote respect for the human person at all stages of life. *But being "right" in such matters can never excuse a wrong choice regarding direct attacks on innocent human life.* Indeed, the failure to protect and defend life in its most vulnerable stages renders suspect any claims to the "rightness" of positions in other matters affecting the poorest and least powerful of the human community. If we understand the human person as the "temple of the Holy Spirit"— the living house of God—then these latter issues fall logically into place as the crossbeams and walls of that house. *All direct attacks on innocent human life, such as abortion and euthanasia, strike at the house's foundation.* These directly and immediately violate the human person's most fundamental right—the right to life. Neglect of these issues is the equivalent of building our house on sand. Such attacks cannot help but lull the social conscience in ways ultimately destructive of other human rights. As Pope John Paul II reminds us, the command never to kill establishes a minimum which we must respect and from which we must start out "in order to say 'yes' over and over again, a 'yes' which will gradually embrace the *entire horizon of the good*" (*Evangelium Vitæ*, 75).

24.   Since the entry of Catholics into the U.S. political mainstream, believers have struggled to balance their faith with the perceived demands of democratic pluralism. As a result, some Catholic elected officials have adopted the argument that, while they personally oppose evils like abortion, they cannot force their religious views onto the wider society. This is seriously mistaken on several key counts. First, regarding abortion, the point when human life begins is not a religious belief but a scientific fact—a fact on which there is clear agreement even among leading abortion advocates. Second, the sanctity of human life is not merely Catholic doctrine but part of humanity's global ethical heritage, and our nation's founding principle. Finally, democracy is not served by silence. Most Americans would recognize the contradiction in the statement, "While I am personally opposed to slavery or racism or sexism I cannot force my personal view on the rest of society." *Real pluralism depends on people*

of conviction struggling vigorously to advance their beliefs by every ethical and legal means at their disposal.

25. Today, Catholics risk cooperating in a false pluralism. Secular society will allow believers to have whatever moral convictions they please—as long as they keep them on the private preserves of their consciences, in their homes and churches, and out of the public arena. Democracy is not a substitute for morality, nor a panacea for immorality. Its value stands—or falls—with the values which it embodies and promotes. *Only* tireless promotion of the truth about the human person can infuse democracy with the right values. This is what Jesus meant when he asked us to be leaven in society. American Catholics have long sought to assimilate into U.S. cultural life. But in assimilating, we have too often been digested. We have been *changed by* our culture too much, and we have changed it not enough. If we are leaven, we must bring to our culture the whole Gospel, which is a *Gospel of life and joy.* That is our vocation as believers. And there is no better place to start than promoting the beauty and sanctity of human life. Those who would claim to promote the cause of life through violence or the threat of violence contradict this Gospel at its core.

26. Scripture calls us to "be doers of the word, and not hearers only . . . [for] faith by itself, if it has no works, is dead" (James 1:22, 2:17). Jesus himself directs us to "Go therefore and make disciples of all nations . . . teaching them to observe all that I have commanded you. . . ." (Matthew 28:19–20). Life in Christ is a life of *active witness.* It demands *moral leadership.* Each and every person baptized in the truth of the Catholic faith is a member of the "people of life" sent by God to evangelize the world.

27. God is always ready to answer our prayers for help with the virtues we need to do his will. First and foremost we need *the courage and the honesty* to speak the truth about human life, no matter how high the cost to ourselves. The great lie of our age is that we are powerless in the face of the compromises, structures, and temptations of mass culture. But we are not powerless. We can make a difference. We belong to the Lord; in Him is our strength and through his grace we can change the world. We also need the *humility* to listen well to both friend and opponent on the abortion issue, learning from each and forgetting ourselves. We need *the perseverance* to continue the struggle for the protection of human life, no matter what the setbacks, trusting in God and in the ultimate fruitfulness of the task

he has called us to. We need *the prudence* to know when and how to
act in the public arena—and also to recognize and dismiss that fear of
acting which postures as prudence itself. And finally we need the
great foundation of every apostolic life: *faith, hope, and charity*.
Faith not in moral or political abstractions, but in the personal presence of God; *hope* not in our own ingenuity, but in his goodness and
mercy; and *love* for others, including those who oppose us, rooted in
the love God showers down on us.

28. These virtues, like the Gospel of life which they help animate,
have serious implications for every Christian involved in any way in
the public life of the nation.

29. As *bishops*, we have the responsibility to call Americans to
conversion, including political leaders, and especially those publicly
identified as Catholic. As the Holy Father reminds us in *The Splendor
of Truth (Veritatis Splendor)*: ". . . [It] is part of our pastoral ministry
to see to it that [the Church's] moral teaching is faithfully handed
down, and to have recourse to appropriate measures to ensure that the
faithful are guarded from every doctrine and theory contrary to it"
(116). As chief teachers in the Church, we must therefore explain,
persuade, correct, and admonish those in leadership positions who
contradict the Gospel of life through their actions and policies.
Catholic public officials who disregard Church teaching on the inviolability of the human person indirectly collude in the taking of innocent life. A private call to conversion should always be the first step
in dealing with these leaders. Through prayer, through patiently
speaking the truth in love, and by the witness of our lives, we must
strive always to open their hearts to the God-given dignity of the
unborn and of all vulnerable persons. So also we must remind these
leaders of their duty to exercise genuine moral leadership in society.
They do this not by unthinking adherence to public opinion polls or
by repeating empty pro-choice slogans, but by educating and sensi-
tizing themselves and their constituents to the humanity of the unborn
child. At the same time we need to redouble our efforts to evangelize
and catechize our people on the dignity of life and the wrongness of
abortion. Nonethe-less, some Catholic officials may exclude themselves from the truth by refusing to open their minds to the Church's
witness. In all cases, bishops have the duty and pastoral responsibility to continue to challenge those officials on the issue in question and
persistently call them to a change of heart. As bishops we reflect particularly on the words of the Office of Readings:

Let us be neither dogs that do not bark nor silent onlookers nor paid servants who run away before the wolf. Instead, let us be careful shepherds watching over Christ's flock. Let us preach the whole of God's plan to the powerful and the humble, to rich and to poor, to men of every rank and age, as far as God gives us the strength, in season and out of season, as St. Gregory writes in his book of Pastoral Instruction.[10]

30. *Priests, religious catechists, Catholic school teachers, family life ministers*, and *theologians* all share, each in their appropriate way, in the Church's task of forming the Catholic faithful in a reverence for the sanctity of life. We call them to a renewed commitment to that task. In their words and example, they should witness loyally and joyfully to the truth that every human life, at every stage of development, is a gift from God. *Physicians, nurses*, and *health care workers* can touch the lives of women and girls who may be considering abortion with practical assistance, counseling, and adoption alternatives. Equally important, they should be conscious evangelizers of their own professions, witnessing by word and example that God is the Lord of life.

31. *Catholics who are privileged to serve in public leadership positions* have an obligation to place their faith at the heart of their public service, particularly on issues regarding the sanctity and dignity of human life. Thomas More, the former chancellor of England who preferred to give his life rather than betray his Catholic convictions, went to his execution with the words, "I die the king's good servant, but God's first." In the United States in the late 1990s, elected officials safely keep their heads. But some will face a political penalty for living their public office in accord with their pro-life convictions. To those who choose this path, we assure them that their course is just, they save lives through their witness, and God and history will not forget them. Moreover, the risk of witness should not be exaggerated, and the power of witness should not be underestimated. In an age of artifice, many voters are hungry for substance. They admire and support political figures who speak out sincerely for their moral convictions. For our part we commend Catholic and other public officials who, with courage and determination, use their positions of leadership to promote respect for all human life.

32.   We urge those Catholic officials who choose to depart from Church teaching on the inviolability of human life in their public life to consider the consequences for their own spiritual well-being, as well as the scandal they risk by leading others into serious sin. We call on them to reflect on the grave contradiction of assuming public roles and presenting themselves as credible Catholics when their actions on fundamental issues of human life are not in agreement with Church teaching. No public official, especially one claiming to be a faithful and serious Catholic, can responsibly advocate for or actively support direct attacks on innocent human life. Certainly there are times when it may be impossible to overturn or prevent passage of a law which allows or promotes a moral evil—such as a law allowing the destruction of nascent human life. In such cases, an elected official, whose position in favor of life is known, could seek legitimately to limit the harm done by the law. However, no appeal to policy, procedure, majority will, or pluralism ever excuses a public official from defending life to the greatest extent possible. As is true of leaders in all walks of life, no political leader can evade accountability for his or her exercise of power (*Evangelium Vitæ*, 73–4). Those who justify their inaction on the grounds that abortion is the law of the land need to recognize that there is a higher law, the law of God. No human law can validly contradict the Commandment: "Thou shalt not kill."

33.   The Gospel of life must be proclaimed, and human life defended, in all places and all times. The arena for moral responsibility includes not only the halls of government, but the voting booth as well. Laws that permit abortion, euthanasia, and assisted suicide are profoundly unjust, and we should work peacefully and tirelessly to oppose and change them. Because they are unjust they cannot bind citizens in conscience, be supported, acquiesced in, or recognized as valid. Our nation cannot countenance the continued existence in our society of such fundamental violations of human rights.

34.   We encourage *all citizens*, particularly Catholics, to embrace their citizenship not merely as a duty and privilege, but as an opportunity meaningfully to participate *in building the culture of life*. Every voice matters in the public forum. Every vote counts. Every act of responsible citizenship is an exercise of significant individual power. We must exercise that power in ways that defend human life, especially those of God's children who are unborn, disabled, or otherwise vulnerable. We get the public officials we deserve. Their virtue—or

lack thereof—is a judgment not only on them, but on us. Because of this, we urge our fellow citizens *to see beyond party politics, to analyze campaign rhetoric critically, and to choose their political leaders according to principle, not party affiliation or mere self-interest.*

35. We urge parents to recall the words of the Second Vatican Council and our Holy Father in *On the Family* (*Familiaris Consortio*), that the family is "the first and vital cell of society" (no. 42).[11] As the family goes, so goes our culture. Parents are the primary educators of their children, especially in the important areas of human sexuality and the transmission of human life. They shape society toward a respect for human life by first *being open to new life themselves*; then by forming their children—through personal example—with a reverence for the poor, the elderly, and developing life in the womb. Families which live the Gospel of life are *important agents of evangelization through their witness.* But additionally, they should organize "to see that the laws and institutions of the state not only do not offend, but support and actively defend the rights and duties of the family," for the purpose of transforming society and advancing the sanctity of life (no. 44).

36. *Women* have a unique role in the transmission and nurturing of human life. They can best understand the bitter trauma of abortion and the hollowness and sterility at the heart of the vocabulary of "choice." Therefore, we ask women to assume a special role in promoting the Gospel of life with a new pro-life feminism. Women are uniquely qualified to counsel and support other women facing unexpected pregnancies, and they have been in the vanguard of establishing and staffing the more than 3,000 pregnancy aid centers in the United States. They, in a way more fruitful than any others, can help elected officials to understand that any political agenda which hopes to uphold equal rights for all, must affirm the equal rights of every child, born and unborn. They can remind us that our nation's declaration of God-given rights, coupled with the command "Thou shalt not kill," are the starting points of true freedom. To choose any other path is to contradict our own identity as a nation dedicated to "Life, Liberty, and the pursuit of Happiness."

37. We commend all *who proclaim and serve the Gospel of life.* By their peaceful activism, education, and prayer, they witness to God's truth and embody our Lord's command to love one another as he loved us. By their service to women who have experienced abortion, they bring his peace and consolation. We urge them to persevere

in this difficult work and not to be discouraged. Like the cross of our Lord, faithful dedication to the Gospel of life is a "sign of contradiction" in our times.

38. As Pope John Paul II has said: "It is a tribute to the Church and to the openness of American society that so many Catholics in the United States are involved in political life." He reminds us that democracy is . . . a moral adventure, a continuing test of a people's capacity to govern themselves in ways that serve the common good and the good of individual citizens. The survival of a particular democracy depends not only on its institutions, but to an even greater extent on the spirit which inspires and permeates its procedures for legislating, administering and judging. *The future of democracy in fact depends on a culture capable of forming men and women who are prepared to defend certain truths and values.*[12]

39. As we conclude the American century and approach a new era for our own nation and the world, we believe that the purpose of the United States remains hopeful and worthy. In the words of Robert Frost, our vocation is to take *"the road less traveled," the road of human freedom rooted in law; law which is rooted, in turn, in the truth about the sanctity of the human person.* But the future of a nation is decided by every new generation. Freedom always implies the ability to choose between two roads: one which leads to life; the other, death (Deuteronomy 30:19). *It is now our turn to choose.* We appeal to all people of the United States, especially those in authority, and among them most especially Catholics, to understand this critical choice before us. We urge all persons of good will to work earnestly to bring about the cultural transformation we need, a true renewal in our public life and institutions based on the sanctity of all human life. And finally, as God entrusted his Son to Mary nearly 2,000 years ago for the redemption of the world, we close this letter today by entrusting to Mary all our people's efforts to witness the Gospel of Life effectively in the public square.

Mary, patroness of America, renew in us a love for the beauty and sanctity of the human person from conception to natural death; and as your son gave his life for us, help us to live our lives serving others. Mother of the Church, mother of our savior, open our hearts to the Gospel of life, protect our nation, and make us witnesses to the truth.

NOTES

[1] Henry Luce, "The American Century," *Life* (February 17, 1941).

[2] Pope John Paul II, Departure from Baltimore/Washington International Airport, Departure Remarks, October 8, 1995; *Origins*, 25:18 (October 19, 1995): 318.

[3] Pope John Paul II, Homily in Giants Stadium, October 5, 1995; *Origins*, 25:18 (October 19, 1995): 305.

[4] Pope John Paul II, Homily in Giants Stadium, October 5, 1995; *Origins*, 25:18 (October 19, 1995): 303.

[5] Pope John Paul II, Arrival in Newark, Airport Remarks, October 4, 1995; *Origins*, 25:18 (October 19, 1995): 301.

[6] In *Planned Parenthood v. Casey*, 505 U.S. 833 (1992), the Supreme Court upheld most of the challenged provisions of a Pennsylvania law regulating abortion. The Court declined, however, to overturn what it called the "central holding" of *Roe v. Wade* and said: "[F]or two decades of economic and social developments, people have organized intimate relationships and made choices that define their views of themselves and their places in society, in reliance on the availability of abortion in the event that contraception should fail." (505 U.S. at 856).

[7] Pope John Paul II, Homily at Camden Yards, "What Freedom Is," October 8, 1995; 25 *Origins*, 25:18 (October 19, 1995): 314.

[8] Pope John Paul II, Remarks on accepting the credentials of the U.S. Ambassador to the Holy See, December 16, 1997; *Origins*, 27 (January 8, 1998): 488 (citing C. Herman Pritchett, *The American Constitution* [New York: McGraw Hill, 1977], p. 2).

[9] Administrative Board, United States Catholic Conference, "Political Responsibility: Proclaiming the Gospel of life, Protecting the Least Among Us, and Pursuing the Common Good" (Washington, DC: United States Catholic Conference, 1995), p. 12.

[10] Boniface, Ep. 78: MGH, Epistolæ, 3, 352, 354; from *Liturgy of the Hours According to the Roman Rite,* vol. III (New York: Catholic Book Publishing Co. 1976), 1457.

[11] Cf. also *Decree on the Apostolate of Lay People* (*Apostolicam Actuositatem*), (Washington, DC: United States Catholic Conference, 1965), 11.

[12] Pope John Paul II, *Ad Limina* Remarks to the Bishops of Texas, Oklahoma and Arkansas (June 27, 1998); *Origins*, 28:16 (October 1, 1998), 282.

Living the Gospel of Life:
A Challenge to American Catholics
Within the Hispanic Community

Arturo Pérez Rodríguez

The American dream has driven people of other lands to leave their homes and families and risk great hazards to find a new life in America. This dream is the motivational force on which the United States is founded. The dream changes perspectives depending upon the dreamer: some people dream of religious freedom; others, of living freely to pursue their lives without persecution; and still others build a new dream while they settle into a new life. For all peoples, the American dream has been defined as living successfully, fully, and freely in this land.

When Pope John Paul II called a synod of the bishops of the Americas, he underscored the link that exists between the countries of this hemisphere. Just as it is erroneous to equate America only with North America, thereby excluding the Central and South American nations and in reality sidelining Canada, so it is erroneous to equate the American dream only with prosperity and success. The countries of the Americas are linked not only geographically but also by the hopes and dreams that motivate people to leave their homelands in search of a better life. For the Hispanic person, the dream is often contextualized in the words *el norte*. *El norte* was not only the geographic destination where dreams would be fulfilled; *el norte* was the Promised Land, filled not only with milk and honey, but also with the riches that would provide for their families the necessities of life so lacking in their own countries. Stories of success were told and retold. Returning *norteños* displayed their success by driving fancy cars and trucks, building new homes, and freely spending their money.

The dream changed into a myth that all who crossed the border would achieve success without much effort. The only price they had to pay to live the dream was to cross the border into the United States, leaving everything else behind. For some persons, crossing the border is a legal, bureaucratic process of filling out numerous forms, getting copies of bank statements, and signing affidavits. They come legally because of marriages, funerals, and annual family visits. For others, crossing the border is a hazardous journey into a long night of eluding border patrols, working with unscrupulous coyotes—smugglers of people—and facing the dangers of the desert. If they successfully crossed the border, either legally or by hazarding all the dangers of the trip, reality soon burst the Promised-Land myth of easy success.

The dream faded as they confronted the harsh realities of their new lives. The true American dream has always been built on sacrifice and faith. These are the foundation stones for anyone building a new life. This sacrifice demands not only leaving behind the support of a known culture, language, and way of life, but also having the faith to put one's life into God's hands. Sacrifice and faith become the foundation, the undercurrent, and the motivation to cross the border *para el norte* and succeed in this land.

Dreams always have to become realities. The decision to choose life and not death is the everyday experience of many Hispanics. It is in the ordinary day-to-day existence that Pope John Paul's encyclical, *The Gospel of Life*, takes root and becomes both a support and a challenge to Hispanics. The words of this encyclical shatter the false illusion of the American dream by soundly promoting a firm foundation for building a life on the gospel principles of sacrifice and faith. These principles support life. Living the Gospel of life implicitly asks the question, "What is real and what is an illusion?" This question encourages and challenges the Hispanic person to remember, to bring to heart their most noble values, and not to buy into the pressures of a materialistic, consumerism society. It is today's translation of being "in the world, but not of the world."

God's Word brings to light that which is life-giving while identifying the shadows of that which takes away life. This chapter offers three specific points for reflection on how the bishops' document, *Living The Gospel of Life: A Challenge to American Catholics*, makes sense and pertains to the Hispanic community of the United States. It seeks to illuminate the shadows with the light of the gospel. What is presented are points of departure for homilists to develop further, based on the life experiences and examples of their local community of faith.

First Reflection: Competition

Competition is one of the basic principles of American society. The business community is based on this principle. Through competition companies rise and fall. Competition is fostered as a principle of life though schools, associations, and societies. Competing and becoming number one, almost at any cost, measures success. Tinkering with the life of the unborn, incapacitated, and terminally ill (no. 4) because they are not "useful" turns them into obstacles to "success." If we can manipulate life to fit our goals, then we can succeed over others. Competition puts us at odds with one another.

Those who have no voice become the American *anawim*—the biblical "poor ones"—of today. We remember that God not only hears the cry of the poor but also chooses the poor as prophets to announce God's Word of Life and denounce the injustice being perpetrated. In terms of this document, the poor are the ones who announce a culture of life while denouncing the culture of death.

Many Hispanics suffer needlessly because of competition that relegates them to being victims of unfair labor practices and inadequate medical attention, and limits their rights to due process of law. They fear that if they speak out, rocking the boat of their business' labor practices, they will be marked as troublemakers. In standing up for their rights, they fear they will jeopardize their legal status. They often stay in the shadows where they are unjustly treated. They are the *anawim* who cry out to the church and society to choose life and believe in the gospel. The bishops emphatically state, "We live the Gospel of life when we live in solidarity with the poor of the world, standing up for their lives and dignity." (no. 5) While competition often separates people from one another, the Gospel of Life builds bridges for all people to see one another as brothers and sisters on the same journey. We become family to one another by bearing the burdens of our neighbor.

Second Reflection: Self-Evident Truths

The U.S. Declaration of Independence speaks great words when it states:

> We hold these truths to be self-evident, that all men [sic]
> are created equal, that they are endowed by their Creator

with certain inalienable rights, that among these are Life,
Liberty, and the pursuit of Happiness . . . .

"What is truth?" Pilate asked Jesus. What is truth for we Hispanics
who are part of the American experience? Truth does not change from
person to person, from moment to moment, nor does truth change
when one crosses a geographic border. There are "unchanging truths
about the human person" (no. 13) that are self-evident. The Gospel of
Life as well is not hidden, but self-evident. It breaks through any illu-
sions of power a society may have of itself. The Gospel of Life casts
its light on the false idols of genetic scientific experimentation,
manipulation of life in any form, or the principle of complete self-
determination over one's own body. Idolatry exists when we create
idols in our own image and likeness and are willing to sacrifice the
truth for them.

The Hispanic community lives out of a family experience. Much
has been written that reminds us that Hispanic families are extended
families. This extension also includes the "parish family." These are
the people who make up the local worshiping, sacramental community. These are the people who come together as a family of faith that
seeks to promote the rights of all of its members. We do this best
when we look out for those who are the most vulnerable among us:
the unborn, the elderly, the mentally challenged, the physically incapacitated. These are the obvious and self-evident truths by which we
live.

The Gospel of Life also sheds its light on the shadows of our
Hispanic family. We are also in need of purification. There exist idols
of power that curtail our development, challenge our faith, and call us
to lead a more just life. Any aspect of domestic violence, addictive
behaviors, gang involvement, and social discrimination among us are
obvious obstacles to living the Gospel of Life that promotes being
fully alive in Christ Jesus. Forgetting our religious traditions, irregu-
lar attendance at Sunday worship, and infrequent participation in the
sacraments opens us up to behaviors that dim the gospel life. We must
choose that which gives life, and refrain from anything that diminishes life and takes away our humanity.

Third Reflection: American Catholics

As members of the Hispanic community, we share in the life and
death experience of our neighbors. We do not live in private worlds.

The tragic events of September 11, 2001, when so many innocent people died, remind us that we all share a common patrimony. The exact number of Hispanic persons hoping to live out the American dream who died in that event is unknown. Yet the pain and sorrow of one family is shared by the human family if we can, through the suffering, bridge our lives together to promote the common good. "Our witness to respect for life shines most brightly when we demand respect for each and every human life, including the lives of those who fail to show that respect for others. The antidote to violence is love, not more violence" (no. 22).

In order for our Hispanic community to be a beacon of light, truth, and hope amidst the extraordinary challenges of the American society, we first seek to live and proclaim the Gospel of Life among ourselves. As members of the Catholic Church, we look into the mirror and face the reality that confronts us. Though often times poor, "human dignity must seriously address the issues of racism, poverty, hunger, employment, education, housing, and health care." (no. 23) We, as Hispanics, become a prophetic people when, as committed baptized persons and part of the Catholic community, we commit ourselves to being a voice that cries out not so much in the wilderness but on the streets of America, in the legislative halls of our government, and in the churches of our neighborhoods.

> Life in Christ is a life of *active witness*. It demands *moral leadership*. Each and every person baptized in the truth of the Catholic faith is a member of the "people of life" sent by God to evangelize the world. (no. 26)

Our people for centuries have undergone great obstacles that could have brought us down and turned us away from the Church. Yet in all times we have remained faithful, trusting in God's great Providence for us. This trust that God is always with us has been our strength. Our grandparents have handed this trust in God down to us as our inheritance. Our religious leaders, catechists, and pastoral ministers have taught us by word and example that we are "God's beloved." Now as the Hispanic community develops its political consciousness and our leaders move into the halls of political influence, we must make a difference in American society. We support those politicians who most promote life in all of its different forms.

All of us—through whatever vocation God has called us, from whatever state of life we live, from all areas of the country—proclaim the Gospel of Life. Our own rich religious traditions bind us to the Passion, death, and Resurrection of Jesus. Through our religious practices that highlight Mary, the mother of all people, through the *Las Posadas* (the traditional celebration commemorating Mary and Joseph's journey in search of shelter) and Living Stations of the Cross processions that reenact the gospel, we proclaim that sacrifice and faith are still part of our dream to live a life more justly. We seek to share a new American dream where all people can sit at one table, where all are welcomed as family, and where life is celebrated to its fullest.

> We urge all persons of good will to work earnestly to bring
> about the cultural transformation we need, a true renewal
> in our public life and institutions based on the sanctity of
> all human life. (no. 39)

We seek to live the Gospel of Life as a Hispanic community that unites the Church of the Americas in this common effort.

Living the Gospel of Life (1998)
Suggestions for Civil/Liturgical Occasions

Rev. Raúl Gómez

The principal subject of this pastoral statement is the dignity and sanctity of human life. As such, its thoughts are easily incorporated into various civil and liturgical occasions throughout the year. Here are some of the most obvious.

Most apt are civil occasions emphasizing American values of human liberty, rights, or this country's founding principles. These include Sundays near July 4 as well as the anniversary of the September 11 terrorist attacks. Also, Thanksgiving and the anniversary of the U.S. Supreme Court ruling on abortion, *Roe v. Wade*, every January provide opportune moments for preaching that includes passages from the bishops' statement.

With their emphasis on the Incarnation and new life, the Christmas and Easter seasons lend themselves to preaching the dignity and sanctity of human life. The Feasts of the Holy Family in December and the Presentation of the Lord on February 2 also provide opportunities. Respect Life Sunday most clearly embodies the concepts of the bishops' statement.

Consider occasions touching on the family and human development. Principal among these are marriage and baptismal preparation as well as the celebrations of these sacraments. Blessings of mothers and newborns, *presentaciones, quince años*, Masses with Anointing of the Sick, and funerals allow for the incorporation of the theme in the words said by the presider. The gospel passage about the least of Jesus' brothers and sisters or the creation stories from Genesis also provide good points of departure for preaching on this pastoral statement.

Living the Gospel of Life:
A Challenge to American Catholics
Suggested Liturgical Texts

Rev. José A. López

Reference: United States Conference of Catholic Bishops, Lectionary for Mass, Second Typical Edition, Vol. I–IV. Chicago: Liturgy Training Publications, 2002.

Texts

II:220	Deuteronomy 30:15–20
IV:827	Isaiah 56:1, 6–7
IV:829	Psalm 98
IV:828–1	Acts 2:42–47
IV:828–2	1 Corinthians 12:3b–7, 12–13
IV:828–6	1 Peter 2:4–9
I:131	James 2:14–18
IV:831–4	John 15:1–8
IV:831–6	John 21:15–17

The texts above were chosen out of the call to choose life (Deut. 30:19) and to live it out to the fullest. The Hispanic family, its values, and its love of children and the elderly are life itself, but are in danger of being absorbed into a culture that in some respects denies not only death in its quest for youth and self-interest through any means possible, but also denies life through self-absorption in abortion, euthanasia, neglect of the elderly, and other life problems. Here is where the preacher is called to be a forceful witness, loyally and joyfully, to the Gospel of Life. The stories of the Hispanic need to be told and preached in light of the story of life as revealed by God in Scripture. Too often life seems to be of less value in the reality of poverty and powerlessness, yet that is where Jesus strengthens life.

CHAPTER VI

Call for Help: Domestic Violence

When I Call for Help:
A Pastoral Response to Domestic
Violence Against Women
Tenth Anniversary Edition

Secretariat for Family, Laity, Women and Youth
United States Conference of Catholic Bishops
3211 4th Street, N.E., Washington, DC
20017-1194 (202) 541-3000
November 13, 2002

A Statement of the U.S. Catholic Bishops

In the beginning, I was young . . . he was handsome. He said I was beautiful, smart, worthy of love . . . made me feel that way. And so we were married, walking joyfully together down a church aisle, our union blessed by God.

Then came the angry words . . . the verbal tearing apart. . . . Now I was made to feel ugly, unintelligent, unworthy of any love, God's or man's.

Next came the beatings . . . unrelenting violence . . . unceasing pain. I shouldn't stay, but this is my husband . . . promised forever. He says I deserve it . . . maybe I do . . . if I could just be good. I feel so alone . . . doesn't God hear me when I cry out silently as I lie in bed each night?

Finally came the release, the realization. It's not me . . . it's him. . . . I am worthy of love, God's and man's. One spring morning, my heart was filled with hope and with fear now only of starting over on my

own. And so again I walked . . . down the hallway of
our apartment building . . . never again to be silent
. . . never again to live with that kind of violence, to
suffer that kind of pain.

—A battered wife[1]

Introduction

As pastors of the Catholic Church in the United States, we state as
clearly and strongly as we can that violence against women, inside or
outside the home, is *never* justified. Violence in any form—physical,
sexual, psychological, or verbal—is sinful; often, it is a crime as well.
We have called for a moral revolution to replace a culture of violence.
We acknowledge that violence has many forms, many causes, and
many victims—men as well as women.[2]

The Catholic Church teaches that violence against another person
in any form fails to treat that person as someone worthy of love.
Instead, it treats the person as an object to be used. When violence
occurs within a sacramental marriage, the abused spouse may question, "How do these violent acts relate to my promise to take my
spouse for better or for worse?" The person being assaulted needs to
know that acting to end the abuse does not violate the marriage promises. While violence can be directed towards men, it tends to harm
women and children more.

In 1992 we spoke out against domestic violence. We called on the
Christian community to work vigorously against it. Since then, many
dioceses, parishes, and organizations have made domestic violence a
priority issue. We commend and encourage these efforts.

In this update of our 1992 statement, we again express our desire
to offer the Church's resources to both the women who are abused
and the men who abuse. Both groups need Jesus' strength and healing.[3]

We focus here on violence against women, since 85 percent of the
victims of reported cases of non-lethal domestic violence are
women.[4] Women's greatest risk of violence comes from intimate
partners—a current or former husband or boyfriend.[5]

Violence against women in the home has serious repercussions for
children. Over 50 percent of men who abuse their wives also beat
their children.[6] Children who grow up in violent homes are more
likely to develop alcohol and drug addictions and to become abusers

themselves.[7] The stage is set for a cycle of violence that may continue from generation to generation.

The Church can help break this cycle. Many abused women seek help first from the Church because they see it as a safe place. Even if their abusers isolate them from other social contacts, they may still allow them to go to church. Recognizing the critical role that the Church can play, we address this statement to several audiences:

> *To women* who are victims of violence and who may need the Church's help to break out of their pain and isolation;

> *To pastors*, parish personnel, and educators, who are often the first responders for abused women;

> *To men* who abuse and may not know how to break out of the cycle of violence; and

> *To society*, which has made some strides towards recognizing the extent of domestic violence against women.

We recognize that violence against women has many dimensions. This statement is not meant to be all-inclusive, but rather to be an introduction, along with some practical suggestions of what dioceses and parishes can do now.

An Overview of Domestic Violence

Domestic violence is any kind of behavior that a person uses to control an intimate partner through fear and intimidation. It includes physical, sexual, psychological, verbal, and economic abuse. Some examples of domestic abuse include battering, name calling and insults, threats to kill or harm one's partner or children, destruction of property, marital rape, and forced sterilization or abortion.[8]

According to a U.S. government survey, 53 percent of victims were abused by a current or former girlfriend or boyfriend. One third of all victims were abused by a spouse, while 14 percent said that the offender was an ex-spouse. Women ages 16 to 24 are nearly three times as vulnerable to attacks by intimate partners as those in other age groups; abuse victims between ages 35 and 49 run the highest risk of being killed.[9]

While abuse cuts across all ethnic and economic backgrounds, some women face particular obstacles. Women of color may not view the criminal justice system as a source of help. Additionally, in some cultures women feel pressured to keep problems within the home and to keep the family together at all costs. Some fear that they will lose face in the community if they leave. Immigrant women often lack familiarity with the language and legal systems of this country. Their abusers may threaten them with deportation.

Women in rural communities may find themselves with fewer resources. The isolation imposed by distance and lack of transportation can aggravate their situation. Isolation can also be a factor for women who do not work outside the home. They may have less access to financial resources and to information about domestic violence. Women with disabilities and elderly women are also particularly vulnerable to violence.

Some who suffer from domestic violence are also victims of stalking, which includes following a person, making harassing phone calls, and vandalizing property. Eight percent of women in the United States have been stalked at some time in their lives, and more than one million are stalked annually.[10] Stalking is a unique crime because stalkers are obsessed with controlling their victims' actions and feelings. A victim can experience extreme stress, rage, depression, and an inability to trust anyone.

Domestic violence is often shrouded in silence. People outside the family hesitate to interfere, even when they suspect abuse is occurring. Many times even extended family denies that abuse exists, out of loyalty to the abuser and in order to protect the image of the family. Some people still argue—mistakenly—that intervention by outside sources endangers the sanctity of the home. Yet abuse and assault are no less serious when they occur within a family. Even when domestic violence is reported, sometimes there are failures to protect victims adequately or to punish perpetrators.

Why Men Batter

Domestic violence is learned behavior. Men who batter learn to abuse through observation, experience, and reinforcement. They believe that they have a right to use violence; they are also rewarded, that is, their behavior gives them power and control over their partner.

Abusive men come from all economic classes, races, religions, and occupations. He may be a "good provider" and a respected member of his church and community. While there is no one type, men who abuse share some common characteristics. They tend to be extremely jealous, possessive, and easily angered. A man may fly into a rage because his spouse called her mother too often or because she didn't take the car in for servicing. Many try to isolate their partners by limiting their contact with family and friends.

Typically, abusive men deny that the abuse is happening, or they minimize it. They often blame their abusive behavior on someone or something other than themselves. They tell their partner, "You made me do this."

Many abusive men hold a view of women as inferior. Their conversation and language reveal their attitude towards a woman's place in society. Many believe that men are meant to dominate and control women.

Alcohol and drugs are often associated with domestic violence, but they do not cause it. An abusive man who drinks or uses drugs has two distinct problems: substance abuse and violence. Both must be treated.

Why Women Stay

Women stay with men who abuse them primarily out of fear. Some fear that they will lose their children. Many believe that they cannot support themselves, much less their children.

When the first violent act occurs, the woman is likely to be incredulous. She believes her abuser when he apologizes and promises that it will not happen again. When it does—repeatedly—many women believe that if they just act differently they can stop the abuse. They may be ashamed to admit that the man they love is terrorizing them. Some cannot admit or realize that they are battered women. Others have endured trauma and suffer from battered woman syndrome.

REMEMBER: Some battered women run a high risk of being killed when they leave their abuser or seek help from the legal system. It is important to be honest with women about the risks involved. If a woman decides to leave, she needs to have a safety plan, including the names and phone numbers of shelters and programs. Some victims may choose to stay at this time because it seems safer. Ultimately, abused women must make their own decisions about staying or leaving.

The Church Responds to Domestic Violence

Scripture and Church Teachings

Religion can be either a resource or a roadblock for battered women. As a resource, it encourages women to resist mistreatment. As a road-block, its misinterpretation can contribute to the victim's self blame and suffering and to the abuser's rationalizations.

Abused women often say, "I can't leave this relationship. The Bible says it would be wrong." Abusive men often say, "The Bible says my wife should be submissive to me." They take the biblical text and distort it to support their right to batter.

As bishops, we condemn the use of the Bible to support abusive behavior in any form. A correct reading of Scripture leads people to an understanding of the equal dignity of men and women and to rela-tionships based on mutuality and love. Beginning with Genesis, Scripture teaches that women and men are created in God's image. Jesus himself always respected the human dignity of women. Pope John Paul II reminds us that "Christ's way of acting, the Gospel of his words and deeds, is a consistent protest against whatever offends the dignity of women."[11]

Men who abuse often use Ephesians 5:22, taken out of context, to justify their behavior, but the passage (v. 21–33) refers to the mutual submission of husband and wife out of love for Christ. Husbands should love their wives as they love their own body, as Christ loves the Church.

Men who batter also cite Scripture to insist that their victims for-give them (see, for example, Matthew 6:9–15). A victim then feels guilty if she cannot do so. Forgiveness, however, does not mean for-getting the abuse or pretending that it did not happen. Neither is pos-sible. Forgiveness is not permission to repeat the abuse. Rather, for-giveness means that the victim decides to let go of the experience and move on with greater insight and conviction not to tolerate abuse of any kind again.

An abused woman may see her suffering as just punishment for a past deed for which she feels guilty. She may try to explain suffering by saying that it is "God's will" or "part of God's plan for my life" or "God's way of teaching me a lesson." This image of a harsh, cruel God runs contrary to the biblical image of a kind, merciful, and lov-ing God. Jesus went out of his way to help suffering women. Think of the woman with the hemorrhage (Mark 5:25–34) or the woman caught in adultery (John 8:1–11). God promises to be present to us in our suffering, even when it is unjust.

Finally, we emphasize that no person is expected to stay in an abusive marriage. Some battered abused women believe that Church teaching on the permanence of marriage requires them to stay in an abusive relationship. They may hesitate to seek a separation or divorce. They may fear that they cannot remarry in the Church. Violence and abuse, not divorce, break up a marriage. We encourage abused persons who have divorced to investigate the possibility of seeking an annulment. An annulment, which determines that the marriage bond is not valid, can frequently open the door to healing.

First Responders: Priests, Deacons, and Lay Ministers

Many church ministers want to help abused women but worry that they are not experts on domestic violence. Clergy may hesitate to preach about domestic violence because they are unsure what to do if an abused woman approaches them for help.

We ask them to keep in mind that intervention by church ministers has three goals, in the following order:

> *Safety* for the victim and children;
>
> *Accountability* for the abuser; and
>
> *Restoration* of the relationship (if possible), or mourning over the loss of the relationship.

We also encourage church ministers to see themselves as "first responders" who:

> *Listen* to and believe the victim's story,
>
> *Help* her to assess the danger to herself and her children,
>
> *Refer* her to counseling and other specialized services.

Church ministers should become familiar with and follow the reporting requirements of their state. Many professionals who deal with vulnerable people are required to report suspected crimes, which may include domestic abuse.

In dealing with people who abuse, church ministers need to hold them accountable for their behavior. They can support the abusive person as he seeks specialized counseling to change his abusive behavior. Couple counseling is not appropriate and can endanger the victim's safety.

What You Can Do to Help

We offer the following practical suggestions for several audiences.

For Abused Women

Begin to believe that you are not alone and that help is available for you and your children.

Talk in confidence to someone you trust: a relative, friend, parish priest, deacon, religious sister or brother, or lay minister.

If you choose to stay in the situation, at least for now, set up a plan of action to ensure your safety. This includes hiding a car key, personal documents, and some money in a safe place and locating somewhere to go in an emergency.

Find out about resources in your area that offer help to battered women and their children. The phone book lists numbers to call in your local area. Your diocesan Catholic Charities office or family life office can help. Catholic Charities often has qualified counselors on staff and can provide emergency assistance and other kinds of help.

The National Domestic Violence Hotline provides crisis intervention and referrals to local service providers. Call 800-799-SAFE (7233) or 800-787-3224 (TTY). E–mail assistance is available at ndvh@ ndvh.org. In some communities, cell phones programmed to 911 are made available to abused women.

For Men Who Abuse

Admit that the abuse is your problem, not your partner's, and have the manly courage to seek help. Begin to believe that you can change your behavior if you choose to do so.

Be willing to reach out for help. Talk to someone you trust who can help you evaluate the situation. Contact Catholic Charities or other church or community agencies for the name of a program for abusers.

Keep in mind that the Church is available to help you. Part of the mission Jesus entrusted to us is to offer healing when it is needed. Contact your parish.

Find alternative ways to act when you become frustrated or angry. Talk to other men who have overcome abusive behavior. Find out what they did and how they did it.

For Pastors and Pastoral Staff

Make your parish a safe place where abused women and abusive men can come for help. Here are some specific suggestions:

Include information about domestic violence and local resources in parish bulletins and newsletters and on websites..

Place copies of this brochure and/or other information—including local telephone numbers for assistance—about domestic violence, in the women's restroom(s).

Keep an updated list of resources for abused women. This can be a project for the parish pastoral council, social justice committee, or women's group.

Find a staff person or volunteer who is willing to receive in-depth training on domestic violence; ask this person to serve as a resource and to help educate others about abuse.

Provide training on domestic violence to all church ministers, including priests, deacons, and lay ministers. When possible, provide opportunities for them to hear directly from victims of violence.

Join in the national observance of October as "Domestic Violence Awareness Month." Dedicate at least one weekend that month to inform parishioners about domestic abuse. During that month, make available educational and training programs in order to sensitize men and women, girls and boys to the personal and social effects of violence in the family. Help them to see how psychological abuse may escalate over time. Teach them how to communicate without violence.

Use liturgies to draw attention to violence and abuse. Here are some specific suggestions:

In homilies, include a reference to domestic violence when appropriate. Just a mention of domestic violence lets abused women know that someone cares. Describe what abuse is, so that women begin to recognize and name what is happening to them. Watch the video *When You Preach, Remember Me* (see Resources).

In parish reconciliation services, identify violence against women as a sin.

Include intercessions for victims of abuse, people who abuse, and those who work with them.

If you suspect abuse, ask direct questions. Ask the woman if she is being hit or hurt at home. Carefully evaluate her response. Some women do not realize they are being abused, or they lie to protect their spouses. Be careful not to say anything that will bolster her belief that it is her fault and that she must change her behavior.

Have an action plan in place to follow if an abused woman calls on you for help. This includes knowing how and where to refer her for help. This will be easier if you have already established contact with local shelters and domestic violence agencies.

Include a discussion of domestic violence in marriage preparation sessions. If violence has already begun in the relationship, it will only escalate after marriage.

In baptismal preparation programs, be alert that the arrival of a child and its attendant stress may increase the risk of domestic violence.

When I Call for Help: A Prayer

One source of healing we have in our lives as Christians is prayer.
Psalm 55 may be an especially apt prayer for women who are dealing with abusive situations. With all of you we pray these verses:

> Listen, God, to my prayer;
>> do not hide from my pleading;
>> hear me and give answer.
>
> If an enemy had reviled me,
>> that I could bear;
> If my foe had viewed me with contempt,
>> from that I could hide.
> But it was you, my other self,
>> my comrade and friend,
> You, whose company I enjoyed,
>> at whose side I walked
>> in procession in the house of God.
>
> But I will call upon God,
>> and the LORD will save me.
> At dusk, dawn, and noon
>> I will grieve and complain,
>> and my prayer will be heard.
>> —Psalm 55:2–3, 13–15, 17–18

RESOURCES

Websites

Center for the Prevention of Sexual and Domestic Violence: www.cpsdv.org

National Domestic Violence Hotline: www.ndvh.org

National Coalition Against Domestic Violence: www.ncadv.org

Family Violence Prevention Fund: www.endabuse.org

Videos

When You Preach, Remember Me, United States Conference of Catholic Bishops, No. 680–8; phone ordering: 800–235–8722

Broken Vows: Religious Perspectives on Domestic Violence, Center for the Prevention of Sexual and Domestic Violence; phone: 206–634–1903; fax: 206–634–0115; e-mail: cpsdv@cpsdv.org

Wings Like a Dove: Healing for the Abused Christian Woman, Center for the Prevention of Sexual and Domestic Violence

Publications

Walk in the Light: A Pastoral Response to Child Sexual Abuse, United States Conference of Catholic Bishops, No. 5–000; phone ordering: 800–235–8722.

Pope John Paul II, *On the Dignity and Vocation of Women* (*Mulieris Dignitatem*). Available on the Vatican's website at www.vatican.va.

Pope John Paul II, *The Gospel of Life,* United States Conference of Catholic Bishops, No. 316–7; phone ordering: 800–235–8722.

Pope John Paul II, *On the Genius of Women*, United States Conference of Catholic Bishops, No. 5–113.; phone ordering: 800–235–8722.

Catechism of the Catholic Church, United States Conference of Catholic Bishops, No. 5–110.; phone ordering: 800–235–-8722.

Archdiocese of St. Paul-Minneapolis, Domestic Violence Committee of the Commission on Women, *When You Are Called For Help: A Guide for Clergy on Responding to Domestic Violence Situations.* Available from the Commission on Women, 328 W. Kellogg Blvd., St. Paul, MN 55102; phone: 651–291–4495.

Bishop Ricardo Ramirez, CSB, Diocese of Las Cruces, *Speaking the Unspeakable: A Pastoral Letter on Domestic Violence.* Available from the diocesan Pastoral Center, 1280 Med Park Drive, Las Cruces, NM 88005; phone: 505–523–7577;. www.dioceseoflascruces.org.

Rev. Marie M. Fortune, *Keeping the Faith: Guidance for Christian Women Facing Abuse* (San Francisco: Harper Collins, 1995).

Rev. Al Miles, *Domestic Violence: What Every Pastor Needs to Know* (Minneapolis: Augsburg Fortress Press, 2000).

Carol J. Adams, *Woman-Battering* (Minneapolis: Augsburg Fortress Press, 1994).

The original document *When I Call for Help: A Pastoral Response to Domestic Violence Against Women* was developed by the Committee on Women in Society and in the Church and the Committee on Marriage and Family of the United States Conference of Catholic Bishops (USCCB), approved for publication by the Administrative Committee in September 1992, and affirmed by the full body of U.S. Catholic bishops at its November 1992 General Meeting. This revised tenth anniversary edition was approved by the full body of U.S. Catholic Bishops at its November 2002 General Meeting and has been authorized for publication by the undersigned.

Msgr. William P. Fay, General Secretary, USCCB

Opening excerpt from Christopher News Notes. Used with permission.

Scriptural texts are taken from the New American Bible, copyright © 1970, 1986, 1991 by the Confraternity of Christian Doctrine, Inc., Washington, D.C. Used with permission. All rights reserved. No part of the New American Bible may be reproduced by any means without permission in writing from the copyright holder.

When I Call for Help: A Pastoral Response to Domestic Violence Against Women (Tenth Anniversary Edition) is available in print editions in English and Spanish and may be ordered by calling toll–free 800–-235–-8722. Ask for publication number 5–509 (English), 5–888 (Spanish).

Para ordenar este recurso en español, llame al 800–235–8722 y presione 4 para hablar con un representante del servicio al cliente, en español.

NOTES

1. Excerpted from "When Home is Where the Hurt Is," Christopher News Notes, no. 326.

2. *Confronting a Culture of Violence: A Catholic Framework for Action.* A Pastoral Message of the U.S. Catholic Bishops (Washington, DC: United States Conference of Catholic Bishops, 1994).

3. See Pope John Paul II, *The Gospel of Life* (Washington, DC: United States Conference of Catholic Bishops, 1995), nos. 2, 23, and 99.

4. National Crime Victimization Survey, 1992–1996. www.cdc.gov/ncipc/fact-sheets/ipvfacts.htm.

5. Full Report of the Prevalence, Incidence, and Consequences of Violence Against Women, Findings from the National Violence Against Women Survey (November 2000). www.ncjrs.org.

6. "Developments in the Law—Legal Responses to Domestic Violence," Harvard Law Review 106 (1993):7: 1608–9. Cited in Carol J. Adams, *Woman-Battering* (Minneapolis: Fortress Press, 1994), 22. In 1995 the National Conference of Catholic Bishops (now United States Conference of Catholic Bishops) addressed one form of child abuse: child sexual abuse in a home or family setting. See *Walk in the Light: A Pastoral Response to Child Sexual Abuse* (Washington, DC: United States Conference of Catholic Bishops, 1995).

7. www.cdc.gov/ncipc/factsheets/ipvfacts.htm.

8. In regard to sexual abuse, see *Catechism of the Catholic Church* (Washington, DC: United States Conference of Catholic Bishops, 2000), no. 2356; *The Gospel of Life*, nos. 3, 23 and 99; and Pope John Paul II's "Letter to Women" no. 5, and "Welcome to Gertrude Mongella, Secretary General of the Fourth World Conference on Women," no. 7, in Pope John Paul II on *The Genius of Women* (Washington, D.C.: United States Conference of Catholic Bishops, 1997). In regard to verbal abuse, see Catechism nos. 2477, 2479, 2482–2487, and 2507–2509.

9. U.S. Bureau of Justice Statistics, "Intimate Partner Violence and Age of Victim, 1993–99" (NCJ–187635). www.ojp.usdoj.gov/bjs/abstract/ipva99.htm.

10. "Stalking in America: Findings from the National Violence Against Women Survey," Joint report from the National Institute of Justice and the National Center for Injury Prevention and Control (April 1998).

11. Pope John Paul II, *On the Dignity and Vocation of Women* (Mulieris Dignitatem), no. 15.

Preaching "When I Call for Help" to U.S. Hispanic Assemblies

Bishop Ricardo Ramírez, C.S.B.

In November, 1991, Bishop Matthew Clark, then chairman of the standing Committee on Women in Society and the Church of the National Conference of Catholic Bishops, proposed that the committee write a brief statement on domestic violence, which, in his words, "has become a high-profile issue." Members of the staff at the Secretariat for Laity and Family Life had received written requests from many people wondering what the position of the U.S. bishops was on the issue of domestic violence.

Members of the Committee on Women included Archbishops Thomas Murphy and John Roach and Bishops Joseph Imesch, John Snyder, David Fellhauer, Joseph Francis, and me. We decided to cosponsor the statement in conjunction with the Bishops' Committee on Marriage and Family Life. It was developed in 1992, and that September it was presented to the Administrative Committee of the conference, which subsequently approved the statement for publication. It was introduced to the rest of the bishops with these words: "The statement comes in response to numerous requests from women that bishops use their position of leadership to point out that the abuse of women is not justified." *When I Call for Help* was published in the fall of 1992 in English and Spanish. That November, the body of bishops affirmed the statement. It is presently being revised and updated by the United States Conference of Catholic Bishops Committees on Women in Society and the Church and Family Life.

I. The Reality of Domestic Violence

Hispanic communities, first of all, should not be singled out for having more instances of domestic violence than other groups. Neither should the poor nor those who suffer social and economic pressures be stereotyped as being more prone to domestic violence. Domestic violence transcends economic and social class. Perpetrators and victims come from every walk of life—from the very poor to the very rich—and from social outcasts to the most respected citizens of our communities. The problem crosses all socio-economic, cultural, religious, and ethnic boundaries.

For generations, violence in the home has been a hidden topic. It was not until recently that what was previously "unspeakable" was more and more in the public forum. We cannot ignore the ugly violence that affects families and, most often, women in our society. The high prevalence of violence against women brings them into regular contact with physicians: at least one in five women seen in emergency departments has symptoms related to abuse. It shocks us further to learn that currently one woman in four will be sexually assaulted in her lifetime.

Domestic violence is manifested in various forms: degrading comments, manipulation of financial resources to intimidate, the use of physical strength to bully and, ultimately, to injure and even kill. This list does not exhaust its many manifestations. While the form of domestic violence varies, the result is always the same: it exchanges the natural bonds of love and nurturing for the unnatural relationships of aggressors violating the dignity, rights, and aspirations of those they promised to love, cherish, and respect.

Some experts estimate that as many as four million women suffer some kind of battering every year. If we take that number of women affected by violence, and we further note that the average family size is 2.2 persons per household, we can project that at least 8.8 million Americans are affected annually by this tragic evil. Domestic violence is the most common form of violence in our society and the least reported crime.

What adds to the tragedy is the fact that in homes where domestic violence happens, 50 to 55 percent of the children residing in those homes are themselves victims of physical or sexual abuse. The "nights of terror" and other horrors experienced by children contribute to lifelong difficulties with self-esteem.

Connected with the violence suffered by children is the pattern that violence in the home is a learned behavior and is passed on from one generation to the next. This learned behavior is often triggered by alcohol or drugs. In many cases, men who become abusive and the women who are abused grew up in homes where violence occurred. A child can grow up believing that violence is acceptable behavior; boys learn that it is a way to feel powerful.

Men who abuse women often convince themselves they have a right to do so. They could even reach the wrongful conclusion that violence is a way to dissipate tension and solve problems—a view society too often supports. Abusive men tend to be extremely jealous, possessive, and easily angered.

II. What Scripture Teaches on Violence

Scripture can give us the spiritual and moral insight to understand the sinfulness of domestic violence and hear the call to redemption and conversion. The Book of Genesis tells us the human person is made in the image and likeness of God and is endowed with an inherent dignity that demands respect. Furthermore, Genesis makes it clear that man and woman enjoy the same and equal dignity. They both reflect the divine glory and complement one another. Both derive their inherent dignity, personal goodness, and original beauty from the Creator who delights in them and affirms their existence by exclaiming that it is good (Genesis 1:31).

Violence in any of its forms gravely offends that dignity and is, at the same time, an offense against God. Abuse, whether physical, verbal, mental, or sexual, must be denounced as a horrible offense against the dignity of the human person.

When sin entered the world through our first parents, it gave way to broken relationships, insecurity, and fear. Original sin transformed the paradise that God created for man and woman into barrenness and desolation. Man and woman were banished from the happiness of the Garden of Eden to a life in which the most basic needs for sustaining life and bringing forth new life would now be achieved only through work, effort, and suffering (Genesis 3:16–19).

The result of sin, according to the Bible, is immediately seen in the story of Cain and Abel. Jealousy, anger, and hatred became hardened in Cain. He then turned against his brother and killed him (Genesis 4:8). This is the example Scripture uses to teach that violence and death are born within the human heart wounded by insecurity and fear. It further tells us that violence, at its very core, is a spiritual malaise and can only be fully eradicated through personal conversion leading to ongoing transformation.

III. The Call to Conversion in Jesus Christ

The possibility of conversion and transformation is precisely why Jesus Christ, the eternal Word of God made flesh, came into the world. Through him and in him, we become sons and daughters of

God. Through him we become intimately united with God and with every human being. When we enter into a personal relationship with Jesus Christ, we enter into solidarity with all other human beings. This happens not so much by what we do, but by what Jesus himself does in reaching out to us in his loving embrace of forgiveness and taking upon himself the burden of our sinfulness. He who has no sin has come to free us from the slavery of sin, death, and all the consequences of sin. "It is in Christ and through his love that we have been redeemed and our sins forgiven, so immeasurably generous is God's favor to us" (Ephesians 1:7).

So powerful and all-embracing is the redemption of Christ that he is able to touch every aspect of human experience and can bring about a transformation of the human heart. Because of him, and his having poured out his love for us on the cross, we are no longer ruled by the wounds of sin and hatred. Those ruled by Christ's love do not seek domination through violence. Human violence, rooted in insecurity and fear, can now be healed by the love of God that has been poured into our hearts (Romans 5:5).

Our relationships are restored in Christ, and because of his grace we are able to look on all others with respect, trust, and love, a love devoid of all selfishness and one that seeks only the good of the other. This is the foundation of all our relationships, especially the relationship in Christian marriage and family life.

IV. Scripture on Marriage and the Family

The Church teaches that from the point of view of God, marriage is an intimate community of the whole of life based on love. Married persons give themselves to one another in the consent they exchange at their wedding, and this consent is one to be lived out until death. Christian marriage reflects God's unconditional and ever-faithful love, and just as marriage is a sacred bond, so family life is sacred, because in the family persons can experience intimately the love of God. As Pope John Paul states:

> the family has the mission to become more and more what it is, that is to say, a community of life and love in an effort that will find fulfillment, as will everything created and redeemed, in the reign of God.

What makes violence in the family so insidious is the severe limitation it puts on the possibility for a family to fulfill its mission to further God's reign of justice and peace.

Hispanic peoples take great pride in claiming that the family is of paramount value in our cultures. Yet each family must examine whether the way its members relate to one another reflects the ideal the Church teaches. We can never be proud of allowing domestic violence to break the inner peace and harmony of our families. Domestic violence is a shameful exercise of power against those whose lives are entwined by ties of blood and family. For this reason, the bishops of the United States and other groups unequivocally teach that "violence in any form—physical, sexual, psychological, or verbal—is sinful; many times it is a crime as well." Violence inflicted in the family on spouses, parents, children, or siblings is intolerable and unconscionable. When it occurs in homes and in the family, it becomes especially grievous because the home and the family are meant to be places of sanctuary for all persons. Domestic violence can never be justified, for it is a sacrilege that poisons the sacred relationships in marriage and takes away from the family as the first and most important school of love.

Scripture can be misused to justify the domination of husbands over their wives. The passage found in Saint Paul's Letter to the Ephesians, "wives be submissive to your husbands" (5:22), has been misunderstood and misused. This passage has to be seen in its historical context, for it was shaped by the times and culture of Paul and reflects the highly hierarchical household that was part of the Greco-Roman empire in which Paul lived and wrote. In that society, just as slaves had to submit to their masters, wives had to submit to their husbands. Ours is a very different culture, wherein all persons are considered equal. Moreover, if we continue reading the rest of Chapter 5 of Ephesians, we will understand Paul's full message, which exhorts all spouses to love one another as Christ loves the Church (5:25). In Christian marriage, spouses give their lives as Christ gave his life for the Church. Husbands and wives love each other in the way in which they consider and treat each other as equals. This parallels the teaching in the Book of Genesis about the equality both man and woman enjoy.

V. The Church and its Pastoral Response

The reality of marriage, both in the past and in the present, very often does not reflect this ideal. Compounding this situation is the fact that we in leadership positions have not always handled marriages involving domestic violence in the best way. Too often, women are exhorted to forgive and forget spousal abuse. Clergy and others in counseling situations tell those who have been abused to resume marital life, and what follows is the further victimization of the abused spouse. In so doing, we fail to recognize spousal abuse for what it is, and contribute to continued abuse. We pastoral ministers can be well-meaning in our efforts to maintain and protect the marriage bond. Nonetheless, to encourage a victim to return to an environment of violence without the benefit of qualified professional help is irresponsible. When such errors are made or sinful actions are excused in God's name, the fault on the part of the clergyman or counselor becomes more lamentable.

Unfortunately, neither the Church nor society has responded adequately to the social problem of domestic violence. The concentration of power and privilege in the hands of men leads to the control and subordination of women, causing social inequality between the sexes. We are becoming increasingly aware that Church ministers have failed at times to recognize domestic violence for what it is because of the way we ourselves exercise power. For this, we need to seek forgiveness.

The Statement of the U.S. Bishops, *When I Call for Help: A Pastoral Response to Domestic Violence Against Women*, is most timely. We live in an age of enormous violence and disrespect for life. Music and video games, as well as the media and the world of entertainment, seem to glorify violence. There is hardly a film or a television program that is devoid of some form of violence. Our children spend more time watching television than they do in school. We hear the alarming stories of children inflicting violence on other children, and even of children killing children.

VI. Practical Conclusions

Much education on the issue of domestic violence needs to be done. Besides the above suggestions, information should be given, especially to women, about the federal Violence Against Women Act

(VAWA), which protects the rights of undocumented women victims of domestic violence.

Men who abuse must be challenged to have the courage to look honestly at their actions at home, especially towards their wives. The first step is to begin to believe they can change their behavior if they choose. They also need to acknowledge the fact that abuse is *their* problem and not their wife's. A man who abuses needs to reach out for help and talk to someone of trust. Many dioceses and local agencies offer services by way of counseling and rehabilitation.

Our message for abused women is that they recognize they are not alone and that many women, in reaching out for help, have found a way to a new life for themselves and their children. They, too, should talk to someone they can trust—a relative, a friend, a parish priest, a deacon, a sister, a lay minister, or a *comadre*. From a practical point of view, an abused woman should hide a car key somewhere outside the house, keep a small amount of money in a safe place, and locate a place to go in an emergency. In practically every area of the country there are resources that offer help to abused women and their children. These resources can be located through a local diocese or by simply calling 911 or 1–800–799–SAFE (7233).

Violence-free homes are a goal for all of us together to achieve. Let us constantly pray for peace and search for ways in which the evil of domestic violence can someday be eradicated. Let us recall the words of a famous leader of Mexico, Benito Juárez, who said, *"El respeto al derecho ajeno es la paz"* ("Peace is the result of respect of the rights of others").

When I Call for Help: A Pastoral Response to Domestic Violence Against Women (1992) Suggestions for Civil/Liturgical Occasions

Rev. Raúl Gómez

This pastoral letter advises pastors and pastoral staffs to dedicate at least one weekend in October, which is "Domestic Violence Awareness Month," to educate parishioners about abuse. It also advocates the inclusion of intercessions for victims, abusers, and for those who help both victims and abusers.

The letter also suggests addressing the topic of domestic violence on three other important occasions. First, marriage preparation can be an important "teachable moment" regarding the interpretation of Scripture, because couples often misinterpret the context of passages that use traditional language common to the social order of bygone eras. Second, baptismal preparation is a good occasion to address the issue of domestic violence, because the stress of the arrival of a child can be a trigger for violent behavior. Third, as the letter notes, prayer is a key source of healing. The official prayer of the Church, the liturgy, lends itself to addressing this issue, especially in terms of the patronal feast days of the Virgin as well as during reconciliation services and the celebration of the sacrament of Anointing of the Sick.

When I Call for Help: A Pastoral Response to Domestic Violence Against Women Suggested Liturgical Texts

Rev. José A. López

Reference: United States Conference of Catholic Bishops, Lectionary for Mass, Second Typical Edition, Vol. I–IV. Chicago: Liturgy Training Publications, 2002.

Texts

IV:801	Genesis 2:18–24
IV:877	Isaiah 41:8–10, 13–14
III:489	Ephesians 5:21–33
I:51	Revelation 7:9–10, 14b–17
IV:901	Matthew 5:20–24
I:94	Matthew 10:26–33
II:251	John 8:1–11

The texts selected do not directly address the issue of battered women but do address God's protection, strength, promises, and assurances to God's loved ones. The preacher is usually not inclined to speak to this concern, yet one needs to reflect on how the effects of violence extend beyond the home, because the system of violence contains within itself alcoholism, drugs, gangs, and all the problems that infest the home and extend their tentacles throughout the community. In the Hispanic community, these situations are, sadly, a daily occurrence.

Always present, violence against women does not have to be a delicate topic. Fortified with Scripture, with the available resources in the community, and with this document from the bishops, the preacher need not fear to speak with a prophetic voice. Our preaching needs to respond with ready resources to help battered women. The document gives excellent suggestions and direction for action in the parish.

This pastoral statement needs to be made known to the Hispanic community, to be discussed, and to be explained in our preaching. The violence in the community toward the poor and neglected cannot be addressed separately from the whole. But abused and battered women need to hear this welcoming word from the pulpit: that there is help, hope, and a way out. If they are not present to hear our words, the word will come to them in one way or another. The words of Isaiah are assuring: "For I am the Lord, your God, who grasps your right hand; it is I who say to you, fear not, I will help you" (41:13).

CHAPTER VII

Welcoming the Stranger Among Us

Welcoming the Stranger Among Us
Unity in Diversity

Office of Migration and Refugee Services
United States Conference of Catholic Bishops
3211 4th Street, N.E., Washington, DC
20017-1194 (202) 541-3000
November 10, 2002

A Statement of the U.S. Catholic Bishops

Summary

On June 2, 2000, the Jubilee Day for Migrants and Refugees, Pope John Paul II celebrated the Eucharist in St. Peter's Square for over 50,000 migrants, refugees, people on the move, and their chaplains from all over the world. The Eucharist drew that great diversity of people into unity in the communion of Father, Son, and Holy Spirit, realizing a Jubilee Year hope for the Church: "to gather into one the dispersed children of God," "to sum up all things in Christ, in heaven and on earth" (John 11:52, Ephesians 1:10).

Unity in diversity is the vision that we bishops, as pastors of the Church in the United States, offer to our people as they welcome the new immigrants and refugees who come to our shores. In the past thirty-five years the number and variety of immigrants coming to the United States have provided a great challenge for us as pastors. Previous immigrants had come predominantly from Europe or as slaves from Africa, but many of the new immigrants come from Latin America and the Caribbean, Asia and the Pacific Islands, the Middle East, Africa, Eastern Europe, and the former Soviet Union and Yugoslavia. Though a good number come as skilled workers and professionals, the greater number come as refugees and immigrants on

149

the edge of survival; large numbers join families already here; others arrive without proper documents. Many were forced to leave their homeland because of a well-founded fear of persecution. This diversity of ethnicity, education, and social class challenges us as pastors to welcome these new immigrants and help them join our communities in ways that are respectful of their cultures and in ways that mutually enrich the immigrants and the receiving Church.

To pursue this vision of unity in diversity, we have chosen the way marked out by Pope John Paul II as he stood beneath the figure of Our Lady of Guadalupe in Mexico City on January 22, 1999, and announced the summary of *Ecclesia in America*: namely, the call to conversion, communion, and solidarity.

The presence of so many people of so many different cultures and religions in so many different parts of the United States has challenged us as a Church to a profound conversion so that we can become truly a sacrament of unity. We reject the anti-immigrant stance that has become popular in different parts of our country, and the nativism, ethnocentricity, and racism that continue to reassert themselves in our communities. We are challenged to get beyond ethnic communities living side by side within our own parishes without any connection with each other. We are challenged to become an evangelizing Church open to interreligious dialogue and willing to proclaim the Gospel to those who wish to hear it. The new immigrants call most of us back to our ancestral heritage as descendants of immigrants and to our baptismal heritage as members of the body of Christ. "For in one Spirit we were all baptized into one body, whether Jews or Greeks, slaves or free persons, and we are all given to drink of one Spirit" (1 Cor 12:13).

The call to communion goes out to all members of the Church—bishops, priests, deacons, religious, lay leaders, and parishioners—to prepare themselves to receive the newcomers with a genuine spirit of welcome. Simple, grace-filled kindness and concern on the part of all parishioners to newcomers are the first steps. This can be accompanied by language and culture study as well as constant and patient efforts at intercultural communication. The integration of incoming groups is complex because of multiple Mass schedules and lack of personnel or resources, but if the receiving parish staffs and parishioners are open to the newcomers and provide a bridge to join cultures to one another, the newcomers themselves will provide the leadership and show the way to a healthy integration. Both on parish and diocesan levels, the presence of brothers and sisters from different cultures should be celebrated as a gift to the Church through well-prepared liturgies, lay leadership development programs inclusive of all, the appointment of prepared leaders of immigrant communities to parish and diocesan positions, and special efforts to help youth find their way as they experience themselves often torn between two cultures.

One successful model of unity in diversity was Encuentro 2000: Many Faces in God's House, the National Conference of Catholic Bishops' Celebration for the Jubilee Year. In the materials prior to the celebration, Encuentro 2000 offered a discussion method called the "mutual invitation process," which maximizes intercultural participation. In the celebration itself, Encuentro 2000 was an experience of the exuberance and vitality, the profound faith and devotional life of the participants. Encuentro 2000 also demonstrated that communion in a multicultural Church is a true possibility for the new millennium.

The call to solidarity can be summed up in Pope John Paul II's *Message for World Migration Day 2000*: "The Church hears the suffering cry of all who are uprooted from their own land, of families forcefully separated, of those who, in the rapid changes of our day, are unable to find a stable home anywhere. She senses the anguish of those without rights, without any security, at the mercy of every kind of exploitation, and she supports them in their unhappiness" (no. 6). We bishops commit ourselves and all the members of our Church communities to continue the work of advocacy for laws that respect the human rights of immigrants and preserve the unity of the immigrant family. We encourage the extension of social services, citizenship classes, community organizing efforts that secure improved housing conditions, decent wages, better medical attention, and appropriate educational opportunities for immigrants and refugees. We advocate reform of the 1996 immigration laws that have undermined some basic human rights for immigrants. We join with others of good will in a call for legalization opportunities for the maximum number of undocumented persons, particularly those who have built equities and otherwise contributed to their communities.

In *Ecclesia in America*, Pope John Paul II calls for a "new evangelization" centered on the person of Jesus Christ. "'The encounter with the living Jesus Christ' is 'the path to conversion, communion and solidarity'" (no. 7). Such an encounter, so central to all our

Jubilee Year activities, leads to a daily vision of the risen Lord, present and active in the world, especially in the poor, in the stranger, and in the migrant and refugee. These immigrants, new to our shores, call us out of our unawareness to a conversion of mind and heart through which we are able to offer a genuine and suitable welcome, to share together as brothers and sisters at the same table, and to work side by side to improve the quality of life for society's marginalized members. In so doing, we work to bring all the children of God into a fuller communion, "the communion willed by God, begun in time and destined for completion in the fullness of the Kingdom" (*Ecclesia in America*, no. 33).

Introduction: An Immigrant Church, Then and Now

> For I was hungry and you gave me food, I was thirsty and you gave me drink, a stranger and you welcomed me.
>
> (Matthew 25:35)

On June 2, 2000, the Jubilee Day for Migrants and Refugees, Pope John Paul II looked out over a sunlit crowd of pilgrims gathered in St. Peter's Square from all nations: migrants, refugees, seafarers, Gypsies,[1] foreign students, circus and carnival workers, airport workers, truckers, all varieties of people on the move with their bishop promoters, their chaplains, and spiritual directors. The pope celebrated the Eucharist, which drew that great diversity of people into unity in the communion of Father, Son, and Holy Spirit. He reminded them that in the Church they are meant to experience this trinitarian communion. In the Church their diversity is to be grounded in a profound unity. Through the members of the Church, solitary migrations are to end in the embrace of solidarity.

This jubilee vision of Pope John Paul II is the vision guiding us, the bishops of the United States, as we respond to the new immigrants who have recently come to our shores.

Twenty years ago in *Beyond the Melting Pot: Cultural Pluralism in the United States*, we the bishops of the United States noted that cultural pluralism was the common heritage of all Americans. As the new millennium unfolds, the "new immigration" from all the continents of the world calls attention to the reality of the United States as largely a "nation of immigrants" and to the diversity of national and ethnic origins of all people of this country. In this new context, the Catholic community is rapidly reencountering itself as an "immigrant Church," a witness at once to the diversity of people who make up our world and to our unity in one humanity, destined to enjoy the fullness of God's blessings in Jesus Christ. This unity in diversity was celebrated at Encuentro 2000, sponsored as the National Conference of Catholic Bishops' principal jubilee celebration, highlighting "many faces in God's house."

A century ago, the Church responded generously to the needs of immigrants: building parishes and schools, establishing a vast array of charitable institutions, evangelizing newcomers, and being evangelized in turn by immigrant Catholics with distinctive traditions of worship and often a deep spirituality of their own. Members of the Eastern Catholic Churches arrived during the same period. They were not always understood by their fellow Catholics, although they were received and did develop as members of the Church in America. Despite the attacks of "nativists" and the criticisms made by English-speaking Catholics, national parishes were established that provided a safe haven where newcomers were able to pray and hear the word of God in their own languages, begin the education of their children in the language of the home, and so adapt to their new society with the security of community and faith. The Church embraced these immigrants, supporting them in their striving to build a better life and encouraging the efforts of many of them to help build a labor movement that could represent them in that struggle. And then, as now—despite the predictions of critics—immigrants and their children quickly became vital participants in American society, acquiring proficiency in English by the second and third generations, rising in the educational system, and contributing in thousands of ways to the economic growth and social, political, and spiritual life of the country.

Who Are the New Immigrants?

The "new" immigration to the United States stems from global changes—both economic and political—over the past forty years, and from legal changes starting with the 1965 Immigration Act. The latter abolished the quota system that had systematically favored immigrants from Western Europe and had largely cut off immigration from Asia, Africa, and the Middle East after 1920. Meanwhile war, economic distress, the desire to be reunited with families, and the new legal opportunities since the 1960s have prompted a diverse immigration from Latin America and the Caribbean, Asia and the Pacific Islands, the Middle East, Africa, Eastern Europe, and the former Soviet Union and Yugoslavia.

While the new immigrants include many unskilled workers who perform difficult and menial tasks as in the past, the new immigrants also include many skilled workers, recruited to fill specialized positions as nurses, computer professionals, and scientists. The United States is thus beneficiary of the years of education, training, and experience that come with these new workers. While we welcome all the new immigrants and recognize that our Church, like the United States as a whole, has come to depend upon the many talents and profound energy of newcomers, we must also remind our government that the emigration of talented and trained individuals from the poorer countries represents a profound loss to those countries. And we remind heads of government around the world that emigration of all kinds—but especially that of those fleeing war and persecution, famine and economic distress—is a sign of the failure of the whole international community to guarantee the security and welfare of all people in their homelands.

The ultimate resolution of the problems associated with forced migration and illegal immigration lies in changing the conditions that drive persons from their countries of origin. Accordingly, we urge the governments of the world, particularly our own government, to promote a just peace in those countries that are at war, to protect human rights in those countries that deny them, and to foster the economic development of those countries that are unable to provide for their own peoples. We also urge the governments of the "receiving" countries to welcome these immigrants, to provide for their immediate needs, and to enable them to come to self-sufficiency as quickly as possible.

The Migration for Survival

We must never forget that many immigrants come to this country in desperate circumstances. Some have fled political persecution, war, and economic devastation, particularly from Southeast Asia in the 1970s, Central America and the Caribbean in the 1980s, and the former Yugoslavia, the former Soviet Union, and Africa in the 1990s. Others have wagered on finding a better life in this country in the face of economic desperation at home. As Pope John Paul II has noted, "In many regions of the world today people live in tragic situations of instability and uncertainty. It does not come as a surprise that in such contexts the poor and the destitute make plans to escape, to seek a new land that can offer them bread, dignity and peace. This is the migration of the desperate . . . . Unfortunately, the reality they find in host nations is frequently a source of further disappointment" (*Message on World Migration Day 2000*, no. 4).

Some refugees[2] have enjoyed the sanction and support of the U.S. government, while others have been denied attention and systematically deported, and some have been subjected to humiliating incarceration under deplorable conditions. Increasing numbers of refugees from the conflicts of the 1980s have seen their status adjusted to that of permanent residency; but disparities in treatment, complicated and drawn-out asylum procedures, and long waits for service contribute to the already difficult process of adjustment that individuals and families in flight have to face. Both individual lay people and church agencies have worked alongside secular organizations to correct these situations and address the sufferings of those caught up in the complex and bureaucratic U.S. immigration system, whose policies often lead to the fragmenting of families, but more needs to be done.

Undocumented Immigrants

One reality remains constant in the American experience of immigration: the demand of the U.S. economy for unskilled labor—and the corresponding entrance of immigrants seeking work—in labor-intensive industries such as agriculture, construction, food processing, and services. Undocumented immigrants face special hardships in such areas. The Immigration and Naturalization Service estimates that three to four million undocumented workers hold jobs in this country, many of which are poorly paid, insecure, and dangerous. They face discrimination in the workplace and on the streets, the constant threat of arrest and deportation, and the fear that they or their children will be denied medical care, education, or job opportunities. Many have lived in the United States for years, establishing roots in their communities, building their families, paying taxes, and contributing to the economy. If arrested and deported, they leave behind children and sometimes spouses who are American citizens. While the changes in the law over the last several years have enabled many in this situation to adjust their status to that of permanent resident, the 1996 immigration legislation made this option more difficult for the vast majority. Without condoning undocumented migration, the Church supports the human rights of all people and offers them pastoral care, education, and social services, no matter what the circumstances of entry into this country, and it works for the respect of the human dignity of all—especially those who find themselves in desperate circumstances. We recognize that nations have the right to control their borders. We also recognize and strongly assert that all human persons, created as they are in the image of God, possess a fundamental dignity that gives rise to a more compelling claim to the conditions worthy of human life. Accordingly, the Church also advocates legalization opportunities for the maximum number of undocumented persons, particularly those who have built equities and otherwise contributed to their communities.

Immigrant Families and Their Communities

The vast majority of the 600,000 to 900,000 immigrants admitted annually to this country enter as immediate relatives of U.S. citizens or legal permanent residents, a trend that coincides with the Church's teaching supporting family reunification. At the same time, the family preference system continues to experience considerable backlogs, prolonging the separation of families. The 1996 immigration laws have torn apart families that have established themselves in the United States over many years, sometimes on the basis of minor criminal offenses duly punished years ago.

Over a third of the new immigrants have become naturalized citizens, and the longer immigrants remain here the more likely they will become citizens; but here, too, the Church views with grave concern recent legislation[3] that has withdrawn basic benefits from legal residents who are not yet citizens and threatened the ability of many hard-working immigrants to remain in this country.

Immigrants experience the tensions of their new situation much more than the society around them does. They have settled in a foreign land with laws, customs, and a language that they must master sooner or later, often at great personal cost. They struggle to build community among themselves in hopes of providing the sense of continuity and security they need in order to face the new world they have chosen or were forced to accept. They do not want to give up all that they value in their own ways of life—nor do they want their children to grow up without those traditions. Thus, many households carry on, to one degree or another, the cultures of immigrant parents, and today, one in five Americans enjoys immediate ties to a heritage beyond our borders.

These realities ensure that few Americans have not encountered recent immigrants to this country in their neighborhoods and workplaces. Long Beach, California is home to more Cambodians than Phnom Penh. Los Angeles ranks just behind Mexico City and Guadalajara in the number of residents of Mexican origin. Chicago at times has had more persons of Polish extraction than Warsaw. At the same time, rural towns and small cities throughout the country have begun to feel a presence of immigrants in their communities not seen since the great wave of immigration at the end of the nineteenth century.

The New Immigration and the Church

Many of the new immigrants are Catholics. Probably more than 80 percent of Hispanic immigrants were raised in the Catholic faith. By some estimates, Hispanic Catholics—including the United States' large Puerto Rican and Mexican-American populations[4]—could make up the majority of U.S. Catholics within the next twenty years. But other immigrant populations also include large numbers of Catholics. Filipinos, who represent almost 5 percent of the immigrant population, are overwhelmingly Catholic. Some 350,000 of the 1.4 million Vietnamese immigrants in this country are Catholic. These Catholics are joined by thousands of Eastern Catholics coming from the former Soviet Union, the Middle East, and India. A smaller but still significant number of the Chinese, Korean, Japanese, Laotian, Sri Lankan, Indonesian, Tongan, Samoan, and Asian-Indian immigrants are also Catholic. Among the increasing numbers of immigrants from Africa, many are Catholics, raised in the vibrant Catholic culture of the Church's fastest growing region.

Throughout the country, the liturgy and church decor increasingly reflect the cultural gifts of the new immigrants, with their own images of Mary and the saints, their songs, and their distinctive celebrations taking their place alongside those of older generations of immigrants. And immigrant communities provide a growing percentage of the vocations to the priesthood and religious life as well as lay leadership at the service of the Church in the United States today. The profile provided regarding the new immigrants who are Catholic should not minimize the Church's overwhelming concern for all new arrivals, regardless of their religious tradition or lack of one.

The Calling of the Church

In this context of opportunity and challenge that is the new immigration, we bishops of the United States reaffirm the commitment of the Church, in the words of Pope John Paul II, to work "so that every person's dignity is respected, the immigrant is welcomed as a brother or sister, and all humanity forms a united family which knows how to appreciate with discernment the different cultures which comprise it" (*Message for World Migration Day 2000*, no. 5). We call upon all people of good will, but Catholics especially, to welcome the newcomers in their neighborhoods and schools, in their places of work and worship, with heartfelt hospitality, openness, and eagerness both to help and to learn from our brothers and sisters, of whatever race, religion, ethnicity, or background.

A Tradition of Welcome and Pastoral Concern

This call is based on the rich heritage of Scripture and the Church's teaching. The patriarchs themselves were nomads. Settled by the hand of God in the time of Abraham, they soon migrated to Egypt, where they suffered oppression and were delivered once again by God's hand. From this experience comes a deep appreciation for the plight of the migrant, underlined in the words of Scripture: "You shall not oppress an alien; you well know how it feels to be an alien, since you were once aliens yourselves in the land of Egypt" (Exodus 23:9). "You shall treat the stranger who resides with you no differently than the natives born among you, have the same love for him as for yourself; for you too were once strangers in the land of Egypt" (Leviticus 19:33–34). The Torah made special provisions for immigrants with the reminder that "you too were once slaves in Egypt" (Deuteronomy 16:9–12): "At the end of every third year you shall bring out all the tithes of your produce for that year and deposit them in community stores, that the Levite who has no share in the heritage with you, and also the alien, the orphan and the widow who belong to your community, may come and eat their fill; so that the LORD, your God, may bless you in all that you undertake" (Deuteronomy 14:28–29).

Indeed, the experience of exile, oppression, and deliverance to the Promised Land is the central act of the drama of salvation for Judaism. In honor of God's deliverance of his people, Israel was enjoined to show justice towards all: "For the LORD, your God, is the God of gods, the LORD of lords, the great God, mighty and awesome, who has no favorites, accepts no bribes; who executes justice for the orphan and the widow, and befriends the alien, feeding and clothing him. So you too must befriend the alien, for you were once aliens yourselves in the land of Egypt" (Deuteronomy 10:17–19). Jesus echoes this tradition when he proclaims prophetically, "For I was hungry and you gave me food, I was thirsty and you gave me drink, a stranger and you welcomed me" (Matthew 25:35).

The Church has remained faithful to this call to care for migrants of all kinds and has responded accordingly over the centuries. The apostolic constitution *Exsul Familia*, promulgated by Pope Pius XII in 1952, takes its name from its evocation of the "émigré Holy Family of Nazareth, fleeing into Egypt," to which the pope pointed as "the archetype of every refugee family." Pope Pius XII recalls a long tradition of papal solicitude for immigrants and refugees, noting the hospitality to strangers and refugees traditionally provided by the Holy See and recalling the words of the Fourth Lateran Council of 1215: "We find in most countries, cities, and dioceses people of diverse languages who, though bound by one Faith, have varied rites and customs. Therefore we strictly enjoin that the Bishops of these cities or dioceses provide the proper men, who will celebrate the Liturgical Functions according to their rites and languages." The pope cites with pride, as one proof of the Church's constant solicitude in this respect, the provisions for the establishment of "national parishes" in the United States in the nineteenth century to accommodate the immigrants of that era.

The Second Vatican Council likewise called on the national bishops' conferences to pay special attention to those who "are not adequately cared for by the ordinary pastoral ministry of the parochial clergy or are entirely deprived of it," including "the many migrants, exiles and refugees," and to devise solutions for them (*Christus Dominus*, no. 18), a call endorsed by Pope Paul VI in approving a revision of church norms regarding pastoral care for immigrants. His *Instruction on the Pastoral Care of People Who Migrate* affirmed that "migrating people carry with them their own mentality, their own language, their own culture, and their own religion. All of these things are parts of a certain spiritual heritage of opinions, traditions, and culture which will perdure outside the homeland. Let it be prized highly everywhere" (no. 11).

These words should apply with special force to members of the numerous Eastern Catholic Churches, who preserve ancient traditions of worship and practice reaching back to the days of the apostles. In full communion with the Catholic Church, they are the bearers of the authentic teachings of the Church, each according to their own traditions. Because of political upheaval, war, and religious persecution, the twentieth century saw an unprecedented emigration—one that continues today—of Eastern Catholics who are a minority in their countries of origin, and who must struggle to maintain their faith and their traditions in the United States in the context of the predominant Latin Church.

Pope John Paul II urges in his apostolic letter *Orientale Lumen* that a "conversion is . . . required of the Latin Church, that she may respect and fully appreciate the dignity of Eastern Christians, and accept gratefully the spiritual treasures of which the Eastern Catholic Churches are the bearers, to the benefit of the entire catholic Communion" (no. 21).

The immigrants among us thus bring a richness that we are bound to embrace, for their sake and for our own. As Pope Paul VI noted, in words recently recalled by Pope John Paul II, "The Church can regard no one as excluded from its motherly embrace, no one as outside the scope of its motherly care. It has no enemies except those who wish to make themselves such. Its catholicity is no idle boast. It was not for nothing that it received its mission to foster love, unity, and peace among men" (*Ecclesiam Suam*, no. 94). The way to achieve this mission was presented on January 22, 1999, when Pope John Paul II stood beneath the image of Our Lady of Guadalupe in Mexico City and delivered to the whole Church the post-synodal apostolic exhortation *Ecclesia in America—On the Encounter with the Living Jesus Christ: The Way to Conversion, Communion, and Solidarity in America.* This is the way we will follow in this document.

A Call to Conversion

Though we celebrate the diversity within our communities, we bishops must also confess that today, as in the past, the treatment of the immigrant too often reflects failures of understanding and sinful patterns of chauvinism, prejudice, and discrimination that deny the unity of the human family, of which the one baptism is our enduring sign. Such patterns, in the words of Pope John Paul II, "show the urgent need for a transformation of structures and a change of mentality, which is what the Great Jubilee of the Year 2000 asks of Christians and every person of good will" (*Message for World Migration Day 2000*, no. 1). For Catholics especially, a recognition of failures in the face of the opportunities and challenges of the new immigration should serve as a call to a renewal of baptismal vows, through repentance and a sharing in the mercy of the one Lord who would gather all to himself in the unity of the children of God.

We bishops must confess, as well, that recent immigrants have not always encountered welcome in the Church. Today, immigrants of all sorts too often face prejudice within the Church. At times their legitimate desire to worship in their own language, according to their own traditions, has not been satisfied. Some have been turned away by pastors or find their petition for a Mass in their own language and a share in parish facilities opposed by members of the parish community. For those who live far from concentrated populations of people who share their heritage, there is often no alternative but to struggle through the English Mass while the deepest expressions of their spirit cry out silently in another language. Where the Church has not been welcoming, many have turned to other sources of community and religious fulfillment, but at the expense of abandoning the riches of their Catholic faith and native traditions.

Forgetful of Our Heritage

Perhaps the greatest obstacle to welcoming the stranger is that many Americans have forgotten their immigrant past. "Nativism" assumes that there is just one image of a "real American" and that immigrants either cannot live up to it or willfully refuse to do so. Originally directed against Catholics of all sorts, today such nativism can be seen in a campaign against "multiculturalism" in all its forms, on the premise that reverence for distinctive traditions and histories undermines the unity of American society. Like the Catholic "Americanizers" of the nineteenth century, who opposed the establishment of national parishes, the critics of multiculturalism today want immigrants and other distinctive groups to shed their languages, customs, and identities as quickly as possible, to become Americans "just like the rest of us." But "the rest of us" are, in fact, a culturally plural society—Catholics, Protestants, Jews, and Muslims; believers and nonbelievers; Southerners and Northerners; Irish, Italian, and Mexican—proud of our heritages and proud to be Americans, all at once.

A kind of nativism appears in the Church itself when established members insist that there is just one way to worship, one set of familiar hymns, one small handful of familiar devotions, one way to organize a parish community, one language for all—and that immigrants must adapt to that way of doing things. In doing so, such nativists forget not only that their ancestors spoke different languages and worshiped in different ways not long ago, but that their devotions and familiar saints, even their patterns of church organization, sprang from encounters between differing traditions within the Church.

Competition for Resources

Competition for resources and recognition among the ethnic groups of the parish often centers on specifics such as Mass times, the use of facilities, and the attention of priests; but such conflicts can reflect vague fears that one group will somehow displace a long-established one. Established parishioners, used to thinking of their parish practices and religious traditions as the norm, may cling to their control over the parish council or "prime" Sunday Mass times. They may find themselves increasingly a minority and may react with fear to protect the parish where they were raised and where they saw their children baptized and educated in the faith. African-American Catholics, who have their own history of having been excluded and discriminated against in the larger Church, as in society in general, now face newcomers in many of their parishes, newcomers who threaten their hold on the few institutions where they have come to feel at home. In some cases, multiple immigrant groups compete with one another within a single parish. In other cases, immigrant clergy struggle with their bishop or pastor for control over the finances of an immigrant group or for final authority over the congregation. While such competition can be destructive of community life, the issues involved are often real, and they require wisdom, much charity, and careful mediation to reach solutions that respect the legitimate concerns of all sides.

Cultural Fears

The fears associated with encounters between groups are often difficult to overcome precisely because they are unacknowledged or unclear. Some are afraid because they do not know how to behave with others of a different culture. Others—in ignorance, relying on stereotypes—are convinced that those who are different are also somehow inferior: less educated, "dirty," or dangerous. Negative images and derogatory jokes and remarks readily merge with racism, America's "original sin," reinforcing the fear of the unknown in many people's minds by creating stereotypes about people whose facial features or skin color identify them as Asian, Arab, African, or Mexican. In some instances, racism has been so deeply ingrained that an institutional racism prevails. Racist attitudes can linger in subtle ways, even when people get to know one another in parish activities, unless we vigorously educate ourselves about our neighbors, learn to appreciate their heritages, encounter their own images of us, and strive to work with them on behalf of common causes.

Some of our fears are tied to what we see as defense of our own culture or way of life. Many people cling—rightfully so—to their distinctive culture. They fear the loss of their own familiar ways of doing things as they encounter new images and practices of community life and worship that are foreign to them. Immigrants themselves often fear other groups and worry that their children will lose the values of the homeland, come to show disrespect towards their parents and elders, and exchange their own culture for the consumer values of the surrounding society. Such concerns are well-founded, and they compound the difficulties of adaptation to a new setting as both host and immigrant react, each against the other, in fear of change.

Change, however, is inevitable as immigrants set down roots in this country, enriching American culture while adopting aspects of it themselves. Indeed, it would be a mistake to regard any culture as fixed and immutable. All cultures are in constant processes of change as their members seek new ways to address individual and group needs and as they encounter new situations and other cultures. Indeed, no culture is either permanent or perfect. All constantly need to be evangelized and uplifted by the good news of Jesus Christ. The encounter between cultures that is an everyday affair in the incorporation of immigrants into the Church and the communities of the United States should provoke not only adaptation on both sides, but a critical discernment of the strengths and failings of each culture in the light of the Gospel.

Institutional Obstacles

Institutional inadequacies have also impeded the full-fledged welcome and communion to which the Church is called. Parish and diocesan structures have not always been flexible enough to accommodate sudden influxes of new groups. Parishes have found themselves serving faith communities that draw members from far outside parish boundaries, raising questions about the sources and limits of parish resources. And regrettably, some parishes have found that their parishioners have imbibed the post-1960s societal attitude of exclusion of new immigrants. In many cases, immigrant Catholics have been attracted to evangelical and Pentecostal churches, leaving behind their Catholic faith.

Many pastors struggle to accommodate separate worship communities who celebrate their faith in their native tongues within the same parish. Pastors strive to meet the needs of multiple culturally diverse groups who are too small to support their own Eucharist and specialized programs. Similarly, pastors who wish to serve whoever approaches the altar may lack the experience or the models to know how to reach out to newcomers who are not Catholic, or whose Catholicism has not included a regular liturgical life or whose faith is tied more closely to home and family than to the parish community.

Immigrant communities must find priests willing and able to minister in their language and a place to gather for worship and community activities. They are often at a loss as to how to supply themselves with liturgical texts and educational materials and how to develop a sense of communion with a diocese whose language is not their own. They struggle to balance the competing demands of U.S. schools and the larger culture on their youth with their own desires to benefit their children with traditional values and culture. Immigrant priests may find themselves jealous of their own autonomy and better able to relate to their own priests' associations and dioceses of origin than to the priests and diocese of their U.S. home, where they may feel a lack of welcome.

The tensions and debates occasioned by such concerns can sometimes lead to greater understanding within the Church. But they can also lead, in the extreme, to painful schisms and the alienation of the faithful from the Church. Taken together—and despite the efforts of many dioceses—such tensions make clear that the Church has not adequately addressed the host of questions that surround pastoral ministry to the new immigrants. In this and the other respects mentioned above, the Church of the twenty-first century requires a profound conversion in spirit and in its institutions to reflect its own cultural pluralism, to address the needs of the whole Catholic community, and to further a genuine communion and solidarity among the diverse members of the Body of Christ.

This debate on the effective and adequate response of current church institutions to the new immigrant reality echoes the discussion in the Synod of America and *Ecclesia in America* on the effectiveness of parish structures:

> Because of the particular problems they present, special attention needs to be given to parishes in large urban areas, where the difficulties are such that normal parish structures are inadequate and the opportunities for the apostolate are significantly reduced. The institution of the parish, however, retains its importance and needs to be preserved. For this, there is a need "to keep looking for ways in which the parish and its pastoral structures can be more effective in urban areas" (no. 41).

A Call to Communion

As Catholics we are called to take concrete measures to overcome the misunderstanding, ignorance, competition, and fear that stand in the way of genuinely welcoming the stranger in our midst and enjoying the communion that is our destiny as children of God. We commit ourselves, accordingly, to working to strengthen understanding among the many cultures that share in our Catholic faith, to promoting intercultural communication among our people, and to seeing that those in ministry to our communities gain the language and cultural skills necessary to minister to the immigrants in our midst.

Coming to Understand Others as the First Form of Hospitality

Time and time again, Pope John Paul II has echoed the teachings of his predecessors and of the Second Vatican Council that "it is one of the properties of the human person that he can achieve true and full humanity only by means of culture" (*Gaudium et Spes*, no. 53) and that to take away a person's culture is therefore to damage human dignity grievously. Communion does not abolish differences but brings together one family, diverse and united in the one Lord. Pope Paul VI urged that: "it must be avoided that these diversities and adaptations in accordance with the various ethnical groups, even though legitimate, result in harm to that unity to which all are called in the Church" (*Pastoralis Migratorum Cura*). Thus, the Church's norms for the pastoral care of immigrants attempt to balance the legitimate rights of immigrants with their duty to look to the common good of both their communities of origin and their host community (*Instruction on the Pastoral Care of People Who Migrate*, nos. 5–11).

The Church embraces the rich cultural pluralism of this immigrant nation—what some call its "multicultural" reality.[5] Pope John Paul II insists that "the immigrant members of the Church, while freely exercising their rights and duties and being in full ecclesial communion in the particular churches, feeling themselves Christians and brothers towards all, must be able to remain completely themselves as far as language, culture, liturgy and spirituality, and particular traditions are concerned" (Address for World Migrants' Day, July 16, 1985). Indeed, the pope warns repeatedly against attempting to rush a process of assimilation or cultural adaptation in the name of unity, because the goal is the mutual enrichment of peoples, not their assimilation to one way of being human. Thus the pope reached out to refugees in the camp at Phanat Nikon, Thailand in November 1984, saying: "My heart is with you. Have faith in yourselves. Don't forget your identity as a free people with your own legitimate place in this world. Don't lose your distinctive personality as a people! Remain firmly rooted in your respective cultures. The world needs to learn more from you and to join in appreciation of your uniqueness."

The pope teaches that immigrants must guard their cultures for the enrichment of the world. But the cultures of immigrants will only be able to enrich this country when all Americans—recent immigrants and those long settled in this country—open their hearts and minds to their neighbors and come to appreciate the diverse cultures that make up this society. Knowledge of cultures cannot just come from books, but must come from the concrete efforts of individuals to get to know their neighbors, in all their diversity.

The welcome and hospitality that we ask our parishes to extend to newcomers must include active efforts on the part of the pastor and

parish staff, individuals and families, parish councils, liturgy committees, social concern entities, youth groups, and other parish organizations to undertake the special effort necessary to learn about the
cultures in their midst, and to exchange visits with worship communities and parishes where different cultural groups make their homes.
Special events such as international dinners, common social events,
and multicultural parish feasts can help to introduce the various members of the parish to other cultures, and can lead to greater exchanges
between groups. The parish is encouraged to sponsor forums in which
members of different cultures can openly share their unique backgrounds and identify areas of unity.

The eucharistic celebration is central to church life and to our
communion as Catholics with one another in the one Lord. Whenever
the diverse cultures of parish and diocese are able to share the
Eucharist in special celebrations that reflect the cultural riches of the
participants, the Church demonstrates in the sacrament of our unity
the multicultural face of the Church, proclaiming "with joy and firm
faith that God is communion, Father, Son, and Holy Spirit, unity in
distinction, and that he calls all people to share in that same
Trinitarian communion" (*Ecclesia in America*, no. 34).

Intercultural Communication

Efforts to learn and worship together may come to nothing at all—or
even reinforce prejudices—unless they are carried out with a spirit of
openness and charity. Not everything in one culture will meet with
the approval of another. There may be disagreements about child-
rearing practices, the place of women in the liturgy, styles of preaching, or suitable expressions of piety. Such differences are inevitable
even within one culture. But in cross-cultural encounters, disagreements must be informed by understanding the roots of people's attitudes and practices and with respect for their right to find their own
way within the one Gospel. Understanding will come with a growing
knowledge of the history, values, and experiences of others. Respect
must be born of charity and faith in the ultimate unity in Christ of all
humanity.

Intercultural communication—sustained efforts, carried out by
people of diverse cultures, to appreciate their differences, work out
conflicts, and build on commonalities—will thus be an important
component of coming to know and respect the diverse cultures that

make up today's Church. The dominant culture in the United States stresses the individual and his or her feelings and decisions. In less individualistic cultures, individuals may feel hesitant to express their own opinions openly, even in a friendly setting, without reinforcement from the group. Among immigrants of the same group, too, divisions along lines of social class or educational background can erect barriers to understanding, with some members adapting to the procedures and practices of parish life more readily than others. Often, culturally sensitive intermediaries are needed to facilitate exchanges, mediate conflicts, and promote genuine participation by all.

Integration will be facilitated when all parties maintain an open spirit. Integration cannot be forced, and those who host newcomers must be especially aware of the vulnerabilities of immigrants and the impulse many immigrants feel to withdraw from interaction. Pastors and lay leaders who are aware of these dynamics of adaptation and communication among cultures will lead the way in facilitating the full, equal incorporation of all members of the community into the life of the Church.

Languages for Ministry

Special efforts to acquire the languages of the new immigrants by all church ministers constitute an essential, concrete step towards a full and effective welcome. In some cases, immigrant groups have brought with them significant numbers of priests and religious. This is true of the Vietnamese community, which has continued to produce vocations in large numbers in this country. In other cases, the home country's Church is sufficiently strong to send priests and religious to the United States to minister to immigrant communities from that country, as was the case in earlier waves of migration to this country. In many cases today, however, there are many immigrants but few priests, and dioceses must make special provisions to find or train priests, religious, and lay people capable of ministering to the newcomers in their own languages and cultures. Missionary orders have contributed magnificently to filling this need. In some dioceses, every seminarian is required to master a language other than English relevant to ministry to local immigrant communities. This practice should be encouraged throughout the United States. Priests, seminarians, religious, and lay ministers should all be encouraged to learn a language and acquire cultural knowledge relevant to their ministry.[6] Study abroad is generally the best way to do this, and it should be widely encouraged.

Especially in the case of some of the smaller immigrant groups, priests may have only a rudimentary knowledge of the language of the group they serve. Then they must depend upon religious, lay leaders, deacons, and trained catechists to ensure an effective ministry. And even where priests with the necessary language skills are available, it is important that other members of the larger community acquire the ability to communicate with immigrants in their own languages as part of a wider effort to develop more inclusive relations at the parish and diocesan levels, carry on the necessary work of evangelization, and promote diocesan programs capable of genuinely uniting diverse communities. The clergy and lay leaders should acquire a proficiency in English as quickly as possible and continue to improve their public speaking skills in English so as to further the communion of their communities with the wider Church in the United States. Parishes should provide opportunities for immigrants, including the elderly, to acquire proficiency in the English language.

Ministry in a Multicultural Church

Language acquisition on behalf of intercultural communication and effective ministry is just one practical step towards the fuller incorporation of the new immigrants into our communities. The Church as an institution needs to undertake other practical steps at national, diocesan, and parish levels.

National or Regional Level

At the national or regional level, efforts must be made to provide liturgical and catechetical materials for communities who do not have ready access to such materials in their language. Most dioceses lack the resources to provide such materials for more than one or two groups. Similarly, diocesan seminaries and lay ministry training programs are often ill-equipped to provide priests, religious, and lay leaders with the full range of linguistic, cultural, and intercultural communication training necessary to serve even local needs.

Efforts to redress these problems could be furthered by the creation of regional pastoral centers, serving the needs of one or several immigrant ethnic communities and financed by the dioceses they serve. Such centers could encourage theological reflection based on the traditions and experience of the various national churches represented in our immigrant communities. They could provide the translation services mentioned above and serve as a source for liturgical and catechetical materials for the communities they represent, as well as develop training materials for pastors, religious, and lay leaders in these communities. And they could offer training for all those involved in ministry to specific groups within the dioceses of their regions, extending the range of possibilities of language education, intercultural communication training, and education for ministry in a multicultural Church more generally.

Diocesan Level

Dioceses are the best equipped to address the multiple needs of the contemporary Church at the local level. The bishop as pastor of a diverse people has the care for all that concerns their life together. Thus, in developing diocesan policies and programs responsive to the reality of today's immigrant Church, bishops must take care to both respect the dignity of the diverse communities of the diocese and draw them to unity in the one Church, striking that balance between the legitimate rights of immigrants to worship according to their own traditions and the concern for the common life of the Church in the United States. Diocesan authorities must decide when and how to honor the desire of immigrant groups for their own chapel, mission, or personal parish; how to foster a spirit of openness and welcome towards immigrant communities within parishes; how to promote the effective evangelization of all members of the local church and of those outside the Church; and how to bring together peoples of all the diverse cultures of the Church into one community.

We bishops commit ourselves with renewed energy to display a spirit of welcome, and we encourage all those involved in ministry to share in that spirit. We will look to the successful models of the past, such as the national parish, or contemporary practices in other dioceses, and adapt them to the needs and circumstances of our own dioceses. In each of our dioceses we will build up programs of ministry to immigrants and support them with new resources to the extent possible, in recognition of the growing contributions of our immigrant communities to the larger Church, and we will insist that pastors lend their support. Our diocesan seminaries must prepare seminarians for ministry to the Church of the twenty-first century. At the same time, we will devote resources to developing programs of cultural understanding and intercultural communication for religious and lay ministers. We bishops have a special responsibility to address questions of social justice for migrants of all sorts, participating in national and local efforts to combat discrimination and ensure equitable treatment under the law to all.

In the past, personal parishes were established successfully in some places to accommodate the needs and desires of strong, local immigrant communities. At the same time, not all groups have had the financial resources or numbers to sustain a parish of their own. Dioceses may need to develop guidelines to help parishes or deaneries respond to smaller or more dispersed groups so that they sense that they are welcome and have facilities appropriate to their needs.

Most dioceses have already provided modest resources to offices of ethnic ministry. The more these offices can be led by members of the communities being served, the better. In some cases, the bishop has appointed a vicar in charge of ministry to larger or more dispersed groups. In a few dioceses, Hispanic ministry in particular has been integrated into all of the offices of the diocese, providing constant feedback on how to address the needs of the Hispanic community within the various diocesan programs. In many dioceses, offices of ethnic ministry are able to ensure that parish positions are filled so as to serve the immigrant communities within the diocese. And many dioceses have designed diocesan–wide events to bring together the various cultures of the Catholic community. All of these efforts need to be studied and strengthened as the Church in the United States strives to celebrate the many gifts that immigrant communities bring to the Church in America.

Parish Level

Immigrants will experience the Church's welcome most personally at the level of the parish. Pastors and parish staff, accordingly, must be filled with a spirit of welcome, responding to a new and perhaps little-understood culture. They will be able to do so precisely to the extent that they have received the support of the diocese and the training that should go with it. A pastor with an open and welcoming spirit who insists that the whole parish participate in such a spirit can make a tremendous difference in relations among different groups.

Pastors need to know about effective models for accommodating multiple cultural groups within a single parish structure. At the same time, the effort to mediate competing demands for facilities and lingering rivalries among groups requires sensitivity to the needs and styles of both cultures, as well as patience, charity, and communications skills. Pastors should make every effort to assist and encourage Eastern Catholics to find parishes that offer pastoral care according to their own traditions and rites. In the past, immigrants belonging to Eastern Catholic churches were lost to those churches because of the lack of Eastern Catholic clergy, churches, and services. Sometimes they were joined to the Latin Church, regrettably because of social and demographic pressures. Membership in a particular church of the immigrant (e.g., Eastern Catholic Church) must be respected.

Reaching out to immigrants who are not Catholics or who, though Catholic, have not yet participated fully in the life of the parish requires language and cultural skills, as well as an evangelical zeal that will need to be developed among more pastors, associates, religious, and lay people through outreach committees or census programs. Lay people, especially those who share language and cultural background with the immigrant group, can be invaluable bridges in efforts to incorporate immigrant communities into the life of the parish and reach out to non-believers among the new immigrants. In many of the countries from which the new immigrants come, it was the lay catechist who led people to conversion or a deeper appreciation of the faith. Lay catechists were the leaders and evangelizers of their people. Their ministry needs to be reaffirmed and strengthened in the new context.

Catholic Charities offers comprehensive services in most dioceses. Pastors can look to Catholic Charities for help in their response to new immigrants. Social service, legal assistance, and adult education programs—including English as a second language, parenting, job training programs, and citizenship classes—can serve as valuable outreach to newcomers. The parish can also provide immigrants with forums for addressing social, emotional, and economic needs. Models and methods of a genuinely evangelical parish life need to be developed and disseminated so that pastors and lay leaders may choose among those best adapted to providing effective outreach to newcomers. In some cases, individual pastors or consortia of parishes, sometimes in conjunction with congregations of other faiths or secular organizations, can create immigration and social service agencies to serve particular neighborhoods.

At the same time, parishes can become sites for dialogue and cooperation, not only with the Protestant denominations that share our common Christian faith, but also with Buddhists, Hindus, Muslims, Jews, and others. Despite differences, all share common goals of providing for the religious and material needs of immigrant communities, and all have much to gain by working together.

Today's immigrants bring a vast richness of gifts, from new spiritual movements to a renewal of devotion to Mary in the great variety of national devotions, such as that to Our Lady of Guadalupe. In many dioceses, a renewal of vocations to the priesthood and religious life is one evident fruit of the new immigration, while lay participation in ministry has blossomed in many ethnic ministries.

The Special Needs of Youth

Of special concern are the youth of immigrant communities. Some are themselves immigrants, who despite a facility for acquiring English may feel especially torn between their original culture and that of their new home—fully at home in neither one culture nor the other. Others were born in this country, and though their first language may have been that of their parents, they quickly acquire the fluency of a native not only in the English language but in the prevailing culture in their schools and neighborhoods. In either case, young people may find themselves frequently in conflict with their parents and elders over ways of behaving and speaking, values, and beliefs, as they become "American" while living within an immigrant household and community that retain the country of origin's culture. Such conflicts are painful for both sides, and one or the other may call upon the Church to defend its particular claims and values. Young people can also experience conflict with their peers who—because of insecurity or insensitivity—cause unnecessary division.

The Church recognizes the centrality of the family in the upbringing of the young and cherishes the great value that many immigrant cultures place upon the family. At the same time, it also has a duty to provide for the young as they struggle for their own identity and their own adaptation within the larger culture. Recreational, educational, and spiritual programs for youth can provide opportunities for helping them to understand and accommodate the claims of their parents while accepting what is wholesome in the culture around them. These programs can also help young people live in harmony with their peers. Everyday pastoral care and special programs for parents can help them understand and accept the struggles of their children, even as they reinforce the confidence that their children have already assimilated much of what they have to teach them despite the dissensions of the moment. Religious education programs can play a special role here in attempting to bridge the gap between cultures within the context of the one faith, and to help the young deal positively with the tensions and difficulties they face.

In some instances, families are drawn to the parish precisely to take advantage of the school. Their immersion in their children's education puts them into regular contact with parish personnel and members of other cultural groups. In other cases, immigrants have had no experience of Catholic schools in their country of origin and require the encouragement (and often financial aid) of the parish to take advantage of this opportunity. Catholic schools can provide the children of immigrants with opportunities to adapt to American culture in a context permeated by the faith and in an atmosphere of hospitality to all cultures, and they can do much to promote cultural understanding and respect among parents and students alike. Catholic schools can also be powerful instruments of evangelization for immigrant communities who, though outside the Church, find in the schools a welcoming and supportive environment for the education of their children. But for a great many immigrants, none of this can be accomplished unless Catholic schools are made affordable for the poorer members of the community, a goal to which the diocese may have to contribute through sister—parish arrangements or outright grants of diocesan funds.

The Call to Solidarity

The Gospel calls us to solidarity with those who are suffering, vulnerable, and in need. In this spirit we recall the words of Pope John Paul II, who proclaimed, "The Church hears the suffering cry of all who are uprooted from their own land, of families forcefully separated, of those who, in the rapid changes of our day, are unable to find a stable home anywhere. She senses the anguish of those without rights, without any security, at the mercy of every kind of exploitation, and she supports them in their unhappiness" (*Message for World*

Migration Day 2000, no. 6). Among today's immigrants, those who have fled war, famine, civil unrest, and economic desperation deserve our special understanding and support; but seafarers, those in the aviation world, and migrant workers, too, suffer uprootedness, discrimination, and injustice, along with all people on the move: circus and carnival workers, truckers, tourists, pilgrims, Gypsies, and Irish travelers.

In an age of economic globalization, a special concern of a culture of solidarity must be the migrant worker, both rural and urban. These laborers are vital to our agricultural, construction, service, and tourist industries. From the time they leave their homes to the time they arrive at their place of work, these migrant workers—forced to search for a basic livelihood for their families—face hazardous border crossings. (In the past five years, more than 500 have died at the U. S.-Mexico border because of increased border enforcement.) They are vulnerable to exploitation and abuse in transit, in border regions, and in the workplace. We bishops pledge ourselves, in the spirit of *Ecclesia in American*, to work in solidarity with the bishops of the migrants' countries of origin to provide for the safety, the basic needs, the human rights, and the effective pastoral care of these migrant workers. One of the propositions of the Synod of America asserts, "The Church in America must be a vigilant advocate, defending against any unjust restriction the natural right of individual persons to move freely within their own nation and from one nation to another. Attention must be called to the rights of migrants and their families and to respect for their human dignity, even in cases of non-legal immigration" (*Ecclesia in America*, no. 65).

Solidarity with migrants and refugees will take many forms, from participating in efforts to ensure that the U.S. government respect the basic human rights of all immigrants, to providing direct assistance to immigrants through diocesan and parish programs. Particularly vulnerable are the immigrant elderly who often find themselves isolated in their new country, lacking in language skills and in the family and community support system that they enjoyed in their country of origin.

Community organizing efforts can also be important vehicles for addressing the needs of immigrant communities and incorporating immigrants into civic life. Such efforts can provide the basis for achieving improved housing conditions, a living wage, better medical attention, and enhanced educational opportunities for all, and for empowering local communities. The United States Catholic Conference supports many such efforts through the Catholic Campaign for Human Development. The local church's participation in such efforts is important, both for the direct good that community organizing can do for individuals and groups, and as part of a broader evangelization that proclaims God's care for all his children and the Church's special responsibility for the poor, the persecuted, and the stranger.

The call to solidarity is also a call to promote the effective recognition of the rights of immigrants and to overcome all discrimination based on race, culture, or religion. "It means bearing witness to a fraternal life based on the Gospel, which respects cultural differences and is open to sincere and trustful dialogue" (Pope Paul VI, *Octogesima Adveniens*, no. 17). Especially since World War II, the Church has devoted special efforts on behalf of the human rights of migrants and refugees throughout the world, and in the United States in particular. At the national level the U.S. Bishops' Office of Migration and Refugee Services has addressed these issues through participation in public policy debates, special programs for refugees, and aid to dioceses. Diocesan officials and parish leaders often participate as well in city—or region—wide bodies aimed at gaining recognition for immigrants in local affairs and combating discrimination.

We Catholic bishops commit ourselves to continue to work at the national level to promote recognition of the human rights of all, regardless of their immigration status, and to advance fair and equitable legislation for refugees and prospective immigrants. Present efforts need to be strengthened and supported with new initiatives, both at the local level and at the national level, as U.S. immigration law and practice change in the face of changing political pressures and social realities. In particular, Catholic lay people, diocesan officials, and bishops should continue to work together with community organizations, labor unions, and other religious bodies on behalf of the rights of immigrants in the workplace, schools, public services, our legal system, and all levels of government. The Catholic Church in the United States through the National Conference of Catholic Bishops, many of the state Catholic conferences, individual bishops, and other Catholic organizations have been meaningfully involved in social advocacy on behalf of migrant workers and other immigrants.

We encourage others to place a higher priority on public social policies that impact this special population.

Conclusion: A Call to a New Evangelization

In *Ecclesia in America*, Pope John Paul II calls for a "new evangelization" centered on the person of Jesus Christ: "'The encounter with the living Jesus Christ' is 'the path to conversion, communion and solidarity'"(no. 7). This personal encounter with the risen Lord, so abundantly recounted in the Gospels, Epistles, and Acts of the Apostles, leads to a daily vision of the Lord present and active in the world, especially in the poor, in the stranger, and in the migrant and refugee. Those most in need draw the members of the Church out of their unawareness to a conversion of heart, through which they are able to offer a genuine and suitable welcome, to share together as brothers and sisters at the same table, and to work side by side to improve the quality of life for society's most vulnerable members. All of this is an expression of the Spirit of the risen Jesus being poured out again on his followers.

The Holy Spirit made manifest at Pentecost enabled people of diverse languages and cultures to understand the one message of salvation. The new evangelization means openness to the gifts of the Spirit wherever they might appear. Our response to the new immigration thus is informed by a renewed vision of what it is to be Church, and by a new spirituality, informed by the Spirit of Pentecost present in the sacrament of confirmation, which gives the power to discern the one message of the kingdom in the diverse customs and languages of our immigrant brothers and sisters.

Immigrant communities give ample witness to what it is to be Church—in their desire to worship as a people, in their faith, in their solidarity with one another and with the weakest among them, in their devotion and their faithfulness to the Church of their ancestors. For the Church in the United States to walk in solidarity with newcomers to our country is to live out our catholicity as a Church. The Church of the twenty-first century will be, as it has always been, a Church of many cultures, languages, and traditions, yet simultaneously one, as God is one—Father, Son, and Holy Spirit—unity in diversity.

The new immigration is a reminder of the pilgrim state of the Church, made up of all those, regardless of race or class or national origin, who have been called to the wedding banquet and have responded (Luke 14:23). As a pilgrim, the Church encompasses in itself all the reality of human suffering and all the glory of the human spirit infused with the grace of Christ. With its diverse pilgrim peoples, the Church in the United States has known uprootedness and loss, persecution and flight, the search for a better life, and the difficulties and disappointments of that search. The Church has known God's grace as it lifts spirits in times of despair, sustains hope in the face of hopelessness, and revives love despite evils and human frailties. In the one baptism, the Church acknowledges God's call to conversion, while in the sacrament of the Eucharist, she enjoys prefigured the glorious communion of Father and Son in the Holy Spirit. At the Eucharist the Church prefigures the revelation of "a great multitude . . . from every nation, race, people, and tongue" (Revelation 7:9).

In such a Eucharist, on that sunlit Jubilee Day of Migrants and Refugees in St. Peter's Square, Pope John Paul II summed up the challenge and hope for the Church in the United States as it welcomes the immigrants of the new millennium in a very simple but profound image:

> Like the disciples of Emmaus, believers, supported by the living presence of the risen Christ, become in turn the traveling companions of their brothers and sisters in trouble, offering them the word which rekindles hope in their hearts. With them they break the bread of friendship, brotherhood and mutual help. This is how to build the civilization of love. This is how to proclaim the hoped-for coming of the new heavens and the new earth to which we are heading. (no. 4)

NOTES

[1] "In keeping with linguistic convention, the term Romani (also spelled Romany in the literature) is used to refer to any or all of the Romani dialects or languages. We use 'Gypsies' to refer to the totality of all groups except the Irish and Scottish Travelers, and where the identity of the group is unverified." (Taken from *Gypsies and Travelers in North America: An Annotated Bibliography*, William G. Lockwood and Sheila Salo [Cheverly, Md.: The Gypsy Lore Society, 1994].)

[2] In international and U.S. law, "refugees" are those who have fled past persecution or have a well-founded fear of future persecution on account of race, religion, nationality, membership in a particular social group, or political opinion. While the United States may grant asylum or special consideration to some refugees, the process of

obtaining such recognition is often fraught with difficulties, and many refugees must deal with the immigration system on the same terms as other immigrants.

3 Congress enacted three major laws in 1996 that have had an adverse impact on immigrants: (1) the Illegal Immigration Reform and Immigrant Responsibility Act (IIRIRA), (2) the Anti-Terrorism and Effective Death Penalty Act (AEDPA), and (3) the Personal Responsibility and Work Opportunity Reconciliation Act (PRWORA). Taken together, these laws have undermined due process protections for immigrants and driven more immigrant families into poverty. The combined effect of IIRIRA and AEDPA have subjected immigrants who committed minor crimes in their past and have served their sentence to mandatory detention and deportation, separating them indefinitely from their loved ones. IIRIRA also removed judicial discretion for individual cases and increased the standard for immigrants to obtain relief from deportation. It further included provisions that allow the summary exclusion of asylum seekers from this country without the benefit of review of their asylum claims by an immigration judge, and bars immigrants who reside in the country in an undocumented status for more than one year from returning to the United States for ten years. PRWORA, the federal welfare law, eliminated all legal immigrants from eligibility for public benefits. While some of these benefits have been restored, virtually all legal immigrants who entered the United States after 1996 remain ineligible for benefits.

4 Puerto Ricans, of course, are not immigrants, but many of them face the same challenges as recent immigrants. Much of the Hispanic population of the southwestern United States, likewise, can trace its ancestry in what is now the United States back many years before the appropriation of these territories by the U.S. government. While having much in common in language and culture with recent immigrants, the Hispanos of New Mexico and many Mexican-Americans throughout the country today welcome the newcomers in their midst as long established residents of this country. At the same time, they have often experienced the discrimination and disadvantage associated with representing a subordinate culture in the United States, on a par with the experiences of recent immigrants.

5 The term "multicultural," like others surrounding the question of immigration, has been much disputed in the United States. Like "cultural pluralism," "multicultural" may describe a society in which multiple cultures exist peaceably side by side, interacting in common social, economic, and political practices, while remaining distinct in others; respecting one another; learning from one another; and each changing at its own pace accordingly. The call for "incorporation" articulated in this letter shares in this spirit. It is not a call for "assimilation" or the disappearance of one culture into another, but for continuing cooperation in pursuit of the common good and with proper respect for the good of each cultural tradition and community.

6 In February 1986 the Pontifical Commission for the Pastoral Care of Migrants and the Congregation for Catholic Education wrote a joint letter on the place of "Human Mobility in the Formation of Future Priests."

The pastoral statement *Welcoming the Stranger Among Us: Unity in Diversity* was developed by the National Conference of Catholic Bishops' Committee on Migration. It was approved by the full body of bishops at their November 2000 General Meeting as a Statement of the National Conference of Catholic Bishops and is authorized for publication by the undersigned.

Reflections on Migration

Rev. Virgil Elizondo

Ibelieve that the theme of this reflection is one of the great themes that will be the distinguishing feature of the Catholic tradition in this century that has just begun. If in the last century we Catholics distinguished ourselves by not eating meat on Fridays, I hope that as this century proceeds, we may be recognized by our commitment to the social mission of the gospel as we acknowledge that Jesus Christ came to save us, not just as individuals, but also as a people.

The whole biblical tradition invites us to concern ourselves with others. We are a family, we are a body—the body of Christ. We must appreciate more and more this profound biblical teaching: each of us is connected to the other. Although we may not realize it, we are connected to the brother or sister who is suffering on the high plateau of Peru or in the local neighborhoods of San Antonio, Chicago, or Moscow. We are connected, wherever we are, and if others suffer, we must do something.

One of the things that will most characterize the Catholic tradition is precisely the evolution of the social teaching of the Church, which had its solid beginnings with Pope Leo XIII, continued through the years, and became stronger with each pope who has come after him. Our Holy Father Pope John Paul II, the bishops, and the committees of bishops see more and more each day that the preferential option for the poor, for the person who suffers, is not just another option for Christians, but is part of the very essence of being Christian. The bishops asked at a recent synod whether the theology of liberation would not have been rejected if so much attention had not been paid to it. In an insightful reply, Archbishop Daniel Pilarczyk of Cincinnati said that in fact it had not been rejected, but that its extremes had been corrected, and that the essence of what it stood for has been accepted to such an extent that now it is hardly ever mentioned by name.

The essence of being Christian is the preferential option for the poor. It is the basis of Scripture, which moves from the poor who suffer to the God who listens to their cry, sees their misery, and says, "I am going to rescue my people." This is the constant biblical foundation: a God who is not distant, who is not indifferent to the suffering of people; a God who takes the initiative, who does not wait for us to come to ask for help, but takes the initiative to meet each person. This is the point of view I wish to develop in relationship to the topic of immigration.

When we study the history of different peoples, we see they have all at some time been in process of immigration. The history of humanity is the history of immigration. In a way, the most natural thing about being human is the movement from one territory to another, sometimes as a result of conflict, other times as a cause of conflict. To migrate is part of human nature. I am of the opinion that today this insight is gaining an urgency of gigantic proportions, especially according to Pope John Paul II, in the way we perceive the immigrant.

At the present time, we see a massive immigration from poor countries towards developed countries. We observe in the United States and across Latin America the constant crossing of frontiers: from Paraguay to Argentina, from Argentina to Brazil, from Guatemala to Mexico, from the Latin American countries to the United States, from Africa to Spain, from Nigeria to France, from Turkey to Germany, from Indonesia to Holland, from Ethiopia to Italy. The different migrations are massive, and they are not only a question for the United States. The massive migration of peoples is one of the great phenomena in the world today. If the developed countries are sending their products and their sellers to the rest of the world, the rest of the world is sending its peoples to those countries that are sending them their merchandise. There is a constant exchange taking place all over the world.

In promoting their products, rich countries—the majority of them formed by immigrants—in one way or another, perhaps without even realizing it, invite the people of those countries that are potential exporters of immigrants to come to them. They do not regard their advertisements as invitations, but they are stimulating the migration of other peoples by causing them to believe they should come to the source of all the products. Those who formerly were quite happy where they were, now want to come to the source, just as the same commercial world, in a certain way, exploits the consumer, and in seeking to develop trade further invites the potential consumer to come to the source. As a result, people are willing to take any risk to come and live the good life these products promote: the promised land, the promised heaven on earth that is offered to them.

The film *El Norte* deals with poor immigrants who come to the U.S. with the dream of glory. But what do they find? Many of you know the answer better than I. So many people who come with big hopes, with big dreams, encounter instead a tragedy of incredible misery. Pope John Paul II speaks of this situation as a world migratory exodus. It is an exodus in which the people go forth from the slavery of misery, the slavery of violence, the slavery of sickness, the slavery of economic and political oppression. People are desperate for any remedy. Any immigration story you listen to would be sufficient material for a major film: the threats the people endure, the sufferings, the risks. The stories of each immigrant are stories of suffering, of sadness, of tragedy. And the world continues to emigrate.

I see the urgency of an encounter between this moment in history and the teaching of the Church. The attitude today in many Christian countries of Europe, the United States, and Latin America is becoming more and more anti-immigrant. We see today in the Western world an increasing contempt for the immigrant. Immigration laws are becoming harsher than ever. They divide families, sons, daughters, spouses. There is quite an increase in laws destructive of the family, an increase in public opposition to the immigrant.

We find our armed forces being used on the border to protect us from "the enemy." And who is this enemy? Our own brother, the poor person, the poor immigrant. We are seeing our armed forces used to protect us against the poor stranger, the unwanted, the unloved. In many developed nations, we are witnessing the poor man being turned into the enemy, and the rich man wanting to protect himself against the poor immigrant more effectively.

How the whole world celebrated with such great joy when the Berlin Wall fell. But today a great wall is being constructed between Mexico and the United States, the great wall between north and south, so that no poor person can come in. The rich man can enter in his private plane, but the poor man—what happens to him?

Our forebears, both European and Latin American, were part of the greatest wave of immigration in the history of humanity, and were able to enter without problems. And who were the immigrants? Poor people, prisoners, the unemployed, the hungry, the "nobodies." Why do we not want others to have the same opportunity that our forebears had? So often, when we take possession of something, we seek to establish laws so that no one else can enjoy what we have enjoyed; we forget very quickly who we are and where we have come from.

I believe that today's situation is urgent for the Church. First, because the immigrant is a human being, like you and me, who seeks what you and I seek: a house, a piece of land, some work. Second, because our Christian faith impels us to work for peace through justice. Third, because the teachings of the Church show us the privileged place of the immigrant in the mystery of the Church.

I would like to give a quick review of the biblical basis of our teaching: the universal love of God who hears the crying, sees the suffering, and says, "I am going to save my people." This biblical tradition begins in Chapter 18 of Genesis. It is the history of how Yahweh comes to Abraham in the guise of three strangers. Abraham did not realize who they were; he just knew they were three strangers. He offered them hospitality, prepared food, and offered them rest and something to drink. God blessed him for this hospitality. The most important principle in this situation is that God comes in the person of the stranger.

We recall the beautiful Latino Christmas custom of *Las Posadas*, where finally an inn is found for Joseph and Mary, after much rejection. The household that receives them is overjoyed with the same happiness that comes to a house that receives the homeless. Through the homeless, the joy of the Lord comes to those who offer shelter. The beginning of the biblical experience of the stranger is like the coming of God among us, and many times we do not recognize him. The rabbinical literature has stories of how the Messiah comes in the guise of the poorest beggar whom people do not recognize. God comes as the unexpected person. The tradition is found strongly in the Book of Exodus, and this book is the key to biblical thought, the heart of the development of the biblical tradition.

In Exodus 22:20, God speaks to his people and says: "You shall not molest or oppress an alien, for you were once aliens yourselves in the land of Egypt." This refrain becomes constant: "Do not mistreat strangers; remember that you, too, were a stranger in Egypt." If God has chosen you to be a new people, it was not so that you would repeat the mistakes of the past. The same is true for us in this country. We have to remember that we have received a great deal, and that we ought not repeat the mistakes of the past. We should remember the suffering of the past, of our forebears, so that others do not have to suffer the same thing today. The same refrain is heard in Exodus 23:9: "You shall not oppress an alien; you well know how it feels to be an alien, since you were once aliens yourselves in the land of Egypt." A constant reminder will be: do not oppress, remember what you suffered.

Deuteronomy 10:17–19 tells us:

> For the LORD, your God, is the God of gods, the LORD of lords, the great God, mighty and awesome, who has no favorites, accepts no bribes; who executes justice for the orphan and the widow, and befriends the alien, feeding and clothing him. So you too must befriend the alien, for you were once aliens yourselves in the land of Egypt.

The theme continues in Deuteronomy 16. It tells us not only to love the stranger but to invite him to our parties; do not merely tolerate him so as to disregard him later. Deuteronomy 16:11 says:

> In the place which the LORD, your God, chooses as the dwelling place of his name, you shall make merry in his presence together with your son and daughter, your male and female slave, and the Levite who belongs to your community, as well as the alien, the orphan, and the widow among you.

This is the biblical refrain for the unwanted, for the one we generally do not like: the stranger, the orphan, the widow, the person who has nobody to protect him. We are urged to invite them to our parties so that they can enjoy our celebrations with us, and to keep the stranger with us, so as to be part of the family and included in our parties. Finally, the Book of Leviticus 19 tells us we should not oppress strangers because God has called us to be saints, and the holiness of God will be revealed. We should not molest the stranger, we should consider him one of ourselves, and we should love him.

Now let us turn to the New Testament. We read the story of the Good Samaritan: the person who comes to my help is my neighbor and I do not ask him questions. If I have a flat tire at night and someone comes to help me, I do not ask him if he is a Christian; I just think, "How good of you to help me!" The one who comes to my help is my neighbor. And who helps a country more than the stranger, the immigrant? The immigrant is the one who does the work no one else wants to do.

But we also see how the law of Jesus carries us even further than the rest of the Bible: "Love one another. Such as my love has been for you, so must your love be for each other" (Jn 13:34). This love is without limit; it is without restriction. The first Christians who were the first missionaries were themselves strangers. The first Christians were the servants, the domestics, lower-rank members of the military, and when they moved they brought Christianity with them. They formed Christian communities. That is why in the Acts of the Apostles, a Christian community often exists before Paul comes to a place. He does not start it. It is already there and he strengthens it.

What are some of the themes we might use for our preaching today? The birth of Jesus in the manger is an image we can see; so are the stories of the Good Samaritan, the woman giving Jesus a drink at the well, and Peter denying Jesus. Our preaching ought to draw people, but if it is to reach the heart it has to express a sense of humor.

Once four young men came to the rectory. They told me they had just crossed the border and that they were very hungry. I invited them to come in and began to prepare breakfast for them and to talk with them. In the course of the conversation, one of them told me that he had enjoyed my sermon last Sunday, and even quoted what I had said. I thought that he might have seen me speaking on television, given that our Mass is broadcast across the border. But he told me no, that he had been present at the Mass but that the immigration authorities had sent him back to Mexico on Monday. Then, because the other three did not know how to cross the border, he had brought them across. The border patrol had sent one back last week, but four had returned this week. There is both humor and contradiction in this situation.

Other young men who came from Guatemala were thankful to some policemen in Laredo, Texas. They had been exploited and humiliated in many ways in their passage through Mexico. The only ones to help them were two policemen in Laredo. They pointed out the train they should take to arrive safe and sound at their destination without being stopped by immigration officials. What they and I least expected was that these policemen were *gringos*, not Latinos.

On the other hand, we have to talk about the tragedies. On another occasion three young people came, ashen-faced, hardly able to speak, but I was able to get the story of how they came. They had crossed the frontier by the river, near Piedras Negras, trying to hide from the highways. As a result, a rattlesnake bit one of them, and the others did not know what to do. They were afraid to go to the ranchers, because they had heard stories of how the ranchers killed Mexicans. They were afraid of everything. Then they sat down to wait, to see what was going to happen, and the young man died from the snake's bite. They tried to cover him with a little earth, and they left him there. Then they came to me to see if I could contact his mother, who was a widow with 13 children. The young man, the eldest, had come to find work in order to send money to his family so they could live a little better. The task of contacting the mother and letting her know her son was dead fell on me, without my even knowing where the body lay.

These are the sufferings, the tragedies. There are also tales of hope. On another occasion, a Guatemalan mother came with her baby by train. Suddenly the crowd shouted: "The Migra"—the immigration police—"are coming." She picked up the baby and sent it rolling from the train. The baby was hardly bruised, but the mother did not have the same good fortune. She jumped from the train, but it caught her clothing and cut off both her legs. But she is walking now with crutches, and she is organizing sewing classes and doing reasonably well. And the child is beautiful and has turned into a young lady.

There are all kinds of stories. This is the basis of our preaching—not statistics, though these help and are good at times. But stories reach people. You are not going to forget these four stories. I am sure that if you meet me in one, two, five, or ten years, you will tell me these stories. Because the stories remain. It is the stories that get the people to think and analyze. Let our preaching reach the heart and include stories of what is happening so as to move the heart to action.

We can distinguish three of the most important types of preaching: The first is for general audiences. If we preach to this type of audience, our Christian task is to give a positive vision of the immigrant. The world sees the immigrant more and more as the enemy, as the cause of all problems and suffering. I believe it is very important for us, in different ways, to give a positive image of the immigrant. In the final analysis, the most positive image is the theological and biblical idea that God comes as an immigrant to meet with us. Those who close the door of their country to the poor immigrant, close their doors on God. God is not in the churches where the immigrant is not welcome. We need to give a positive image of the immigrant so that it is clear to everyone that what the world says about the immigrant is not true—not only is he not the enemy, but on the contrary, he is the one who will help to build this country.

We also have to preach a new idea of what it is to be "a missionary." Formerly to be missionary meant to go and serve in a foreign country. There is validity in this type of mission today, but the concept of mission has also changed radically for the Western Church. Now mission also means to receive the poor stranger in our homes, in our parishes, in our schools, and in our neighborhoods. This is a much less romantic idea. A lot of people are happy to have someone go "over there" but they do not want others to come "over here" and go to the same schools as their children, play in the same schoolyard as their children; they might become friends and someday want to marry each other!

Today the countries of the West have to develop the spirit of receiving: to receive and to find ways of helping the poor immigrant. The fundamental virtue of the Christian is hospitality. In the parishes and in all the religious centers we must be more hospitable. Many immigrants come alone, without family. If we are preaching to immigrants, we should bring out other important themes. The first theme grows out of a very profound Latin American tradition: Divine Providence. God is always present to us even in the most difficult stages of our lives. God never leaves us alone. We ought never to undervalue the power of faith that impels people to do incredible things and heroic acts. I have been told stories where only faith has saved the persons involved.

We cannot take away all the suffering that the immigrant experiences, even though we would like to do so. But within the context of this suffering, we can give strength so that they survive, so that suffering does not ruin their lives, so that suffering does not turn them into alcoholics, drug addicts, or criminals. We should recover an image that perhaps we have not appreciated enough: the image of Mary, the mother. Mary, as mother, is always with us. This is something that in the United States we are scarcely beginning to appreciate: the profound feeling that I am connected to Mary, my mother.

Another image we have to recover is the love of God, which comes in many ways, including the suffering of Christ. We do not want to glorify suffering, because we do not want suffering to destroy life. The great master of liberating education, Paulo Freire, used to say: "Do not remove the symbols of a suffering God, of a suffering people, without having eliminated first of all suffering itself." There is nothing worse than meaningless suffering. For the people who suffer it is important to know that God is right there with them, at this very moment. This idea does not justify suffering, but it does give strength to go forward.

We have to challenge immigrants to avail themselves of the opportunities this country offers, especially in education. That is why I say to the adults, "Why don't you go back to school, to be an example to your children?" It made me happy last year to be at the University of Texas at San Antonio when a great-grandmother graduated with a master's degree in education. All her grandchildren and great-grandchildren were there. People stood to applaud her. I say to people, "Why do you not give that kind of example to your children?" At 40, 50, or 70 years of age, people are still at the university. One simply has to be challenged. We should not expect less of our people. We have got to have big expectations. Because our people have suffered, we should have great expectations, not small ones, because we can do it. If we hope for little, we will achieve little.

When I finished 12 years of work at the cathedral, a young daughter of poor immigrants who had begun first grade when I arrived at the cathedral completed 12th grade, speaking English, Spanish, French, and German perfectly. And a young lad who began later—he was a sophomore when I left the cathedral—spoke Spanish, English, Russian, and Japanese, although not yet perfectly. These young people can achieve, but we have to challenge and help them. We cannot abandon those who are in the "poor me" category. The immigrant is to be helped also to go beyond himself. After all, they have already risked their lives to come here. Challenge them to take the opportunities offered; let her educate herself, let him acquire good moral values.

Finally, I believe that we, like the recently canonized Juan Diego, have to be daring and to preach to the leaders of the Church. It is not enough to preach only to the public in general but also to those who lead the community. In this respect, we have to challenge the leaders, catechists, liturgy directors, and bishops to be with the people, because it is from here that salvation will come to the rest of the people, like the God who comes to us in unexpected persons and places. I believe salvation can come to the United States through poor immigrants, and this is dependent on the amount of attention which the immigrant experiences in the Church; the immigrant should be a priority; not a remainder but something truly important. Walk with these people who suffer, accompany them in their suffering, and through this suffering begin to walk in a new life. This is probably the greatest challenge to our preaching: not to be afraid to preach, as Saint Paul says, "I charge you to preach the word, to stay with this task whether convenient or inconvenient" (2 Tim 4:2). When the opportune moment presents itself, come forward and say the appropriate words, and be not afraid because God is with you. Who then can be against you? So we have to be the voice that challenges the church we love so much.

The most important challenge we face at this moment is the immigrant. Not because immigrants are more important than others, but because of the suffering they endure at the present moment. If we are faithful to God's call, God will achieve great miracles through us. May the joy of the gospel message be always the source of inspiration to each one of us, and may the words of Jesus be always heard in our message: "Blest are you poor; the reign of God is your" (Luke 6:20).

Welcoming the Stranger Among Us
Suggestions for Civil/Liturgical Occasions

Rev. Raúl Gómez

This pastoral letter contains a wealth of useful data, concepts, and applications. As with the other documents in this book, there are several civil and liturgical occasions lending themselves to the incorporation of their themes. Here are a few to consider.

Ethnic festivals in the United States often provide a context for raising the topic of refugees and migrants. Sometimes they include the Eucharist or ecumenical or interreligious prayer services. Awareness of the peoples comprising one's community and of their history, important holidays, and emblematic celebrations can be a launching pad for addressing the issue of refugees and migrants. For example, the lunar New Year festivities of February–March can be a time to raise this issue in relation to Asians. Columbus Day and St. Patrick's Day can raise this in relation to Italians, Native Americans, Hispanics, Irish, and English. Thanksgiving Day is also key. Nationhood days observed by the different Hispanic/Latino countries, or the anniversaries of the death of labor leader César Chávez on April 23 and the martyrdom of El Salvadoran Archbishop Oscar Romero on March 24 are also opportune moments.

At Pentecost, we see how the gospel is for all and how it leads to the peaceful coexistence of diverse cultures. In addition, the readings about the flight into Egypt and of Matthew 25:31–46 are fitting opportunities. The readings about Abraham's call, the Exodus and the Exile, and the Tower of Babel are also favorable. Consider ways to preach on the memorials of saints such as Kateri Takewitha (July 14), Paul Miki and companions (February 6), Cyril and Methodius (February 14), Casimir (March 4), Toribio de Mogrovejo (March 23), Charles Lwanga and companions (June 3), Rose of Lima (August 23), and Andrew Kim Taegon and companions (September 20), among others. Finally, the patronal feast days of the various Hispanic/Latino groups in the United States can provide a context in which to address the question of one's sisters and brothers.

Welcoming the Stranger Among Us
Suggested Liturgical Texts

Rev. José A. López

Reference: United States Conference of Catholic Bishops, Lectionary for Mass, Second Typical Edition, Vol. I–IV. Chicago: Liturgy Training Publications, 2002.

Texts:

IV:927	Deuteronomy 10:1
	Deuteronomy 24:17–22
III:95	Galatians 3:26–29
IV:928	Romans 9:12–16b
IV:929	Tobit 13:2, 3–4, 6, 7, 8
IV:931–1	Matthew 2:13–15, 19–23
IV:931–2	Matthew 25:31–46

While the selected readings seem to be directed primarily to those who are receiving immigrants, wholeheartedly or reluctantly, Scripture reminds everyone that the "You shall not violate the rights of the alien or of the orphan" (Deut 24:17) and speaks to all who follow his ways. He has called everyone out of the land of Egypt, that land of darkness. Having done that, he now requires all to do that which he had done: "For remember you were once slaves in Egypt, and the Lord, your God, ransomed you from there" (Deut 24:18). The texts also serve to remind immigrants that they, too, must always be welcoming to others. One of the key marks of the preacher is to invite the people to welcome anyone who walks through the church doors as a brother or sister to all.

CONCLUSION

Preacher Exegete Thyself

Preacher Exegete Thyself

Burn all Bibles. Not the Word of God, of course, just the packaging that domesticates that Word with trite subtitles such as "The Prodigal Son," or "The Widow's Mite." Each cliché is an editorial nod and wink that assures everyone of a chummy, shared assumption about the Word.

Did the prophets suffer and apostles die for a script of such conspicuous assumption? Putting subtitles in Scripture is like putting a to-do list on romance.

But romance is alluring only when alluding. So a romance with Scripture as with a spouse is forever fresh only if regularly revelatory. Familiarity breeds contempt, mystery always tempts. The Other is ultimately unknowable and therein lies the unending adventure.

Only strangers have adventures because homebodies never venture beyond the familiar. Because conventional citizens are too cozy in their shared assumptions to see beyond the subtitles to the subtleties, only strangers really appreciate the always-otherness of God's Word.

U.S. Hispanics and the Consequences of Conquest

Many Mexican-Americans feel like strangers in their own land, myriad Puerto Ricans feel like colonists within their own country, and countless Cuban-Americans feel like aliens even when U.S. citizens. United States Hispanics differ in many respects, but hold three things in their collective memory:

1) Catholicism

2) the Spanish language

3) the contemporary consequences of conquest.

Hispanic homiletics, therefore, requires all three members of this triad.

Virtually all Latina/o Christians trace some of their ancestry to Iberian Catholicism. They may also claim indigenous blood and/or African roots, but most are heirs of a combination that includes the faith as well as the language of the Spanish conquerors. The legacy of this first conquest is precisely the violently imposed combination of Native American, Iberian, and enslaved African peoples and traditions that Virgil Elizondo calls the first *mestizaje*. This fusion produced a new people, a new culture, and new religious expressions.

Eventually the United States subjugated the crumbling edges of that colonial Spanish Empire. What is now the southwest U.S. was taken over in the 1840s, Puerto Rico in 1898, and by 1950 the hegemony was so complete that those in the U.S., as well as much of the rest of the world, commonly referred to a single nation with a presumptuous title that more rightfully belongs to an entire hemisphere: "America."

This is a second conquest or *mestizaje* peculiar to U.S. Hispanics. Like the first, it included the usurpation of land, and a newly dominant (civil) religion. This second conquest resulted in Mexican-Americans no longer being Mexican (they now lived in the U. S.), but never quite "American." They were strangers in their own land. Puerto Ricans speak of cultural schizophrenia, Cubans of diaspora, but all of the social dislocation as a consequence of the second conquest. Even Hispanics who no longer speak Spanish and those who no longer practice Catholicism resonate with these strident tones of alienation.

The consequences of the second conquest are profound and easily found. According to a recent survey by the National Community on Latino/a Leadership, of the heirs of the second conquest, up to 57 percent feel politically disenfranchised, 42 percent have an annual household income of less that $20,000, 69 percent hold only a high school degree or less, and 40–50 percent experience discrimination. These are just some of the topics explored by my colleagues in this book.

The literature on the legacy of the dual conquest or double *mestizaje* is enormous, accessible, and details the contemporary social, political, and economic dislocation of U.S. Hispanics. Consequently this single, common datum widely uniting an otherwise heterogeneous community (along with at least a cultural memory of Catholicism and Spanish) should constitute an essential member of a triad informing homiletics among Hispanics. Yet it is on that datum that the triad totters.

Preaching in Spanish

The National Survey of Leadership in Latino Parishes and Congregations (Program for the Analysis of Religion Among Latinos, 2002) notes that Catholic preachers are much less likely than Protestants to "always preach on political topics such as electoral procedures, anti-poverty programs and affirmative action . . . ." Despite the contemporary renewal of Catholic preaching and the U.S. bishops' attention to social justice, Catholics who preach in Spanish in the U.S. virtually ignore the third member of the triad, the contemporary consequences of conquest. Why?

Perhaps because, according to this same survey, Latinos lead only 25 percent of Catholic Hispanic faith communities. By contrast, Protestant preachers are three times more likely to be Hispanic themselves, and also much more likely to preach about the concerns of ordinary Hispanics. They know from their own experience the consequences of conquest; Catholic preachers generally do not. Simply put, a Catholic preacher who is not Hispanic but who labors to learn Spanish and tries with good will to serve the people is nonetheless nearly always male, usually middle-class, and effectively multicultural.

Multicultural? Isn't that the label the U.S. Church uses to describe minorities? How can a white, non-Hispanic be multicultural? Such a question leads to my surmise: White, non-Hispanics fail to seriously consider the consequences of conquest when we fail to seriously consider the captivating consequences of culture. For a non-Hispanic Catholic to preach well, he must first culturally exegete himself.

Captured by Culture

Just as non-Hispanic whites create offices of multicultural ministry without considering that whites too have a culture, so we also often study Hispanic ethnicity without ever considering our own ethnic background. Since we do not sufficiently reflect on our own cultural perspective, we fail to appreciate how limiting that perspective is. Consider everyday examples of our cultural assumptions. Why do advice columnists counsel direct rather than indirect communication? Because our culture values fair competition over group sensibilities.

Why is flying coach class even briefly so challenging? Because our culture values personal space over public familiarity. Why are we all concerned about our 401Ks and social security? Because our culture values independence over family support. Why are we willing to trust a salesman in business dealings even if we know he is disloyal to his spouse? Because our culture values compartmentalized associations rather than interconnected (communal) relationships.

Every culture depends on such common, assumed, in-group values that are so unconscious we are often only aware of them when they are violated. Innocent questions from out-group inquirers, however, show how unreflective of our cultural matrix we are. Consider questions posed to my colleagues and me from sincere foreign clergy: *Why do you only talk to each other during commercials? Why do you put all your grandparents in warehouses?* We sputter in reply because we have always assumed that the underlying assumptions (interrupting someone's entertainment is impolite, nursing homes are required in modern society) were universal certainties rather than our peculiar cultural subtitles. No culture is self-evident to outsiders, but it can be self-imprisoning to insiders.

And it is precisely this lack of an exegesis of our own culture that biases our preaching. We study Spanish. We sincerely serve the people. And we faithfully study "their" culture. All of which is necessary, but insufficient. We need also to exegete our own cultural assumptions (usually we don't even recognize that we have any!) if we are to be a catalyst that charges liturgy with justice, rather than an inert element that preaches the former (inadequately) without the latter.

Perhaps that is why the newest USCCB document on Hispanic ministry, *Encuentro and Mission: A Renewed Pastoral Framework for Hispanic Ministry*, declares:

> However, we must state clearly and loudly that efforts . . .
> must include a clearly understood sensitivity *to* cultures
> being served [and] to *the culture of those men preparing
> for the priesthood or diaconate* . . . .(No. 45, emphasis
> added).

Non-Latinos who preach among U.S. Hispanics often speak Spanish adequately. Many have studied the history and cultures of their Hispanic communities. Few, however, demonstrate a "clearly understood sensitivity" to the imprisoning influence of their own culture.

Therefore, we often unconsciously put our own cultural subtitles on the Scriptures even if we happen to be preaching them in Spanish. In such a case, even when our Spanish is fluent, the idiom and the assembly remain incongruent. In general, we deal sufficiently with two parts of the triad of Hispanic homiletics (language and faith), but wobble on the third, the contemporary consequences of conquest.

Cultural Amphibians

Social dislocation, the experience of being a stranger in a strange land, is a common experience of the otherwise diverse group we (for lack of a better term) call Hispanic or Latino/a. This painful experience also highlights the question of identity. As seen in these pages, the Hispanic contributors wrestle repeatedly with questions of identity and cultural perspective. Perhaps we non-Hispanic preachers can learn from them how to culturally exegete ourselves.

These Hispanic theologians have both a method for and a source of their theology. The source is the lived experience of their people. And their method is *conjunto* or communion in mission. This means that ideally these theologians accompany their people, reflect with them on their common faith experience, and rearticulate that faith in a way that promotes the dignity of the people. What would such a contextual approach to our preaching look like? How specifically might we non-Hispanics culturally exegete ourselves in preparation for preaching in Spanish? Perhaps we can learn from the source and method indicated by U.S. Hispanic theologians such as my present collaborators.

The source of our cultural exegesis is our own cross-cultural experience, and the method is communion in mission. Therefore, what has been our experience?

I have suggested that our experience is like being a frog. A frog is an amphibian. Non-Hispanic preachers who have dedicated themselves to Hispanic ministry are cultural amphibians. If we have learned Spanish and learned to love the people we serve, we can never "go home" or return to a more naïve time when we believed that the church couldn't possibly be racist or nationalistic. Because of our avocation, we are often on the margins of the college of preachers: just look at the tomes they write and the conferences they convene, and see how often they reflect the reality of Hispanic faith communities.

Yet despite our dedication and even the acceptance of our Hispanic congregants, we're still *gringos* after all these years. Our Spanish is accented, our theology educated, our families and colleagues segregated from our ministry by language, geography, and experience. We love the people we serve, but we will never be one of them. And we love the people from our home culture, but we can never again share their segregation. We're cultural amphibians negotiating a niche between the culture of our family of birth and the culture of our family of Church. Yet in both places we are, to a certain extent, always strangers.

Recall, however, that only strangers appreciate the always Otherness of God's Word. Homebodies in their cozy familiarity of shared assumption cannot see beyond their own cultural subtitles to God's subtleties. Hence, it is precisely the perspective of a stranger that provides preachers with a new cultural candidness, because strangers know that we do not exegete God's Word: the Word exegetes us.

Being "strangers before God's Word" therefore means that we are amphibians, frogs hopping between the two cultures of our childhood formation and our preaching vocation. However, since neither wholly defines us, neither wholly confines us. Strangers before the Word endure dislocation, but also enjoy a frog-like freedom. That experience must be the source of our reflection.

Yet we are often not in practical communion. Communion in mission or *conjunto* is a helpful methodology, but difficult because there is only sporadic initial preparation for this ministry and less continuing support.

The USCCB's Secretariat for Hispanic Affairs says that half of the country's seminarians are required to learn Spanish. On a practical level, however, that often means they only learn enough to "read the Mass," and given the increasing age of the average seminarian, even that requirement is sometimes waived.

Those seminarians who go to a Spanish immersion program and/or find a qualified Spanish language professor at the seminary rarely find related courses (e.g., in liturgy or preaching) in the curriculum or professors trained in cross-cultural communication. If one looks past the seminary's public relations to the academic qualifications of the professors charged with Hispanic ministry formation, one rarely finds people with terminal degrees adequate to their field. Although no one would hire a priest without a J.C.D. to teach canon law simply because he is experienced in marriage annulments, seminaries regularly hire professors of Hispanic ministry without corresponding doctorates simply because they have worked in Hispanic parishes. Education is not everything and experience is invaluable, but the combination of the two is ideal. If future preachers are to be taught the skills to culturally exegete themselves, they must have professors qualified to impart those skills. Dismissing the importance of qualified professors imputes unimportance to those same skills. Hopefully such issues will be addressed in the revised *Program for Priestly Formation.*

Professional lay ministry formation, the preparation of permanent deacons, and the continuing education of all preachers lag. Not only do we need to attract and retain more Hispanics to the permanent diaconante and lay ministry, we also need to invest the same kind of resources in the cross–cultural preparation of non-Hispanic lay ministers and permanent deacons, as well as the continuing education of all preachers, that we must have in our seminarians.

Thus, while our own experience as cultural amphibians can be the source of our reflection, the methodology of communion in mission is difficult because we do not have a common and adequate initial preparation or continuing education. Again, however, we can learn from our Hispanic sisters and brothers such as the veteran contributors to this work: *se hace el camino en el andar*—we make the path by walking it.

Can we not gather and reflect on our experience as cross–cultural preachers in *conjunto*? Those of us in large urban areas where many preachers do this ministry could gather to reflect regularly. Those of us in areas where Hispanics are newer and more dispersed might need regional or national gatherings. All of us could lobby the National Organization for Continuing Education of Roman Catholic Clergy, the National Federation of Priests' Councils, schools of theology, and institutes of deacon and lay ministry formation, as well as the various think tanks and professional associations of liturgy and homiletics. But we need to gather our experience in communion if we are to reflect as a Church on our mission to preach among Hispanics.

I am proud to collaborate on this book. Not only does it add to the paucity of works concerning preaching among U.S. Hispanic Catholics, it is unique in its treatment of social justice. Hence it will help correct the previous inattention to the contemporary consequences of conquest without which the triad will still be off-balance.

For the two-thirds of Catholics who preach in Spanish as a second language, our good will and other fine skills are necessary but insufficient. If we do not also seriously consider the captivating consequences of our own culture, we will not adequately address the consequences of conquest. Therefore, we cross-cultural preachers must first exegete ourselves. And such exegesis will best be addressed through a communal consideration of our cross-cultural experience.

Burning bibles is just a metaphorical exaggeration. Blazing new trails to prepare preachers, however, is not hyperbolic but apostolic. And the first step is imperative: Preacher, exegete thyself.

Kenneth G. Davis, O.F.M., Conv.

CONTRIBUTORS

Contributors

Rev. José Aguirre López is a native south Texan. He attended Assumption Seminary and Oblate School of Theology in San Antonio, Texas. He teaches Homiletics and Pastoral Care and Counseling at Oblate School of Theology.

Walter J. Burghardt, S.J., S.T.D., is widely regarded as the Dean of Catholic preaching in the United States. He is also well-known for his work with Preaching the Just Word.

Kenneth G. Davis, O.F.M., Conv., is Associate Professor of Pastoral Studies at Saint Meinrad School of Theology, and General Editor of the *Hispanic Theological Initiative Book Series.*

Rev. Virgil Elizondo is a Diocesan Priest of the Archdiocese of San Antonio, TX. His teaching positions include the Mexican American Cultural Center, University of Notre Dame, Univ. of Texas at San Antonio, and the University of Santa Barbara. He is the author of numerous books and articles.

Sister Angela Erevia, M.C.D.P., is originally from Texas. She is Director of the Hispanic Ministry Office of the Archdiocese of Omaha. She has a B.A. in Religious Studies from Our Lady of the Lake University, 1969, and an M.R.E. from St. Thomas University, 1973. She has written extensively on "quince años," including *Quince Años: Celebrando la Vida*, 2000.

Rev. Raúl Gómez, S.D.S., is originally from southern Arizona. He is Director of the Hispanic Studies Program and Associate Professor of Systematic Studies at Sacred Heart School of Theology, Hales Corners, Wisconsin. He has a B.A. from the University of Arizona, an M.P.A. from California State, Sacramento, an M.Div. from the Franciscan School of Theology, and a Ph.D. in Liturgical Studies from Catholic University of America.

Most Rev. Roberto O. Gonzalez, O.F.M., Archbishop of San Juan de Puerto Rico since 1999. Born in Elizabeth, New Jersey of Puerto Rican parents; professed in the Franciscan Order, 1973; Ordained Priest, 1977; Doctor in Sociology, Fordham University, 1984; Installed Auxiliary Bishop of Boston, 1988; Installed Coadjutor Bishop of Corpus Christi, 1995 and Bishop of Corpus Christi, 1997.

Rev. Leopoldo Pérez, O.M.I., is Associate Professor of Moral Theology at Oblate School of Theology in San Antonio, Texas. He has a B.A. in Psychology from St. Edward's University, Austin, Texas, 1979, an M.Div. from Oblate School of Theology, 1983, and an S.T.L., 1992, and an S.T.D., 1995 in Moral Theology from the Gregorian University, Rome.

Rev. Arturo Pérez Rodriguez is originally from Chicago. He is an Archdiocesan Priest who writes and teaches about Hispanic liturgy and spirituality, as well as being administrator of two Chicagoland parishes, St. Francis de Sales and St. George. He has an M.Div. from St. Mary of the Lake Seminary and an M.A. from the University of Notre Dame, Indiana.

Rev. Jorge L. Presmanes, O.P. is a Dominican Friar of the Province of St. Martin de Porres. He has an M.Div. and an M.A. from the Dominican School, G.T.U., Berkeley. He is Adjunct Professor of Theology for the M.A. in Pastoral Ministry jointly offered through Barry University and the South East Pastoral Institute, and is completing a D.Min. at Barry University. He is Pastor of St. Dominic Parish in Miami.

Most Rev. Ricardo Ramírez, C.S.B., D.D., is Bishop of Las Cruces, New Mexico. He is from Bay City, Texas, and a member of the Congregation of St. Basil. He holds a B.A. from the University of St. Thomas, Houston, 1959; an M.A. from the University of Detroit, 1968. He was ordained a Priest Dec. 10, 1966; ordained Bishop October 27, 1981; named First Bishop of the Diocese of Las Cruces, New Mexico on October 18, 1982.

Rev. Jose Antonio Rubio is a priest of the Diocese of San Jose, Director of Ecumenical and Interreligious Affairs of the Diocese, and Administrator of Five Wounds Portuguese National Parish in San Jose. He has a B.A. from U.C. Berkeley; an M.Div. from St. Patrick Seminary, Menlo Park, California; an M.A. from Santa Clara University; a S.T.L. from Catholic University of America, and is working on S.T.D. at Jesuit School of Theology, Berkeley.

Mark E. Wedig, O.P., is a Dominican Friar of the Province of St. Martin de Porres and Prior of the Dominican community at St. Dominic Parish, Miami. He is Associate Professor and Chair of the Department of Theology and Philosophy at Barry University, Florida. He holds the Ph.D. in Liturgical Studies from the Catholic University of America.

BIBLIOGRAPHY

Bibliography

Alvarez, Carmelo E. "Ecumenism in Transition? Hispanic Responses from the United States." *Journal of Hispanic/Latino Theology* 4, no. 2 (November 1996): 60–74.

Amoros Alicea, José A. "Fe, Desarrollo y Solidaridad: Reflexiones en Torno a la Enciclica Sollicitudo Rei Socialis." *Apuntes* 10, no. 3 (Fall 1990): 51–58.

Aquino, María Pilar. "The Challenge of Hispanic Women." *Missiology* 20, no. 2 (April 1992): 261–268.

_____. "Construyendo la Misión Evangelizadora de la Iglesia: Inculturación y Violencia Hacia las Mujeres.' In Ana María Tepedino and María Pilar Aquino, eds. *Entre La Indignación y La Esperanza*, 63–91. Bogotá: Indo-American Press Service, 1998.

_____. "El 'Des-Cubrimiento,' Colectivo de la Propia Fuerza: Perspectivas Teológicas desde las Mujeres Latinoamericanas." *Apuntes* 13, no. 1 (Spring 1993): 86–103.

_____. "Including Women's Experience: A Latina Feminist Perspective." In Ann O'Hare Graff, ed. *The Embrace of God. Feminist Approaches to Theological Anthropology*, 51–70. Maryknoll: Orbis Books, 1995.

_____. "The Collective 'Discovery' of Our Own Power: Latina American Feminist Theology." In Isasi-Diaz, Ada Maria and Segovia, Fernando, eds. *Hispanic/Latino Theology, Challenge and Promise*, 240–258. Philadelphia: Fortress Press, 1996.

_____. "Latin American Feminist Theology." *Journal of Feminist Studies* 14, no. 1 (Spring 1998): 89–107.

_____. "Economic Violence in Latin American Perspective." In Mary John Mananzan, Mercy Amba Oduyoye, Elsa Tamez, J. Shannon Clarkson, Mary C. Grey, and Letty M. Russell, eds. *Women Resisting Violence: Spirituality for Life*, 100–108. Maryknoll: Orbis Books, 1996.

_____, and Roberto S. Goizueta, eds. *Theology: Expanding the Borders. The Annual Publication of the College Theology Society*. Mystic, Connecticut: Twenty-Third Publications, 1998.

Audinet, Jacques. "Beyond Multiculturalism: A European Perspective." *Listening* 32, no. 3 (Fall 1997): 161–173.

Awalt, Barbe, and Paul Rhetts. "The Images of Nuestra Senora in New Mexican Devotional Art: Traditional and Contemporary." *Marian Studies* 49 (1998): 19–40.

Azevedo, Marcello. "Hispanic Leaders: Faith and Culture in the New Millennium." *Chicago Studies* 36, no. 3 (December 1997): 224–242.

Barber, Janet, IHM. "The Guadalupan Image: An Inculturation of the Good News." *Josephinum Journal of Theology* 4 (Supplement 1997): 65–81.

Barrón, Clemente, CP. "Racism and Religious Life." *Review for Religious* 55, no. 5 (September–October 1996): 494–505.

Bañuelas, Arturo. "U.S. Hispanic Theology." *Missiology* 2 (April 1992): 275–300.

_____, ed. Mestizo Christianity: *Theology from the Latino Perspective*. Maryknoll: Orbis Books, 1995.

Becker, Sister Jean, OSF. "Hispanic Associates: Gift and Challenge." *Sisters Today* 69, no. 6 (November 1997): 454–455.

Borran, George. "Hispanic Catholic Youth in the United States." *Chicago Studies* 36, no. 3 (December 1997): 243–254.

Boff, Leonardo, and Virgil Elizondo, eds. "Editorial." *In Concilium: Ecology and Poverty: Cry of the Earth, Cry of the Poor,* ix–xii. Maryknoll: Orbis Books, 1995.

Buckley, Francis. "Popular Religiosity and Sacramentality: Learning from Hispanics a Deeper Sense of Symbol, Ritual, and Sacrament." *Living Light* 27, no. 4 (Summer 1991): 351–360.

Burgaleta, Claudio M. "A Rahnerian Reading of Santería: A Proposal for a Christian Recovery of the Syncretic Elements of Latin American Popular Religiosity based on Rahner's Concept of 'Anonymous Christianity.' *Apuntes* 13, no. 2 (Summer 1993): 139–150.

_____. "The Theology of José de Acosta (1540–1600): Challenge and Inspiration for Bridging the Gap between the Academy, Society, and the Church." *Theology Today* 54, no. 4 (January 1998): 470–479.

Burghardt, Walter J. "Preaching the Just Word." In Mark Searle, ed. *Liturgy and Social Justice.* Collegeville: Liturgical Press, 1980.

_____. *Let Justice Roll Down like Waters: Biblical Justice Homilies Throughout the Year.* New York: Paulist Press, 1998.

Cadena, Gilbert R. "The Social Location of Liberation Theology: From Latin America to the United States." In Isasi-Diaz, Ada Maria and Segovia, Fernando, eds. *Hispanic/Latino Theology, Challenge and Promise*, 167–182. Philadelphia: Fortress Press, 1996.

Cadena, Gilbert R., and Lara Medina. "Liberation Theology and Social Change: Chicanas and Chicanos in the Catholic Church." In Roberto M. de Anda, ed. *Chicanas and Chicanos in Contemporary Society*, 99–111. Boston: Allyn and Bacon, 1996.

Candelaria, Michael R. *Popular Religion and Liberation: The Dilemma of Liberation Theology.* Albany: State University of New York Press.

Carrasco, David. *Religions of Mesoamerica.* San Francisco: Harper & Row, 1990.

_____. "Those Who Go on a Sacred Journey: The Shapes and Diversity of Pilgrimages." *Concilium* 4 (1996): 13–24.

Casarella, Peter. "The Painted Word." *Journal of Hispanic/Latino Theology* 4, no. 2 (November 1998): 18–42.

Castillo, Ana. *Goddess of the Americans: Writings on the Virgin of Guadalupe.* New York: Riverhead Books, 1996.

Cervantes, Carmen Maria. "Catholic Education for Ministry Among Hispanics." *The Living Light* 27 (Fall 1990): 46–50.

Cervantes, Fernando. "'The Defender of the Indians': Bartolomé de las Casas in Context." *Way* 38, no. 3 (July 1998): 271–281.

Clark, Kevin. "Snapshots from the Edge: A Report from the U. S./Mexican Border." *Salt of the Earth* (May/June 1997): 12–18.

Corona, Ignacio. "Guadalupanism: Popular Religion and Cultural Identity." *Josephinum Journal of Theology* 4 (Supplement 1997): 6–22.

Cunningham, Hilary. *God and Caesar at the Rio Grand: Sanctuary and the Politics of Religion.* Minneapolis: University of Minnesota Press, 1995.

_____. "Sanctuary and Sovereignty: Church and State along the U. S.-Mexican Border." *Journal of Church and State* 40, no. 2 (Spring 1998): 371–386.

D'Antonio, William V., et. al., eds. *Laity: American Catholics Transforming the Church.* Kansas City, Missouri: Sheed & Ward, 1996.

Dalton, Fredrick John. *The Moral Vision of Cesar Chavez.* Maryknoll: Orbis Books, 2003.

Davis, Kenneth G. "A.A.: Making It User Friendly." *Apuntes* 10, no. 2 (Summer 1990): 36–43.

_____. "Father, We're Not in Kansas Anymore." *The Priest* 46, no. 7 (July 1990): 14–16.

_____. "On Being a Frog in My Field." *The Priest* 47, no. 10 (October 1991): 6–7.

_____. "CORHIM: Hispanic Seminars." *Review for Religious* 50, no. 6 (November/ December 1991): 881–887.

_____. "A Return to the Roots: Conversion and the Culture of the Mexican-Descent Catholic," *Pastoral Psychology* 40, no. 3 (January 1992): 139–158.

_____. "What's New in Hispanic Ministry?" *Overheard*, vol. 13 (Fall, 1993): audio recording.

_____. "Las Bodas de Plata de Una Lluvia de Oro." *Revista Latinoamericana de Teologia* 12, no. 37 (April 1996): 79–91.

_____. "A New Catholic Reformation." *Chicago Studies* 36, no. 3 (December 1997): 216–223.

_____. "Challenges to the Pastoral Care of Central Americans in the United States."*Apuntes* 17, no. 2 (Summer 1997): 45–56.

_____. "A Survey of Contemporary U.S. Hispanic Catholic Theology." *Theology Digest* 44, no. 3 (Fall 1997): 203–211.

_____. "A Silver Anniversary and a Rain of Gold." *Listening* 32 no. 3 (Fall 1997): 147–151.

_____. "Sensus Fidelium: Vehículo para la Inculturación en Culturas Concretas." In Rosemarie Kamke, ed. *Abrir Caminos a la Vida,* 120–127. Rome: Institución Teresiana, 1999.

_____. "Cursillo de Cristiandad: Gift of the Hispanic Church." *Chicago Studies* 38, no. 3 (Fall–Winter 1999): 318–328.

_____, and Philip Lampe, Ph.D. "The Attraction and Retention of Hispanics to Doctor of Ministry Programs." *Theological Education* 33, no. 1 (Autumn, 1996): 75–82.

_____. "Child Abuse in the Hispanic Community: A Christian Perspective," *Apuntes* 12, no. 3 (Fall 1992): 127–136.

_____. "Preaching in Spanish as a Second Language." *Homiletic* (Fall 1992): 7–10.

_____. "Encuentros, National Pastoral." In *New Catholic Encyclopedia*, Volume 19 (Supplement 1989–1995): 117–119.

_____. "Pointers for Presiders, Spanish as a Second Language: Part I." *AIM: Liturgy Resources* (Winter 1995): 22–24.

_____. "When a Bilingual Preacher Is Made, Not Born." *AIM:Liturgy Resources* (Winter 1999): 18–19.

Deck, Allan Figueroa. "Chávez, César Estrada." In *New Catholic Encyclopedia*, Volume 19 (Supplement 1989–1995): 77–78.

_____. "La Raza Cósmica: Rediscovering the Hispanic Soul." *Critic* (Spring 1993): 46–53.

_____. "The Hispanic Presence: A Moment of Grace." *The Critic* 45, no. 1 (Fall 1990): 48–59.

_____. "Popular Culture, Popular Religion: Framing the Question." *Way* 73 Supplement (Spring 1992): 24–35.

_____. "The Crisis of Hispanic Ministry: Multiculturalism as Ideology." *America* 163, no. 2 (July 14–21, 1990): 33–36.

_____. "Hispanic Catholic Prayer and Worship." In Justo L. González, ed. *Alabadle! Hispanic Christian Worship*, 29–41. Nashville: Abingdon Press, 1996.

_____. "'A Pox on Both Your Houses': A View of Catholic Conservative-Liberal Polarities from the Hispanic Margin." In Mary Jo Weaver and R. Scott Appleby, eds., *Being Right: Conservative Catholics in America*, 88–104. Bloomington: Indiana University Press, 1995.

_____. "Latino Religion and the Struggle for Justice: Evangelization as Conversion." *Journal of Hispanic/Latino Theology* 4, no. 3 (February 1997): 28–41.

_____, and Christopher Tirres. "Latino Popular Religion and the Struggle for Justice." In Gary Orfield and Holly Lebowitz Rossi, eds. *Religion, Race, and Justice in a Changing America*, 139–210. New York: A Century Foundation Book, 1999.

de Luna, Sister Anita. "One and Many: Cultivating Cultural Diversity." *Church* (Summer 1999): 23–27.

Díaz-Stevens, Ana María. "Aspects of Puerto Rican Religious Experience: A Sociohistorical Overview." In Gabriel Haslip-Viera and Sherrie L. Baver, eds. *Latinos in New York: Communities in Transition*, 159–164. Notre Dame: Notre Dame University Press, 1996.

_____. "In the Image and Likeness: Literature as Theological Reflection." In Isasi-Diaz, Ada Maria and Fernando Segovia, eds. *Hispanic/Latino Theology, Challenge and Promise*, 86–103. Philadelphia: Fortress Press, 1996.

_____. "Syncretism, Popular Religiosity, and Communitarian Spirituality among Puerto Ricans and Hispanics in the United States." *Listening* 33, no. 3 (Fall 1998): 162–174.

Doyle, Dennis M. "Communion Ecclesiology on the Borders: Elizabeth Johnson and Roberto S. Goizueta." In María Pilar Aquino and Roberto S. Goizueta, eds. *Theology: Expanding the Borders*, 200–218. Mystic, CT: Twenty-Third Publications: 1998.

Duin, Julia. "Hispanic Catholics." *New Covenant* (January 1990): 9–11.

Durand, Jorge, and Douglas S. Massey. *Miracles on the Border: Retablos of Mexican Migrants to the United States*. Tucson: University of Arizona Press, 1995.

Elizondo, Virgil. "Métissage: La Naissance d'une Nouvelle Culture et d'une Nouvelle Chrétienté," *Lumiére et Vie* 208 (July 1992): 77–90.

_____. "Guadalupe, Our Lady of." In Richard P. McBrien, ed. *The Harper Collins Encyclopedia of Catholicism*, 594–595. Harper San Francisco, 1995.

_____. "Sanación y Liberación Pentecostales: Respuesta de la Teología de la Liberación." *Concilium* (June 1996): 481–487.

_____. "Pastoral Opportunities of Pilgrimages." *Concilium* 4 (1996): 107–114.

_____. "Guadalupe: An Endless Source of Reflection." *Journal of Hispanic/Latino Theology* 5, no. 1 (August 1997): 61–65.

_____. "The Mexican American Cultural Center Story." *Listening* 32, no. 3 (Fall 1997): 152–160.

_____. "Transformation of Borders: Border Separation or New Identity." In María Pilar Aquino and Roberto Goizueta, eds. *Theology: Expanding the Borders*, 22–39. Mystic, CT: Twenty-Third Publications, 1998.

_____. "Analyse de Racisme." *Concilium* 248 (1993): 69–77.

_____. "Evil and the Experience of God." *Way* 33, no. 1 (January 1993): 34–43.

_____. "Letter to the Church in Italy." *Adista* (Italy) 14 (October 1995): 92–95.

Empereur, James L., S.J. "Popular Religion and the Liturgy: The State of the Question." *Liturgical Ministry* 7 (Summer 1998): 105–120.

Engh, Michael E. *Frontier Faiths: Church, Temple and Synagogue in Los Angeles, 1846–1888*. Sante Fe: University of New Mexico Press, 1993.

_____. "Companion of the Immigrants: Devotion to Our Lady of Guadalupe among Mexicans in the Los Angeles Area, 1900–1940." *Journal of Hispanic/Latino Theology* 5, no. 1 (August 1997): 37–47.

Espín, Orlando O. "The Vanquished, Faithful Solidarity and the Marian Symbol: A Hispanic Perspective on Providence." In Joan Coultas and Barbara Doherty, eds. *On Keeping Providence*, 84–101. Terre Haute, Indiana: St. Mary of the Woods Press, 1991.

_____. "Trinitarian Monotheism and the Birth of Popular Catholicism: The Case of Sixteenth Century Mexico." *Missiology* 20, no. 2 (April 1992): 178–204.

_____. "The God of the Vanquished: Foundations for a Latino Spirituality." *Listening* 27, no. 1 (Winter 1992): 70–84.

_____. "Pentecostalism and Popular Catholicism: The Poor and Tradition." *Journal of Hispanic/Latino Theology* 3, no. 2 (November 1995): 14–43.

_____. "A Multicultural Church? Theological Reflections from Below." In William Cenkner, ed. *The Multicultural Church: A New Landscape in U.S. Theologies*, 54–71. New York: Paulist Press, 1996.

_____. "Popular Catholicism: Alienation or Hope?" In Isasi-Diaz, Ada Maria and Fernando Segovia, eds. *Hispanic/Latino Theology, Challenge and Promise*, 307–324. Philadelphia: Fortress Press, 1996.

Espinosa, Manual J. "The Origin of the Penitentes of New Mexico: Separating Fact from Fiction." *Catholic Historical Review* 79, no. 3 (July 1993): 454–477.

Fandel, Cecilia, OSM. "The Border and Immigration: An Invitation to Posada." *New Theology Review* 2, no. 1 (February 1999): 32–42.

Fernández, Eduardo C., SJ. "La realidad latina en los EEUU: sombras y luces." In Roberto Viola, S.J., *Reflexiones Catequéticas: Encuentro de San Antonio, Texas, Julio 1995*, 175–179. Bogotá: 1996.

_____. "The Contributions of the Jesuit Order in the New Mexico-Colorado-West Texas Area as the Rocky Mountain Mission, 1867–1919." In Thomas J. Steele, S.J., Paul Rhetts, and Barbe Awalt, eds. *Seeds of Struggle, Harvest of Faith*, 135–148. Albuquerque: LPD Press, 1998.

_____. "Seven Tips on the Pastoral Care of U.S. Catholics of Mexican Descent." *Chicago Studies* 36:3 (December 1997): 255—268.

_____."Transformation of Borders: Border Separation or New Identity." In María Pilar Aquino and Roberto S. Goizueta, *Theology: Expanding the Borders*, 22–39. Mystic, CT: Twenty-Third Publications, 1998.

_____. "The Hispanic Liturgical Year: The People's Calendar." *Liturgical Ministry* 7 (Summer 1998): 129–135.

Folliard, Dorothy, OP. "M.A.C.C. as Graced Whirlpool: Some Reflections from a Non-Hispanic." *Listening* 32, no. 3 (Fall 1997): 179–187.

Francis, Mark. "The Challenge of Worship in a Multicultural Assembly." *Liturgy* 14, no. 4 (Winter 1997): 3–9.

Gabriel, Rosemary, ed. *Santos de Palo: The Household Saints of Puerto Rico*. New York: Museum of American Folk Art, 1992.

Galles, Duane, LCM. "The Hispanic Musical Presence in the New Evangelization in the United States!" *Sacred Music* 124, no. 2 (Summer 1997): 6–11.

Garcia, Sixto. "Hispanic Theologians as Actors, Poets, and Prophets of Their Communities." *Journal of Hispanic/Latino Theology* 6, no. 4 (May 1999): 5–18.

_____. "A Matter of Presence." *Journal of Hispanic/Latino Theology* 5, no. 2 (November 1997): 22–53.

Garcia-Rivera, Alejandro. "The Cosmic Frontier: Toward a Natural Anthropology." *Journal of Hispanic/Latino Theology* 3, no. 1 (August 1995): 42–49.

_____. St. Martin de Porres: *The "Little Stories" and the Semiotics of Culture*. Maryknoll: Orbis Books, 1995.

_____. "Border Crossings." *Momentum* 27, no. 2 (April/May 1996): 42–44.

_____. "Creator of the Visible and the Invisible: Liberation Theology, Postmodernism, and the Spiritual." *Journal of Hispanic/Latino Theology* 3, no. 4 (May 1996): 35–56.

_____. "The 'Pilgrim Church' of Vatican II: A Tale of Two Altars." *Concilium* 4 (1996): 92–103.

Goizueta, Roberto S. "In Defense of Reason." *Journal of Hispanic/Latino Theology* 3, no. 3 (February 1996): 16–26.

_____. "Bartolomé de Las Casas, Modern Critic of Modernity: An Analysis of a Conversion." *Journal of Hispanic/Latino Theology* 3, no. 4 (May 1996): 6–19.

_____. "U.S. Hispanic Popular Catholicism as Theopoetics." In Isasi-Diaz, Ada Maria and Fernando Segovia, eds. *Hispanic/Latino Theology, Challenge and Promise*, 261–288. Philadelphia: Fortress Press, 1996.

_____. "The Church and Hispanics in the United States: From Empowerment to Solidarity." In Michael Downey, ed. *Theologies of Empowerment*, 160–175. New York: Crossroad, 1991.

_____. "Nosotros: Toward a U.S. Hispanic Anthropology." *Listening* 27, no. 1 (Winter 1992): 55–69.

_____. "Catholic Theological Education and U.S. Hispanics." In Patrick W. Carey and Earl C. Muller, SJ, eds. *Theological Education in the Catholic Tradition: Contemporary Challenges*, 340–350. New York: Crossroad Publishing Company, 1997.

_____. "The Back Roads: Alternative Catholic Intellectual Traditions." In Sandra Yocum Mize and William Portier, eds. *American Catholic Traditions, Resources for Renewal*, 24–28. College Theology Society Annual 42, 1996.

_____. "San Fernando Cathedral: Incarnating the Theology Born of the Mexican American Cultural Center." *Listening* 32, no. 3 (Fall 1997): 190–202.

_____. "Méstissage Hispanique et Méthode Théologique aux États–Unis." *Concilium* 248 (1993): 35–44.

_____. "The Preferential Option for the Poor: The CELAM Documents and the NCCB Pastoral Letter on U.S. Hispanics as Sources for U.S. Hispanic Theology." *Journal of Hispanic/Latino Theology* 3, no. 2 (November 1995): 65–77.

_____. *Caminemos con Jesús: Toward a Hispanic/Latino Theology of Accompaniment*. Maryknoll: Orbis Books, 1995.

Gómez, Raúl. "Professing Unity in Faith and Love: Hispano-Mozarabic Diptychs." *Liturgy* 13, no. 1 (Spring 1996): 60–63.

_____. "The Day of the Dead: Celebrating the Continuity of Life and Death." *Liturgy* 14, no. 1 (Spring 1997): 28–40.

Gomez-Kelly, Sally. "Pointers for Pastoral Care: Ministering with the Hispanic Community." *AIM: Liturgy Resources* 14, no. 1 (Spring 1996): 6–8.

González, María Elena, RSM. "Parish Restructuring in Multicultural Communities." *Origins* 24, no. 46 (May 1995): 781–788.

González, Rev. Robert A. "The Mariology of the Nican Mopohua." *Josephinum Journal of Theology* 3, no. 1 (Winter/Spring 1996): 42–55.

Gros, Jeffrey, FSC. "An Agenda for the Unity of the Church in the Western Hemisphere: Encounter with the Living Christ: The Way to Conversion, Communion, and Solidarity in America." *Journal of Hispanic/Latino Theology* 4, no. 2 (November 1996): 6–33.

Guerrero, Father José Luis. "El Nican Mopohua: Magistral Ejemplo de Inculturación." *Josephinum Journal of Theology* 4 (Supplement 1997): 23–49.

Gutierrez, Gustavo. "Discovering a People." *Listening* 32, no. 3 (Fall 1997): 174–178.

Hall, Suzanne. "Welcoming the Stranger." *Momentum* 18, no. 3 (August–September 1997): 19–22.

Hammerback, John C. *Rhetorical Career of Cesar Chavez*. College Station: Texas A&M University Press, 1998.

Hanlon, Don. "The Confrontation of Two Dissimilar Cultures: The Adobe Church in New Mexico." *Journal of the Interfaith Forum on Religion, Art, and Architecture* (Winter 1991): 17–20.

Harris, Daniel C.M. and Ray John Marek, O.M.I. "A Public Voice: Preaching on Justice Issues." *Theological Education* 38, no. 1 (2001): 47–59.

Herrera, Marina. "Response to M. Shawn Copeland." In William Cenkner, ed. *The Multicultural Church: A New Landscape in U.S. Theologies*, 24–34. New York: Paulist Press, 1996.

_____. "Meeting Cultures at the Well." *Religious Education* 87, no. 8 (Spring 1992): 173–180.

Hinojosa, Juan-Lorenzo. "Formation in Hispanic Ministry." *Review for Religious* 50, no. 5 (September/October 1991): 722–729.

Hughes, Cornelius. "Views from the Pews: Hispanic and Anglo Catholics in a Changing Church." *Review of Religious Research* 33, no. 4 (June 1992): 364–375.

Isasi-Díaz, Ada María. "Hispanic Women in the Roman Catholic Church." In Melanie A. May, ed. *Women and Church: The Challenge of Ecumenical Solidarity in an Age of Alienation*, 13–17. Grand Rapids, Michigan: Wm. B. Eerdmans, 1991.

_____. "Mujerista Liturgies and the Struggle for Liberation." In Chauvet and Francois Kabasale Lumbala, eds. *Concilium: Liturgy and the Body*, 104–111. Maryknoll: Orbis Books, 1995.

_____. "Mujerista Theology's Method: A Liberative Praxis, a Way of Life," *Listening* 27, no. 1 (Winter 1992): 41–64.

_____. "Defining Our Proyecto Histórico: Mujerista Strategies for Liberation." *Journal of Feminist Studies in Religion* 9, nos. 1–2 (Spring/Fall 1993): 17–28.

_____. "Elements of a Mujerista Anthropology." In Ann O'Hare Graff, ed. *The Embrace of God: Feminist Approaches to Theological Anthropology*, 90–102. Maryknoll: Orbis Books, 1995.

_____. "Mujerista Theology's Method: A Liberative Praxis, A Way of Life." In James D. Whitehead and Evelyn Eaton Whitehead, eds. *Method in Ministry: Theological Reflection and Christian Ministry*, 123–132. Kansas City: Sheed & Ward, 1995.

_____. *Women of God, Women of the People*. St. Louis: Chalice Press, 1995.

_____. *Mujerista Theology: A Theology for the Twenty-First Century*. Maryknoll: Orbis Books, 1996.

_____. "Un poquito de justicia—A Little Bit of Justice." In Isasi-Diaz, Ada Maria and Fernando Segovia, eds. *Hispanic/Latino Theology, Challenge and Promise*, 325–339. Philadelphia: Fortress Press, 1996.

_____. "Afterwords: Strangers No Longer." In Isasi-Diaz, Ada Maria and Fernando Segovia, eds. *Hispanic/Latino Theology, Challenge and Promise*, 367–374. Philadelphia: Fortress Press, 1996.

_____. "The Present-Future of EATWOT: A Mujerista Perspective." *Voices from the Third World* 19, no. 1 (June 1996): 86–103.

_____. "Economic Violence against Minority Women in the USA." In Mary John Mananzan, Mercy Amba Oduyoye, Elsa Tamez, J. Shannon Clarkson, Mary C. Grey, and Letty M. Russell, eds. *Women Resisting Violence: Spirituality for Life*, 89–99. Maryknoll: Orbis Books, 1996.

_____. "Round Table Discussion: Nondiscrimination and Diversity." *Journal of Feminist Studies in Religion* 13, no. 2 (Fall 1997): 87–89.

_____. "Doing Theology as Mission." *Apuntes* 18, no. 4 (Winter 1998): 99–111.

_____, and Robert Schreiter, eds. *Dialogue Rejoined: Theology and Ministry in the United States Reality*. Collegeville: Liturgical Press, 1995.

Jensen, Carol. "Roman Catholicism in Modern New Mexico: A Commitment to Survive." In Ferenc M. Szasz and Richard W. Etulain, eds. *Religion in Modern New Mexico*, 1–26. Albuquerque: University of New Mexico Press, 1997.

Jordan, Brian. "Immigration: Public Policy, Pastoral Practice." *Church* 13, no. 2 (Summer 1997): 20–23.

LaSalle, Don. *Proceedings of the North American Academy of Liturgy*. Annual Meeting, Chicago (January 1997): 69–70.

Lassalle-Klein, Robert. "The Potential Contribution of C.S. Peirce to Interpretation Theory in U.S. Hispanic/Latino and Other Culturally Contextualized Theologies." *Journal of Hispanic/Latino Theology* 6, no. 3 (February 1999): 5–34.

Levitt, Peggy. "Local-level Global Religion: The Case of U. S.-Dominican Migration." *Journal for the Scientific Study of Religion* 37, no. 1 (1998): 74–89.

López, José. "The Liturgical Year and Hispanic Customs." *AIM: Liturgy Resources* 14, no. 2 (Summer 1996): 6–10.

Lovrien, Peggy. "Inculturation and Multiculturalism." *Ministry and Liturgy* 26, no. 7 (September 1999): 12–14.

Loya, Gloria Inés. "Considering the Source/Fuentes for a Hispanic Feminist Theology." *Theology Today* 54, no. 4 (January 1998): 491–498.

Jiménez, Pablo A. "In Search of a Hispanic Model of Biblical Interpretation." *Journal of Hispanic/Latino Theology* 3, no. 2 (November 1995): 44–64.

Lampe, Philip E. "Is the Church Meeting the Needs of Hispanics?" *Living Light* 27, no. 1 (Fall 1990): 51–55.

Levada, William. "Hispanic Ministry's Changing, Face." *Origins* 25, no. 3 (June 1995): 46–48.

Macy, Gary. "Demythologizing 'the Church' in the Middle Ages." *Journal of Hispanic/Latino Theology* 3, no. 1 (August 1995): 23–41.

Maduro, Otto. "Notes toward a Sociology of Latina/o Religious Empowerment." In Isas-Diaz, Ada Maria and Fernando Segovia, eds. *Hispanic/Latino Theology, Challenge and Promise*, 151–166. Philadelphia: Fortress Press, 1996.

Maldonado, Roberto D. "La Conquista? Latin American (Mestizaje) Reflections on the Biblical Conquest." *Journal of Hispanic/Latino Theology* 2, no. 4 (May 1995): 5–25.

Maldonado, Pérez Zaida. "Death and the 'Hour of Triumph': Subversion within the Visions of Saturus and Polycarp." In María Pilar Aquino and Roberto Goizueta, eds. *Theology: Expanding the Borders*, 121–144. Mystic, Conn.: Twenty-Third Publications, 1998.

Martin, Shane, and Ernesto Colin. "The Novels of Graciela Limon: Narrative, Theology, and the Search for Mestiza/o Identity" *Journal of Hispanic/Latino Theology* 7, no. 1 (August 1999): 6–25.

Martínez, German, OSB. "Hispanic-American Spirituality," in Michael Downey, ed., *The New Dictionary of Catholic Spirituality*, 473–476. Collegeville, Minnesota: Liturgical Press, 1993.

_____. "Hispanic Culture and Worship: The Process of Inculturation." *U.S. Catholic Historian* 11, no. 2 (Spring 1993): 79–91.

Matovina, Timothy A. "Liturgy and Popular Expressions of Faith: A Look at the Works of Virgil Elizondo." *Worship* 63, no. 5 (September 1991): 436–444.

_____. "Guadalupan Devotion in a Borderlands Community." *Journal of Hispanic/Latino Theology* 4, no. 1 (August 1996): 6–26.

_____. "Between Two Worlds." In Gerald E. Poyo, ed. *Delano Journey, 1770–1850*, 73–87. Austin: University of Texas Press, 1996.

_____. "New Frontiers of Guadalupanismo." *Journal of Hispanic/Latino Theology* 5, no. 1 (August 1997): 20–36.

_____. "Sacred Place and Collective Memory: San Fernando Cathedral, San Antonio, Texas." *U.S. Catholic Historian* 15, no. 1 (Winter 1997): 33–50.

_____. "San Fernando Cathedral and the Alamo: Sacred Place, Public Ritual, and Construction of Meaning." In *Proceedings of the North American Academy of Liturgy*. Notre Dame, Indiana: North American Academy of Liturgy, 1998.

_____. "Hispanic Faith and Theology." *Theology Today* 54, no. 4 (January 1998): 507–511.

_____. "Religion and Ethnicity in San Antonio: Germans and Tejanos in the Wake of United States Annexation." *Catholic Southwest: A Journal of History and Culture* 10 (1999): 29–49.

_____. "Representation and the Reconstruction of Power: The Rise of padres and Las Hermanas." In Mary Jo Weaver, ed. *What's Left? Liberal American Catholics*. Bloomington: Indiana University Press, 1999.

_____. "Ministries and the Servant Community." *Worship* 67, no. 4 (July 1993): 351–360.

_____. "Lay Initiatives in Worship on the Texas Frontera, 1830–1860," *U.S. Catholic Historian* 12 (Fall 1995).

_____. "Marriage Celebrations in Mexican American Communities." *Liturgical Ministry* 5 (Winter 1996): 22–26.

_____. "The National Parish and Americanization." *U.S. Catholic Historian* 17, no. 1 (Winter 1999): 45–58.

McClure, John S. *Best Advice for Preaching.* Minneapolis: Fortress Press, 1998.

McNally, Michael. "Presence and Persistence: Catholicism among Latins in Tampa's Ybor City, 1885–1985." *U.S. Catholic Historian* 14, no. 2 (Spring 1996): 73–91.

McNamara, Patrick H. *Conscience First, Tradition Second: A Study of Young American Catholics.* Albany: State University of New York Press, 1993.

_____. "Researching Churches in the Southwestern Latino Community: How do the Assumptions, Theories, and Methods of Twenty-Five Years Ago Stand Today?" In Stevens-Arroyo, Anthony M. and Gilbert R. Cadena, eds., *Old Masks, New Faces: Religion and Latino Identities*, 23–32. New York: The Bildner Center for Western Hemisphere Studies, 1995.

Mejido, Manuel Jesús. "Theoretical Prolegomenon to the Sociology of U.S. Hispanic Popular Religion." *Journal of Hispanic/Latino Theology* 7, no. 1 (August 1999): 27–55.

Mendieta, Eduardo. "From Christendom to Polycentric Oikonumé: Modernity, Postmodernity, and Liberation Theology." *Journal of Hispanic/Latino Theology* 3, no. 4 (May 1996): 57–76.

Miranda, J. "Hispanic Churches in America." In Robert D. Linder, et. al., eds., *Dictionary of Christianity in America.* Downers Grove, Illinois: Intervarsity Press, 1990.

Mordey, Aurora. "Spanish Language Instruction at St. John's Seminary." *Seminary Journal* 2, no. 2 (Fall 1996): 42–47.

Muñoz Sepúlveda, Isidro. "Puerto Rico: Idioma e Identidad." *Razón y Fe* (March 1993): 227–287.

Novo Pena, Silvia. "Religion," in Nicolás Kanellos, ed., *The Hispanic-American Almanac*, 367–387. Detroit, Michigan: Gale Research, 1993.

Ostendorf, David L. "Exploiting Immigrant Workers," *Christian Century* (5 May 1999): 492–493.

Palacios, Joseph. *Locating the Social in Social Justice: Social Justice Teaching and Practice in the American and Mexican Catholic Churches.* Ph.D. Diss.. U. C. Berkeley, 2001.

Perez, Leopoldo, O.M.I. "Preferential Option for the Poor: Indications from U.S. Oblate Hispanic Ministry." *Offerings* (2003).

Perez y Mena, Andrés I. "Cuban Santería, Haitian Vodun, Puerto Rican Spiritualism: A Multiculturalist Inquiry into Syncretism." *Journal for the Scientific Study of Religion* 37, no. 1 (1998): 15–27.

Pérez Rodríguez, Arturo. "Mestizo Liturgy: A Mestizaje of the Roman and Hispanic Rites of Worship." *Liturgical Ministry* 6 (Summer 1997): 141–147.

Philibert, Paul, OP, and John Reid. "Su Futuro, Nuestro Futuro." *Touchstone* 14, no. 3 (Spring 1999): 10–11.

Pierce, Brian, "Bartolomé de las Casas and Truth: Toward a Spirituality of Solidarity." *Spirituality Today* 44, no. 1 (1992): 4–19.

Pineda, Ana María. "Evangelization of the 'New World': A New World Perspective." *Missiology* 20, no. 8 (April 1992): 151–161.

_____. "The Colloquies and Theological Discourse: Culture as a Locus for Theology." *Journal of Hispanic/Latino Theology* 3, no. 3 (February 1996): 27–42.

_____. "In the Image and Likeness: Literature as Theological Reflection." In Isasi-Diaz, Ada Maria and Fernando Segovia, eds. *Hispanic/Latino Theology, Challenge and Promise*, 104–116. Philadelphia: Fortress Press, 1996.

_____. "Liberation Theology: Practice of a People Hungering for Human Dignity." *Way* 38, no. 3 (July 1998): 231–238.

_____. "Hospitality." In Dorothy C. Bass, ed. *Practicing Our Faith: A Way of Life for a Searching People*, 29–42. San Francisco: Jossey–Bass, 1997.

Polischuk, P. "Hispanic American Pastoral Care." In Rodney J. Hunter, ed., *Dictionary of Pastoral Care and Counseling*. Nashville: Abingdon, 1990.

Pulido, Alberto L. "Are You an Emissary of Jesus Christ?: Justice, the Catholic Church, and the Chicano Movement." *Exploration in Ethnic Studies* 14, no. 1 (January 1991): 17–34.

_____. "The Religious Dimensions of Mexican Americans." In Julian Samora and Patricia Vandel Simon, eds. *A History of the Mexican-American People* (revised edition), 223–234. Notre Dame, Indiana: University of Notre Dame Press, 1993.

Ramírez, Ricardo. "The Challenge of Ecumenism to Hispanic Christians." *Ecumenical Trends* 21, no. 8 (1992): 1, 11–14.

_____. "Prison Reform and the Ideals of justice." *Origins* 24, no. 37 (March 1995): 612–615.

_____. "The Crisis in Ecumenism among Hispanic Christians." *Origins* 24, no. 40 (March 1995): 660–667.

Riebe-Estrella, Gary. "The Challenge of Ministerial Formation." *Missiology* 20, no. 2 (April 1992): 269–274.

_____. "American Cultural Shifts: Formation for Which Candidates? For Which Church?" *Seminary Journal* 2, no. 2 (Fall 1996): 27–33.

_____. "Movement from Monocultural to Multicultural Congregations." *Review for Religious* 55, no. 5 (September–October 1996): 507–520.

_____. "Sangre llama a sangre: Cultural Memory as a Source of Theological Insight." In Isasi-Diaz, Ada Maria and Fernando Segovia, eds. *Hispanic/Latino Theology, Challenge and Promise*, 117–133. Philadelphia: Fortress Press, 1996.

_____. "Latinos and Theological Education." *Journal of Hispanic/Latino Theology* 4, no. 3 (February 1997): 5–12.

_____. "Latino Religiosity or Latino Catholicism?" *Theology Today* 54, no. 4 (January 1998): 512–515.

_____. "La Virgen: A Mexican Perspective." *New Theology Review* 12, no. 2 (May 1999): 39–47.

Robeck, Cecil M., Jr. "Evangelization or Proselytism of Hispanics? A Pentecostal Perspective." *Journal of Hispanic/Latino Theology* 4, no. 4 (May 1997): 42–64.

Roden-Lucero, Edward. *Parish-Based Community Organizing as a Pastoral Response to Poverty in the Hispanic Community: A Practical Hermeneutic of*

Catholic Social Teaching. D.Min. Diss., San Antonio, Texas: Oblate School of Theology, 2003.

Rodriguez, Edmundo, S.J. "Jesus, Power and the One." *Review for Religious* 56, no. 1 (January–February 1997): 87–94.

Rodriguez-Holguin, Jeanette Y. "Hispanics and the Sacred." *Chicago Studies* 29, no. 2 (August 1990): 137–154.

Rodriguez, Jeannette. "Contemporary Encounters with Guadalupe." *Journal of Hispanic/Latino Theology* 5, no. 1 (August 1997): 48–60.

_____. "U.S. Hispanic/Latino Theology: Context and Challenge." *Journal of Hispanic/Latino Theology* 5, no. 3 (February 1998): 6–15.

Rodriguez, Jesús, BCC, D.Min. "Chaplains' Communication with Latino Patients: Case Studies on Non-Verbal Communication." *The Journal of Pastoral Care* 53, no. 3 (Fall 1999): 309–317.

Romero, Gilbert. "The Bible, Revelation and Marian Devotion." *Marian Studies* 44 (1993).

_____. "Hispanic Theology and the Apocalyptic Imagination." *Apuntes* 15, no. 4 (Winter 1995): 133–137.

_____. "Amos 5:21–24: Religion, Politics, and the Latino Experience." *Journal of Hispanic/Latino Theology* 4, no. 4 (May 1997): 21–41.

Rubio, José A. "El Cristo Latinoamericano." *Living Light* 33, no. 1 (Fall 1996): 30–34.

_____. "Checklist for Multicultural and Multilingual Worship." *Liturgy* 14, no. 4 (Winter 1997): 23–26.

Ruiz, Jean-Pierre. "Contexts in Conversation: First World and Third World Readings of Job." *Journal of Hispanic/Latino Theology* 2, no. 3 (February 1995): 5–29.

_____. "New Ways of Reading the Bible in the Cultural Settings of the Third World." In Beuken, William and Sean Freyne, eds., *Concilium: The Bible as Cultural Heritage,* 73–84. Maryknoll: Orbis Books, 1995.

_____. "Naming the Other: U.S. Hispanic Catholics, the So-Called 'Sects,' and the 'New Evangelization.'" *Journal of Hispanic/Latino Theology* 4, no. 2 (November 1996): 34–59.

_____. "U.S. Hispanic/Latino Theology: 'The Boom' and Beyond." *Catholic Issues* 09/20/98 01:06.

_____. "Four Faces of Theology." In Fernando F. Segovia and Mary Ann Tolbert, *Teaching the Bible,* New York: Orbis Books, 1998.

_____. "Revelation 4:8–11, 5:9–14: Heavenly Hymns of Creation and Redemption." In M. Kiley, ed. *Prayer from Alevader to Constantine,* 244–249. London: Routledge, 1997.

_____. "The Politics of Praise: A Reading of Revelation 19:1–10." In *Society of Biblical Literature: 1997 Seminar Papers.* Atlanta: Scholars Press, 374–393.

San Pedro, Bishop Enrique, SJ. "The Pastor and the Theologian." In William Cenkner, ed. *The Multicultural Church: A New Landscape in U.S. Theologies,* 140–151. New York: Paulist Press, 1996.

Schelkshorn, Dr. Hans. "Discourse and Liberation: Toward a Critical Coordination of Discourse Ethics and Enrique Dussel's Ethics of Liberation." *Journal of Hispanic/Latino Theology* 5, no. 2 (November 1997): 54–74.

Segovia, Fernando F. "A New Manifest Destiny: The Emerging Theological Voice of Hispanic Americans." *Religious Studies Review* 17, no. 2 (April 1991): 101–109.

_____. "Two Places and No Place on Which to Stand: Mixture and Otherness in Hispanic American Theology," *Listening* 27, no. 1 (Winter 1992): 26–40.

_____."Aliens in the Promised Land: The Manifest Destiny of U.S. Hispanic American Theology." In Isasi–Diaz, Ada Maria and Fernando Segovia, eds. *Hispanic/Latino Theology, Challenge and Promise*, 15–42. Philadelphia: Fortress Press, 1996.

_____. "In the World but Not of It: Exile as a Locus for a Theology of the Diaspora." In Isasi-Diaz, Ada Maria and Fernando Segovia, eds. *Hispanic/Latino Theology, Challenge and Promise*, 195–217. Philadelphia: Fortress Press, 1996.

_____."Pedagocial Discourse and Practices in Cultural Studies: Toward a Contextual Biblical Pedagogy." In Fernando F. Segovia and Mary Ann Tolbert, eds. *Teaching the Bible*, 137–168. New York: Orbis Books, 1998.

_____, and Mary Ann Tolbert, eds. "'And They Began to Speak in Other Tongues': Competing Modes of Discourse in Contemporary Biblical Criticism." In Fernando F. Segovia and Mary Ann Tolbert, eds., *Reading from This Place. Vol. 1, Social Location and Biblical Interpretation in the United States*, 1–32. Minneapolis: Fortress Press, 1995.

Sevilla, Bishop Carlos, SJ. "The Ethics of Immigration Reform." *Origins* 27, no. 43 (April 1998): 728–732.

Silva Gotay, Samuel. "El Partido Acción Cristiana: Transfondo Histórico y Significado Sociológico del Nacimiento y Muerte de Un Partido Político Católico en Puerto Rico." *Cristianismo y Sociedad* 108: 95–108.

Sosa, Juan J. "Hispanic Weddings: A Family Affair." *Liturgia y Canción* 7, no. 3 (1996): 5–13.

_____. "Textos Litúrgicos para los Católicos Hispanos en los Estados Unidos (Liturgical Texts for Spanish-speaking Catholics in the United States)." *Liturgia y Canción* 9, no. 3 (Tiempo Ordinario 1, 1998): 12–21.

_____. "Liturgy and Popular Piety: A Marriage Made on Earth." *Church* 15, no. 3 (Fall 1999): 13–16.

Smith, Darren L., ed. *Hispanic Americans Information Directory* 1990–1991. Detroit: Gale Research, Inc., 1990.

Steele, Thomas J., ed. *Archbishop Lamy in his own Words*. Albuquerque, NM: LPD Press, 2000.

Stevens-Arroyo, Antonio M. "From Barrios to Barricades: Religion and Religious Institutions in the History of Latinos/as Since 1960." In David Gutierrez, ed., *The Columbia History of Latinos in the United States*. Columbia University Press: New York, forthcoming, 2003.

_____. "Juan Mateo Guaticabanó: The First to Be Baptized in America." *Apuntes* 16, no. 3 (Fall 1996): 67–77.

_____. "Latino Catholicism and the Eye of the Beholder: Notes Towards a New Sociological Paradigm." *Latino Studies Journal* 6, no. 2 (May 1995): 22–55.

_____. "Puerto Rican Struggles in the Catholic Church." In Clara E. Rodríguez and Virginia Sánchez Korrol, eds. *Historical Perspectives on Puerto Rican Survival in the United States*, 155–165. Princeton: Markus Wiener Publishers, 1996.

_____. "The Evolution of Marian Devotionalism within Christianity and the Ibero-Mediterranean Polity." *Journal for the Scientific Study of Religion* 37, no. 1 (1998): 50–73.

_____. "The Latino Religious Resurgence." *Annals of the American Academy of Political and Social Science* 558 (July 1998): 163–177.

_____, and Andres L Pérez y Mena, eds. *Enigmatic Powers: Syncretism with African and Indigenous Peoples' Religions among Latinos.* Vol. 3, PARAL Series. New York: The Bildner Center for Western Hemisphere Studies, CUNY, 1995.

_____ and Gilbert R. Cadena, eds. *Old Masks, New Faces: Religion and Latino Identities.* Vol. 2, PARAL series. New York: The Bildner Center for Western Hemisphere Studies, CUNY, 1995.

Stiefvater, Robert X. "Qué Viva Cristo Rey! Long Live Christ the King." *Liturgy* 13, no. 2 (Summer 1996): 28–33.

Suarez Rivero, Ruy G. "Teologia en la Frontera: Limite y Encuentro de Dos Mundos." In Maria Pilar Aquino and Roberto Goizueta, eds. *Theology: Expanding the Borders*, 40–59. Mystic, Ct: Twenty-Third Publications, 1998.

Tabares, Fanny. "Pastoral Care of Catholic South Americans Living in the United States." *Chicago Studies* 36, no. 3 (December 1997): 269–281.

Tepedino, Ana María, and María Pilar Aquino, eds. "Introduction." In *Entre la Indignación y la Esperanza*, 7–10. Bogotá: Indo-American Press Service, 1998.

Toomey, Don. "'Bautismo de Jesús,' A Magnificent Bulto by Santero Filimón Agular." *Catholic Southwest* 10 (1999): 51–60.

Trasloheros H., Jorge E. "The Construction of the First Shrine and Sanctuary of Our Lady of Guadalupe in San Luis Potosí, 1654–1664." *Journal of Hispanic/Latino Theology* 5, no. 1 (August 1997): 7–19.

Turek, Doris Mary, SSND. "La Tierra Prometida: A Mother's Sacrifice." *New Theology Review* 12, no. 1 (February 1999): 70–74.

Tweed, Thomas A. "Identity and Authority at a Cuban Shrine in Miami: Santería, Catholicism, and Struggles for Religious Identity." *Journal of Hispanic/Latino Theology* 4, no. 1 (August 1996): 27–48.

United States Catholic Conference, Department of Education. *The Hispanic Experience in the United States: Pastoral Reflections Using the Catechism of the Catholic Church,* 1996.

Urrabazo, Rosendo. "Pastoral Education of Hispanic Adults," *Missiology* 20, no. 2 (April 1992): 258–260.

_____. "Pastoral Ministry in a Multicultural Society," *Origins* 22, no. 23 (November 1992): 386–391.

U.S./Latin American Bishops. "Fostering Ecumenism in the U.S. Hispanic Community." *Origins* 24, no. 40 (March 1995): 657–660.

Valdéz, Jorge Luis. "U.S. Hispanics between the Borders of Catholicism and Protestantism." In María Pilar Aquino and Roberto S. Goizueta, *Theology: Expanding the Borders*, 219–239. Mystic, CT: Twenty-Third Publications, 1998.

Vera, Alexandrina D. "Guitars in Hispanic Liturgy Today." *Pastoral Music* (January 1998): 32–35.

Vidal, Jaime R. "Pilgrimage in the Christian Tradition." *Concilium* 4 (1996): 35–47.

Ward, James Garcia. "Project 13: Hispanic Vocations and Formation." *Apuntes* 10, No. 1 (Spring 1990): 15–16.

Warren, Mark R. *Dry Bones Rattling: Community Building to Revitalize American Democracy.* Princeton: Princeton University Press, 2001.

Wright, Robert E. "Popular Religiosity: Review of Literature." *Liturgical Ministry* 7 (Summer 1998): 141–146.

_____. "Sacred Sites: Building Churches and Communities in 19th Century South Texas." *Heritage* 17, no. 1, 16–20.

Index